# digits™

## Homework Helper

## Grade 7 Volume 2

**PEARSON**

Boston, Massachusetts • Chandler, Arizona • Glenview, Illinois • Upper Saddle River, New Jersey

**Acknowledgments for Illustrations:**
Rory Hensley, David Jackson, Jim Mariano, Rich McMahon, Lorie Park, and Ted Smykal

ISBN-13: 978-0-13-327632-9
ISBN-10: 0-13-327632-5
1 2 3 4 5 6 7 8 9 10 V011 17 16 15 14 13

# Contents

**Unit D: Geometry**

# Authors and Advisors

### Francis (Skip) Fennell
*digits Author*

*Approaches to mathematics content and curriculum, educational policy, and support for intervention*

Dr. Francis (Skip) Fennell is Professor of Education at McDaniel College, and a senior author with Pearson. He is a past president of the National Council of Teachers of Mathematics (NCTM) and a member of the writing team for the Curriculum Focal Points from the NCTM, which influenced the work of the Common Core Standards Initiative. Skip was also one of the writers of the Principles and Standards for School Mathematics.

### Art Johnson
*digits Author*

*Approaches to mathematical content and support for English Language Learners*

Art Johnson is a Professor of Mathematics at Boston University who taught in public school for over 30 years. He is part of the author team for Pearson's high school mathematics series. Art is the author of numerous books, including Teaching Mathematics to Culturally and Linguistically Diverse Students published by Allyn & Bacon, Teaching Today's Mathematics in the Middle Grades published by Allyn & Bacon, and Guiding Children's Learning of Mathematics, K–6 published by Wadsworth.

### Helene Sherman
*digits Author*

*Teacher education and support for struggling students*

Helene Sherman is Associate Dean for Undergraduate Education and Professor of Education in the College of Education at the University of Missouri in St. Louis, MO. Helene is the author of Teaching Learners Who Struggle with Mathematics, published by Merrill.

### Stuart J. Murphy
*digits Author*

*Visual learning and student engagement*

Stuart J. Murphy is a visual learning specialist and the author of the MathStart series. He contributed to the development of the Visual Learning Bridge in enVisionMATH™ as well as many visual elements of the Prentice Hall Algebra 1, Geometry, and Algebra 2 high school program.

### Janie Schielack
*digits Author*

*Approaches to mathematical content, building problem solvers,and support for intervention*

Janie Schielack is Professor of Mathematics and Associate Dean for Assessment and PreK–12 Education at Texas A&M University. She chaired the writing committee for the NCTM Curriculum Focal Points and was part of the nine-member NCTM feedback and advisory team that responded to and met with CCSSCO and NGA representatives during the development of various drafts of the Common Core State Standards.

### Eric Milou
*digits Author*

*Approaches to mathematical content and the use of technology in middle grades classrooms*

Eric Milou is Professor in the Department of Mathematics at Rowan University in Glassboro, NJ. Eric teaches pre-service teachers and works with in-service teachers, and is primarily interested in balancing concept development with skill proficiency. He was part of the nine-member NCTM feedback/advisory team that responded to and met with Council of Chief State School Officers (CCSSCO) and National Governors Association (NGA) representatives during the development of various drafts of the Common Core State Standards. Eric is the author of Teaching Mathematics to Middle School Students, published by Allyn & Bacon.

### William F. Tate
***digits* Author**

*Approaches to intervention, and use of efficacy and research*

William Tate is the Edward Mallinckrodt Distinguished University Professor in Arts & Sciences at Washington University in St. Louis, MO. He is a past president of the American Educational Research Association. His research focuses on the social and psychological determinants of mathematics achievement and attainment as well as the political economy of schooling.

### Randall I. Charles
***digits* Advisor**

Dr. Randall I. Charles is Professor Emeritus in the Department of Mathematics at San Jose State University in San Jose, CA, and a senior author with Pearson. Randall served on the writing team for the Curriculum Focal Points from NCTM. The NCTM Curriculum Focal Points served as a key inspiration to the writers of the Common Core Standards in bringing focus, depth, and coherence to the curriculum.

> *Pearson tapped leaders in mathematics education to develop **digits**. This esteemed author team—from diverse areas of expertise including mathematical content, Understanding by Design, and Technology Engagement—came together to construct a highly interactive and personalized learning experience.*

### Jim Cummins
***digits* Advisor**

*Supporting English Language Learners*

Dr. Jim Cummins is Professor and Canada Research Chair in the Centre for Educational Research on Languages and Literacies at the University of Toronto. His research focuses on literacy development in multilingual school contexts as well as on the potential roles of technology in promoting language and literacy development.

### Grant Wiggins
***digits* Consulting Author**

*Understanding by Design*

Grant Wiggins is a cross-curricular Pearson consulting author specializing in curricular change. He is the author of Understanding by Design published by ASCD, and the President of Authentic Education in Hopewell, NJ. Over the past 20 years, he has worked on some of the most influential reform initiatives in the country, including Vermont's portfolio system and Ted Sizer's Coalition of Essential Schools.

### Jacquie Moen
***digits* Advisor**

*Digital Technology*

Jacquie Moen is a consultant specializing in how consumers interact with and use digital technologies. Jacquie worked for AOL for 10 years, and most recently was VP & General Manager for AOL's kids and teen online services, reaching over seven million kids every month. Jacquie has worked with a wide range of organizations to develop interactive content and strategies to reach families and children, including National Geographic, PBS, Pearson Education, National Wildlife Foundation, and the National Children's Museum.

# Welcome to digits.

## Using the Homework Helper

**digits** is designed to help you master mathematics skills and concepts in a way that's relevant to you. As the title **digits** suggests, this program takes a digital approach. **digits** is digital, but sometimes you may not be able to access digital resources. When that happens, you can use the Homework Helper because you can refer back to the daily lesson and see all your homework questions right in the book.

Your Homework Helper supports your work on **digits** in so many ways!

The lesson pages capture important elements of the digital lesson that you need to know in order to do your homework.

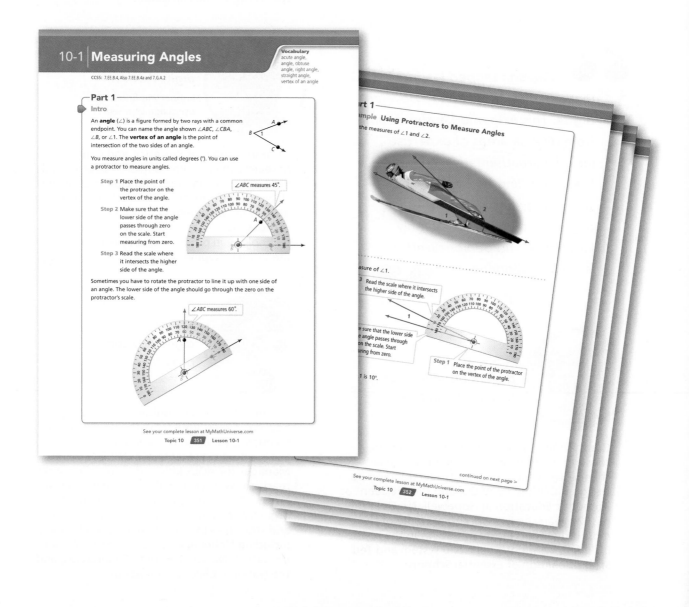

Every lesson in your Homework Helper also includes two pages of homework. The combination of homework exercises includes problems that focus on reasoning, multiple representations, mental math, writing, and error analysis. They vary in difficulty level from thinking about a plan to challenging. The problems come in different formats, like multiple choice, short answer, and open response, to help you prepare for tests.

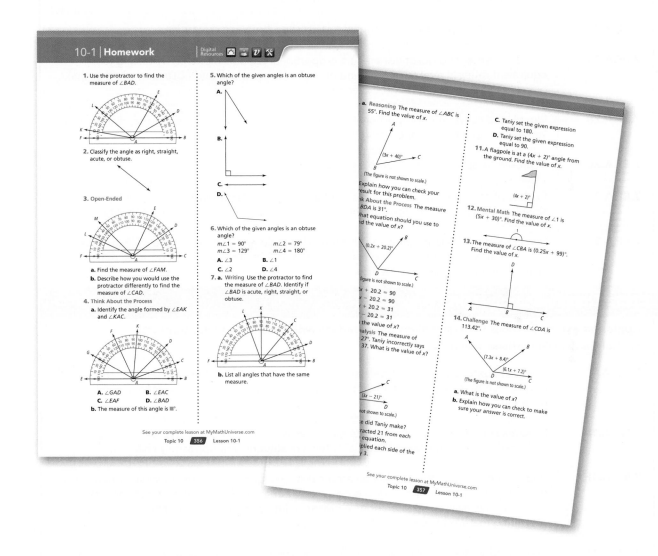

| Number | Standard for Mathematical Content |
|---|---|

## 7.RP  Ratios and Proportional Relationships

**Analyze proportional relationships and use them to solve real-world and mathematical problems.**

| | |
|---|---|
| **7.RP.A.1** | Compute unit rates associated with ratios of fractions, including ratios of lengths, areas and other quantities measured in like or different units. |
| **7.RP.A.2** | Recognize and represent proportional relationships between quantities. |
| **7.RP.A.2a** | Decide whether two quantities are in a proportional relationship, e.g., by testing for equivalent ratios in a table or graphing on a coordinate plane and observing whether the graph is a straight line through the origin. |
| **7.RP.A.2b** | Identify the constant of proportionality (unit rate) in tables, graphs, equations, diagrams, and verbal descriptions of proportional relationships. |
| **7.RP.A.2c** | Represent proportional relationships by equations. |
| **7.RP.A.2d** | Explain what a point $(x, y)$ on the graph of a proportional relationship means in terms of the situation, with special attention to the points $(0, 0)$ and $(1, r)$ where $r$ is the unit rate. |
| **7.RP.A.3** | Use proportional relationships to solve multistep ratio and percent problems. Examples: simple interest, tax, markups and markdowns, gratuities and commissions, fees, percent increase and decrease, percent error. |

## 7.NS  The Number System

**Apply and extend previous understandings of operations with fractions to add, subtract, multiply, and divide rational numbers.**

| | |
|---|---|
| **7.NS.A.1** | Apply and extend previous understandings of addition and subtraction to add and subtract rational numbers; represent addition and subtraction on a horizontal or vertical number line diagram. |
| **7.NS.A.1a** | Describe situations in which opposite quantities combine to make 0. For example, a hydrogen atom has 0 charge because its two constituents are oppositely charged. |
| **7.NS.A.1b** | Understand $p + q$ as the number located a distance $|q|$ from $p$, in the positive or negative direction depending on whether $q$ is positive or negative. Show that a number and its opposite have a sum of 0 (are additive inverses). Interpret sums of rational numbers by describing real-world contexts. |
| **7.NS.A.1c** | Understand subtraction of rational numbers as adding the additive inverse, $p - q = p + (-q)$. Show that the distance between two rational numbers on the number line is the absolute value of their difference, and apply this principle in real-world contexts. |
| **7.NS.A.1d** | Apply properties of operations as strategies to add and subtract rational numbers. |
| **7.NS.A.2** | Apply and extend previous understandings of multiplication and division and of fractions to multiply and divide rational numbers. |

| Number | Standard for Mathematical Content |
|--------|-----------------------------------|

## 7.NS The Number System (continued)

**Apply and extend previous understandings of operations with fractions to add, subtract, multiply, and divide rational numbers.**

| | |
|--------|--------|
| **7.NS.A.2a** | Understand that multiplication is extended from fractions to rational numbers by requiring that operations continue to satisfy the properties of operations, particularly the distributive property, leading to products such as $(-1)(-1) = 1$ and the rules for multiplying signed numbers. Interpret products of rational numbers by describing real-world contexts. |
| **7.NS.A.2b** | Understand that integers can be divided, provided that the divisor is not zero, and every quotient of integers (with non-zero divisor) is a rational number. If $p$ and $q$ are integers, then $\left(\frac{p}{q}\right) = \frac{(-p)}{q} = \frac{p}{(-q)}$. Interpret quotients of rational numbers by describing real-world contexts. |
| **7.NS.A.2c** | Apply properties of operations as strategies to multiply and divide rational numbers. |
| **7.NS.A.2d** | Convert a rational number to a decimal using long division; know that the decimal form of a rational number terminates in 0s or eventually repeats. |
| **7.NS.A.3** | Solve real-world and mathematical problems involving the four operations with rational numbers. |

## 7.EE Expressions and Equations

**Use properties of operations to generate equivalent expressions.**

| | |
|--------|--------|
| **7.EE.A.1** | Apply properties of operations as strategies to add, subtract, factor, and expand linear expressions with rational coefficients. |
| **7.EE.A.2** | Understand that rewriting an expression in different forms in a problem context can shed light on the problem and how the quantities in it are related. For example, $a + 0.05a = 1.05a$ means that "increase by 5%" is the same as "multiply by 1.05." |

**Solve real-life and mathematical problems using numerical and algebraic expressions and equations.**

| | |
|--------|--------|
| **7.EE.B.3** | Solve multi-step real-life and mathematical problems posed with positive and negative rational numbers in any form (whole numbers, fractions, and decimals), using tools strategically. Apply properties of operations to calculate with numbers in any form; convert between forms as appropriate; and assess the reasonableness of answers using mental computation and estimation strategies. |
| **7.EE.B.4** | Use variables to represent quantities in a real-world or mathematical problem, and construct simple equations and inequalities to solve problems by reasoning about the quantities. |
| **7.EE.B.4a** | Solve word problems leading to equations of the form $px + q = r$ and $p(x + q) = r$, where $p$, $q$, and $r$ are specific rational numbers. Solve equations of these forms fluently. Compare an algebraic solution to an arithmetic solution, identifying the sequence of the operations used in each approach. |
| **7.EE.B.4b** | Solve word problems leading to inequalities of the form $px + q > r$ or $px + q < r$, where $p$, $q$, and $r$ are specific rational numbers. Graph the solution set of the inequality and interpret it in the context of the problem. |

| Number | Standard for Mathematical Content |
|--------|-----------------------------------|

## 7.G Geometry

**Draw construct, and describe geometrical figures and describe the relationships between them.**

| Number | Standard for Mathematical Content |
|--------|-----------------------------------|
| **7.G.A.1** | Solve problems involving scale drawings of geometric figures, including computing actual lengths and areas from a scale drawing and reproducing a scale drawing at a different scale. |
| **7.G.A.2** | Draw (freehand, with ruler and protractor, and with technology) geometric shapes with given conditions. Focus on constructing triangles from three measures of angles or sides, noticing when the conditions determine a unique triangle, more than one triangle, or no triangle. |
| **7.G.A.3** | Describe the two-dimensional figures that result from slicing three- dimensional figures, as in plane sections of right rectangular prisms and right rectangular pyramids. |

**Solve real-life and mathematical problems involving angle measure, area, surface area, and volume.**

| Number | Standard for Mathematical Content |
|--------|-----------------------------------|
| **7.G.B.4** | Know the formulas for the area and circumference of a circle and use them to solve problems; give an informal derivation of the relationship between the circumference and area of a circle. |
| **7.G.B.5** | Use facts about supplementary, complementary, vertical, and adjacent angles in a multi-step problem to write and solve simple equations for an unknown angle in a figure. |
| **7.G.B.6** | Solve real-world and mathematical problems involving area, volume and surface area of two- and three-dimensional objects composed of triangles, quadrilaterals, polygons, cubes, and right prisms. |

## 7.SP Statistics and Probability

**Use random sampling to draw inferences about a population.**

| Number | Standard for Mathematical Content |
|--------|-----------------------------------|
| **7.SP.A.1** | Understand that statistics can be used to gain information about a population by examining a sample of the population; generalizations about a population from a sample are valid only if the sample is representative of that population. Understand that random sampling tends to produce representative samples and support valid inferences. |
| **7.SP.A.2** | Use data from a random sample to draw inferences about a population with an unknown characteristic of interest. Generate multiple samples (or simulated samples) of the same size to gauge the variation in estimates or predictions. |

**Draw informal comparative inferences about two populations.**

| Number | Standard for Mathematical Content |
|--------|-----------------------------------|
| **7.SP.B.3** | Informally assess the degree of visual overlap of two numerical data distributions with similar variabilities, measuring the difference between the centers by expressing it as a multiple of a measure of variability. |
| **7.SP.B.4** | Use measures of center and measures of variability for numerical data from random samples to draw informal comparative inferences about two populations. |

**Investigate chance processes and develop, use, and evaluate probability models.**

| Number | Standard for Mathematical Content |
|--------|-----------------------------------|
| **7.SP.C.5** | Understand that the probability of a chance event is a number between 0 and 1 that expresses the likelihood of the event occurring. Larger numbers indicate greater likelihood. A probability near 0 indicates an unlikely event, a probability around $\frac{1}{2}$ indicates an event that is neither unlikely nor likely, and a probability near 1 indicates a likely event. |

| Number | Standard for Mathematical Content |
|---|---|

## 7.SP Statistics and Probability (continued)

**Investigate chance processes and develop, use, and evaluate probability models.**

| | |
|---|---|
| **7.SP.C.6** | Approximate the probability of a chance event by collecting data on the chance process that produces it and observing its long-run relative frequency, and predict the approximate relative frequency given the probability. |
| **7.SP.C.7** | Develop a probability model and use it to find probabilities of events. Compare probabilities from a model to observed frequencies; if the agreement is not good, explain possible sources of the discrepancy. |
| **7.SP.C.7a** | Develop a uniform probability model by assigning equal probability to all outcomes, and use the model to determine probabilities of events. |
| **7.SP.C.7b** | Develop a probability model (which may not be uniform) by observing frequencies in data generated from a chance process. |
| **7.SP.C.8** | Find probabilities of compound events using organized lists, tables, tree diagrams, and simulation. |
| **7.SP.C.8a** | Understand that, just as with simple events, the probability of a compound event is the fraction of outcomes in the sample space for which the compound event occurs. |
| **7.SP.C.8b** | Represent sample spaces for compound events using methods such as organized lists, tables and tree diagrams. For an event described in everyday language (e.g., "rolling double sixes"), identify the outcomes in the sample space which compose the event. |
| **7.SP.C.8c** | Design and use a simulation to generate frequencies for compound events. For example, use random digits as a simulation tool to approximate the answer to the question: If 40% of donors have type A blood, what is the probability that it will take at least 4 donors to find one with type A blood? |

| Number | Standard for Mathematical Practice |
|---|---|
| **MP1** | Make sense of problems and persevere in solving them. |
| **MP2** | Reason abstractly and quantitatively. |
| **MP3** | Construct viable arguments and critique the reasoning of others. |
| **MP4** | Model with mathematics. |
| **MP5** | Use appropriate tools strategically. |
| **MP6** | Attend to precision. |
| **MP7** | Look for and make use of structure. |
| **MP8** | Look for and express regularity in repeated reasoning. |

# Measuring Angles

**Vocabulary**
acute angle,
angle, obtuse
angle, right angle,
straight angle,
vertex of an angle

CCSS: 7.EE.B.4, Also 7.EE.B.4a and 7.G.A.2

## Part 1

### Intro

An **angle** (∠) is a figure formed by two rays with a common endpoint. You can name the angle shown ∠ABC, ∠CBA, ∠B, or ∠1. The **vertex of an angle** is the point of intersection of the two sides of an angle.

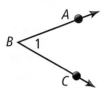

You measure angles in units called degrees (°). You can use a protractor to measure angles.

**Step 1** Place the point of the protractor on the vertex of the angle.

**Step 2** Make sure that the lower side of the angle passes through zero on the scale. Start measuring from zero.

**Step 3** Read the scale where it intersects the higher side of the angle.

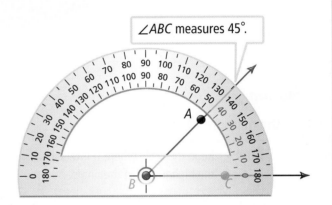

∠ABC measures 45°.

Sometimes you have to rotate the protractor to line it up with one side of an angle. The lower side of the angle should go through the zero on the protractor's scale.

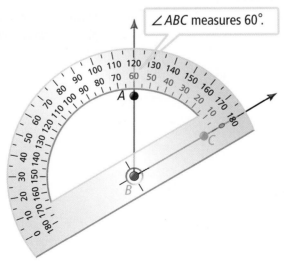

∠ABC measures 60°.

## Example  Using Protractors to Measure Angles

Find the measures of ∠1 and ∠2.

## Solution · · · · · · · · · · · · · · · · · · · · · · · · · · · · · · · · · · · · ·

Find the measure of ∠1.

Step 3  Read the scale where it intersects the higher side of the angle.

Step 2  Make sure that the lower side of the angle passes through zero on the scale. Start measuring from zero.

Step 1  Place the point of the protractor on the vertex of the angle.

The measure of ∠1 is 10°.

continued on next page >

## Part 1

**Solution** continued

Find the measure of ∠2.

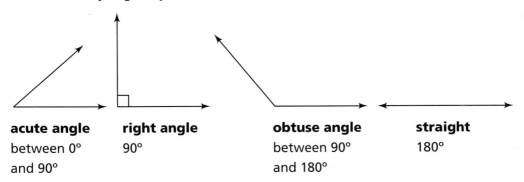

**Step 3** Read the scale where it intersects the higher side of the angle.

**Step 2** Make sure that the lower side of the angle passes through zero on the scale. Start measuring from zero.

**Step 1** Place the point of the protractor on the vertex of the angle.

The measure of ∠2 is 160°.

## Part 2

### Intro

You can classify angles by their measures.

**acute angle**
between 0° and 90°

**right angle**
90°

**obtuse angle**
between 90° and 180°

**straight**
180°

### Example  Classifying Angles by Their Measures

Classify the following angles as *acute*, *right*, *obtuse*, or *straight*.

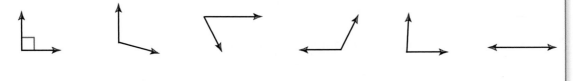

continued on next page >

# Part 2

**Example** continued

**Solution** · · · · · · · · · · · · · · · · · · · · · · · · · · · · · · · · · · · · · · · · · · · · · · · · · · · · · · · · ·

This symbol indicates that the angle is a right angle.

This angle measures 90°. It is a right angle.

This angle is larger than a right angle, but is smaller than a straight angle. It is an obtuse angle.

This angle is smaller than a right angle. It is an acute angle.

This angle is larger than a right angle, but is smaller than a straight angle. It is an obtuse angle.

This angle is smaller than a right angle. It is an acute angle.

This angle looks like a straight line.

This angle is a straight angle.

# Part 3

## Example  Finding Angle Measures Using Algebra

The measure of $\angle 1$ is $(3x - 5)°$. Find the value of $x$.

**Solution** · · · · · · · · · · · · · · · · · · · · · · · · · · · · · · · · · · · · · · · · · · · · · · · · · · · · · · · · · · ·

$\angle 1$ is a right angle, so it has a measure of $90°$.

$$(3x - 15)° = 90°$$
$$3x - 15 + 15 = 90 + 15$$
$$3x = 105$$
$$\frac{3x}{3} = \frac{105}{3}$$
$$x = 35$$

The value of $x$ is 35.

**1.** Use the protractor to find the measure of ∠BAD.

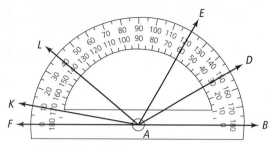

**2.** Classify the angle as right, straight, acute, or obtuse.

**3. Open-Ended**

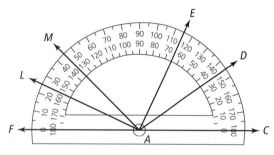

   **a.** Find the measure of ∠FAM.

   **b.** Describe how you would use the protractor differently to find the measure of ∠CAD.

**4. Think About the Process**

   **a.** Identify the angle formed by ∠EAK and ∠KAC.

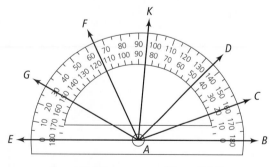

   **A.** ∠GAD        **B.** ∠EAC

   **C.** ∠EAF        **D.** ∠BAD

   **b.** The measure of this angle is ■°.

**5.** Which of the given angles is an obtuse angle?

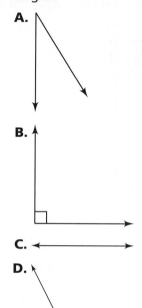

**6.** Which of the given angles is an obtuse angle?

   $m\angle 1 = 90°$        $m\angle 2 = 79°$

   $m\angle 3 = 129°$      $m\angle 4 = 180°$

   **A.** ∠3         **B.** ∠1

   **C.** ∠2         **D.** ∠4

**7. a. Writing** Use the protractor to find the measure of ∠BAD. Identify if ∠BAD is acute, right, straight, or obtuse.

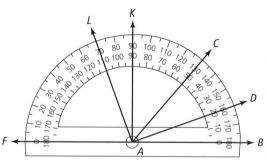

   **b.** List all angles that have the same measure.

**8. a. Reasoning** The measure of ∠ABC is 55°. Find the value of x.

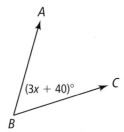

(The figure is not shown to scale.)

**b.** Explain how you can check your result for this problem.

**9. Think About the Process** The measure of ∠BDA is 31°.

**a.** What equation should you use to find the value of x?

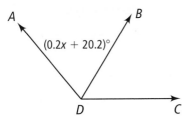

(The figure is not shown to scale.)

**A.** $0.2x + 20.2 = 90$

**B.** $0.2x - 20.2 = 90$

**C.** $0.2x + 20.2 = 31$

**D.** $0.2x - 20.2 = 31$

**b.** What is the value of x?

**10. a. Error Analysis** The measure of ∠DBC is 27°. Taniy incorrectly says that x = 37. What is the value of x?

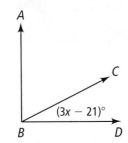

(The figure is not shown to scale.)

**b.** What mistake did Taniy make?

**A.** Taniy subtracted 21 from each side of the equation.

**B.** Taniy multiplied each side of the equation by 3.

**C.** Taniy set the given expression equal to 180.

**D.** Taniy set the given expression equal to 90.

**11.** A flagpole is at a $(4x + 2)°$ angle from the ground. Find the value of x.

$(4x + 2)°$

**12. Mental Math** The measure of ∠1 is $(5x + 30)°$. Find the value of x.

**13.** The measure of ∠CBA is $(0.25x + 99)°$. Find the value of x.

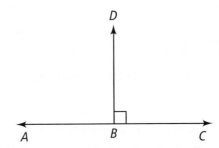

**14. Challenge** The measure of ∠CDA is 113.42°.

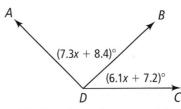

(The figure is not shown to scale.)

**a.** What is the value of x?

**b.** Explain how you can check to make sure your answer is correct.

# 10-2 | Adjacent Angles

**Vocabulary**
adjacent angles

CCSS: 7.G.B.5, Also 7.G.A.2

## Key Concept

Two angles are **adjacent angles** if they share a vertex and a side, but have no interior points in common.

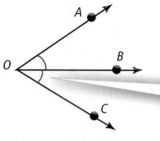

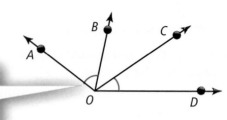

These marks on an angle can make it easier to identify a particular angle.

∠AOB and ∠BOC are adjacent angles.

∠AOB and ∠COD are not adjacent angles.

## Part 1

### Example  Identifying Adjacent Angles

Use the diagram of the roller coaster supports.

**a.** Name an angle adjacent to ∠FAD.
**b.** Name two angles adjacent to ∠BGC.
**c.** Name two angles adjacent to ∠CEH.
**d.** Name two angles adjacent to ∠ABC.

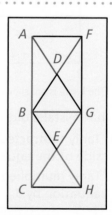

### Solution · · · · · · · · · · · · · · · · · · · · · · · · · · · · · · · · · · · · · · · · · · · · · · · ·

**a.** Name an angle adjacent to ∠FAD.
   ∠DAB
**b.** Name two angles adjacent to ∠BGC.
   ∠DGB, ∠EGH
**c.** Name two angles adjacent to ∠CEH.
   ∠BEC, ∠GEH
**d.** Name two angles adjacent to ∠ABC.
   ∠ABD, ∠CBE or ∠CBH, ∠CBG, ∠ABG, ∠ABE, and ∠CBD

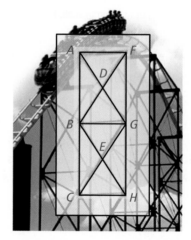

### Example  Using Algebra to Find Measures of Adjacent Angles

The measure of ∠PRS is 80°. What is the value of x?

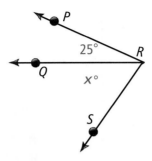

**Solution** · · · · · · · · · · · · · · · · · · · · · · · · · · · · · · · · · · · · ·

∠PRQ and ∠QRS are
adjacent angles.

$$m\angle PRQ + m\angle QRS = m\angle PRS$$
$$25° + x° = 80°$$
$$25 + x - 25 = 80 - 25$$
$$x = 55$$

The value of x is 55.

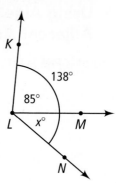
**1.** Select each angle that is adjacent to ∠w.

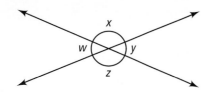

**A.** ∠z      **B.** ∠y

**C.** ∠x

**2.** Which of these is a pair of adjacent angles?

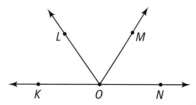

**A.** ∠KOL and ∠MON

**B.** ∠KOM and ∠LON

**C.** ∠LOM and ∠LON

**D.** ∠KOL and ∠LOM

**3.** Given the measure of two of the angles, find the measure of ∠SAP. Simplify your answer.

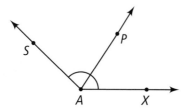

∠SAX = 136

∠PAX = 57

**4.** The measure of ∠POR is $107\frac{7}{12}$°. What is the value of x?

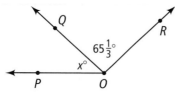

(The figure is not shown to scale.)

**5. Think About the Process**

**a.** What equation should you use to find the value of x in this figure?

---

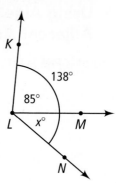

(The figure is not shown to scale.)

**A.** x − 85 = 138

**B.** 85 − x = 138

**C.** 85 + x = 138

**D.** 138 + x = 85

**b.** The value of x is ■.

**6. Think About the Process** The measure of ∠PQS is 142°.

**a.** What equation should you use to find the value of x?

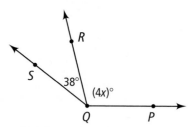

(The figure is not shown to scale.)

**A.** 142 + 38 = 4x

**B.** 4x − 38 = 142

**C.** 4x + 142 = 38

**D.** 4x + 38 = 142

**b.** What is the value of x?

**7. a. Reasoning** Find the value of x in the figure.

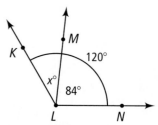

(The figure is not shown to scale.)

**b.** Explain how you know your answer is reasonable.

8. **Street Layout** Three streets, Willow, Ash, and Elm, all share an intersection, labeled O in the figure. The measure of the acute angle between Willow and Ash, ∠POQ, is 50°. The measure of ∠POR is 107°.

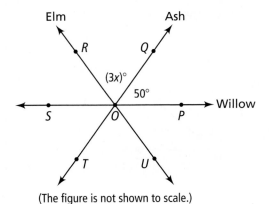

(The figure is not shown to scale.)

**a.** What is the value of x?

**b.** Explain how the measures of the angles let you check your work.

9. **Open-Ended**

**a.** Find each angle in this figure that is adjacent to ∠LOP. Select all that apply.

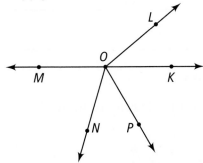

|  |  |
|---|---|
| **A.** ∠LON | **B.** ∠MON |
| **C.** ∠NOP | **D.** ∠KOM |
| **E.** ∠KON | **F.** ∠LOM |
| **G.** ∠KOP | **H.** ∠MOP |
| **I.** ∠KOL |  |

**b.** Draw an example of adjacent angles from your surroundings. Label all adjacent angles in your drawing.

10. The measure of ∠TOW is 145°. What is the value of x? Give the measures of the angles.

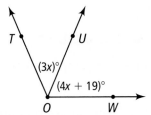

(The figure is not shown to scale.)

11. **a. Challenge** If the measure of ∠NOQ is 152.2°, what is the value of x?

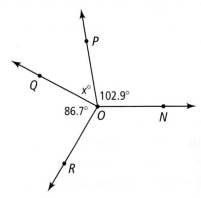

**b.** What are the measures of ∠POR and ∠NOR?

**c.** Explain how you can check to make sure your answers are correct.

CCSS: 7.G.A.2, 7.G.B.5

## Key Concept

Two angles are complementary angles if the sum of their measures is 90°.

Complementary angles that are adjacent form a right angle. ∠AOB and ∠BOC are complementary adjacent angles.

As the measures of the two angles change, the sum of their measures is still 90°.

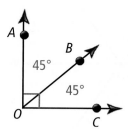

Suppose two complementary angles are not adjacent. Even though ∠AOB and angle ∠BOC are not adjacent, the sum of their measures remains 90° as the measures of the two angles change.

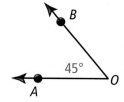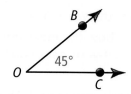

## Part 1

### Example Finding Complements of Angles

Draw an adjacent complement for each angle. What is the measure of each complement?

a. 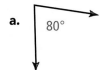   80°

b.   30°

c.   45°

**Solution** · · · · · · · · · · · · · · · · · · · · · · · · · · · · · · · · · · · · · · · · · · · · · · · · · · · · · · · · · · · · · · · ·

a.    80°   or      80°

The measure of the complement is 90° − 80°, or 10°.

continued on next page >

## Part 1

### Solution continued

**b.**

　or　

The measure of the complement is 90° − 30°, or 60°.

**c.**

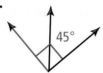　

The measure of the complement is 90° − 45°, or 45°.

## Part 2

### Example  Finding Complementary Angles Using Algebra

∠1 and ∠2 are complementary angles. The measure of ∠1 is 24°, and the measure of ∠2 is $(3x)°$. What is the value of $x$?

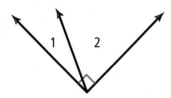

### Solution · · · · · · · · · · · · · · · · · · · · · · · · · · · · · · · · · · · · · · · · · · · · · · ·

The sum of the measures of complementary angles is 90°.

$$24° + 3x° = 90°$$
$$24 + 3x − 24 = 90 − 24$$
$$3x = 66$$
$$\frac{3x}{3} = \frac{66}{3}$$
$$x = 22$$

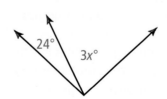

The value of $x$ is 22.

**1.** Which figure shows an adjacent complement for the given angle?

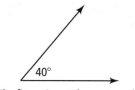

40°

(The figure is not drawn to scale.)

**A.**

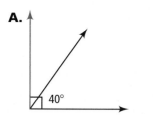

40°

**B.**

40°

**C.**

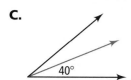

40°

**2. Think About the Process**

**a.** How do you decide if the angles shown are complementary?

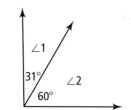

∠1

31° ∠2

60°

(The figure is not drawn to scale.)

**A.** If the sum of the angles is greater than 180°, the angles are complementary.

**B.** If the sum of the angles is 180°, the angles are complementary.

**C.** If the sum of the angles is 90°, the angles are complementary.

**D.** If the sum of the angles is greater than 90°, the angles are complementary.

**b.** Are the angles shown complementary angles? If not, what should the measure of ∠1 be so that the angles are complementary?

**A.** Yes, the angles are complementary.

**B.** No, the angles are not complementary. The measure of ∠1 should be ■°.

**3.** Find the measure of the complement of an 18° angle.

**4. Estimation** ∠1 and ∠2 are complementary angles. The measure of ∠1 is 58°. The measure of ∠2 is $10x°$. Estimate the value of x by rounding the measure of ∠1 to the nearest ten degrees. The figure is not drawn to scale.

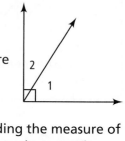

2

1

**5. Think About the Process** ∠1 and ∠2 are complementary angles. The measure of ∠1 is 58°. The measure of ∠2 is $(2x + 16)°$. The figure is not drawn to scale.

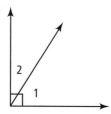

2

1

**a.** What should you do first to find the value of x?

**A.** Write an equation where the difference of the measures of ∠1 and ∠2 is equal to 90°.

**B.** Write an equation where the sum of the measures of ∠1 and ∠2 is equal to 180°.

**C.** Write an equation where the difference of the measures of ∠1 and ∠2 is equal to 180°.

**D.** Write an equation where the sum of the measures of ∠1 and ∠2 is equal to 90°.

**b.** The value of x is ■.

**6. Reasoning** The measure of ∠1 is 39°.

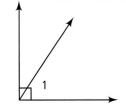

(The figure is not shown to scale.)

**a.** Find the measure of the angle adjacent to ∠1.

**b.** Explain how you know your answer is reasonable.

**7. Street Intersection** Three streets form an intersection. ∠C and ∠D are complementary angles. If the measure of ∠D is x° and the measure of ∠C is 16° greater than ∠D, what is the value of x?

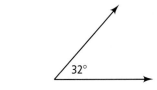

(The figure is not drawn to scale.)

**8. Multiple Representations** Select the 2 adjacent complements for the angle shown. The figure is not drawn to scale.

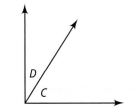

**A.**

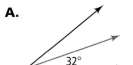

**B.**

**C.**

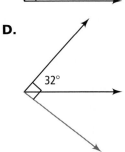

**D.**

**9.** ∠1 and ∠2 are complementary angles. The measure of ∠1 is 55°. The measure of ∠2 is 5(x + 1)°. Find the value of x.

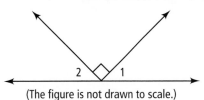

(The figure is not shown to scale.)

**10. Challenge** ∠1 and ∠2 are complementary angles. The measure of ∠1 is (−5x + 45)° and the measure of ∠2 is (11x + 21)°.

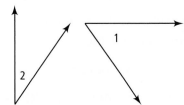

(The figure is not drawn to scale.)

**a.** Find the value of x.

**b.** What is the measure of ∠1?

**c.** What is the measure of ∠2?

See your complete lesson at MyMathUniverse.com

**Vocabulary**
supplementary angles

CCSS: 7.G.A.2, 7.G.B.5

## Key Concept

Two angles are supplementary angles if the sum of their measures is 180°. Supplementary angles that are adjacent form a straight angle. ∠AOB and ∠BOC are supplementary adjacent angles.

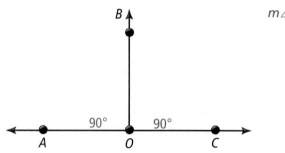

$$m\angle AOB + m\angle BOC = 180°$$
$$90° + 90° = 180°$$

Notice that as the measures of the two angles change, the sum of their measures is still 180°.

Suppose two supplementary angles are not adjacent.

Even though ∠AOB and ∠BOC are not adjacent, the sum of their measures remains 180° as the measures of the two angles change.

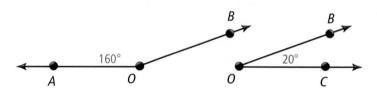

$$m\angle AOB + m\angle BOC = 180°$$
$$160° + 20° = 180°$$

# Part 1

### Example  Finding Adjacent Supplements of Angles

Draw an adjacent supplement for each angle. What is the measure of each supplement?

a.  50°

b. 165°

c.

**Solution** · · · · · · · · · · · · · · · · · · · · · · · · · · · · · · · · · · · · · · · · · · · · · · · · · · ·

a. 50°        or        50°

The measure of the supplement is 180° − 50° or 130°.

b. 165°        or        165°

The measure of the supplement is 180° − 165° or 15°.

c.          or

The measure of the supplement is 180° − 90° or 90°.

# Part 2

### Example Finding Measures of Supplementary Angles

What is the value of *x*?

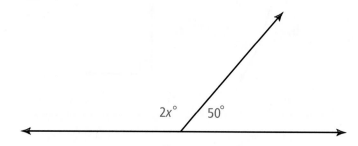

**Solution** · · · · · · · · · · · · · · · · · · · · · · · · · · · · · · · · · · · · · · · · · · · · · · · · · · · · · · · · · · · · · · · · · · · · · ·

The two angles are supplementary.

| | |
|---|---|
| **The sum of the measures of supplementary angles is 180°.** | $(2x)° + 50° = 180°$ |
| **Subtract 50 from each side.** | $2x + 50 - 50 = 180 - 50$ |
| **Simplify.** | $2x = 130$ |
| **Divide each side by 2.** | $\frac{2x}{2} = \frac{130}{2}$ |
| **Simplify.** | $x = 65$ |

The value of *x* is 65.

**1.** Which of the following is a correct drawing of an adjacent supplement of the figure? Select all that apply.

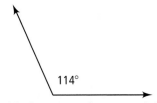

114°

(The figure is not drawn to scale.)

**A.**

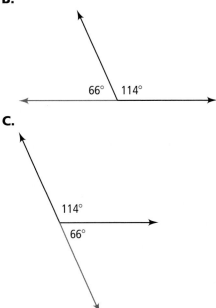

114°
66°

**B.**

66°  114°

**C.**

114°
66°

**2.** Find the supplementary angle of 128.9°.

**3.** Find the value of x using the measures of the two given adjacent supplementary angles.

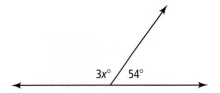

3x°  54°

**4.** If ∠A and ∠B are supplementary angles and ∠A is three times as large as ∠B, find the measures of ∠A and ∠B.

**5. a. Writing** Solve for x if the angles are adjacent supplementary angles.

   **b.** Show how to check that your value of x is correct.

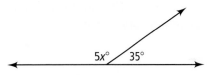

5x°  35°

**6. Error Analysis** In the figure, ∠EOG is a straight angle. Charlie incorrectly says the measure of ∠FOG is 26°.

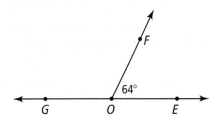

F
64°
G     O     E

**a.** What is the measure of ∠FOG?

**b.** What error might Charlie have made?

   **A.** Charlie found the complement instead of the supplement.

   **B.** Charlie found the supplement instead of the complement.

   **C.** Charlie found the measure of ∠EOF instead of ∠FOG.

**7. Street Intersection** Two streets form an intersection. $\angle C$ and $\angle D$ are supplementary angles. If the measure of $\angle C$ is 140° and the measure of $\angle D$ is two times the value of $x$, what is the value of $x$?

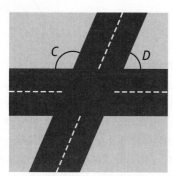

(The figure is not shown to scale.)

**8. Mental Math** The angles are adjacent supplementary angles.

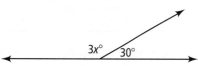

**a.** What is the value of $x$?

**b.** Find the measure of each angle.

**c.** Explain how the angle measures allow you to check your work.

**9. a. Think About the Process** Which equation should you solve to find the value of $x$ in this figure?

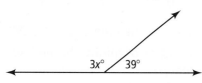

**A.** $3x° = 39°$

**B.** $3x° + 39° = 90°$

**C.** $3x° + 39° = 180°$

**D.** $x° + 39° = 180°$

**b.** What is the value of $x$?

**10. Think About the Process** The given angles $Y$ and $Z$ are supplementary angles. The measure of $\angle Z$ is 96°. The measure of $\angle Y$ is four times the value of $x$.

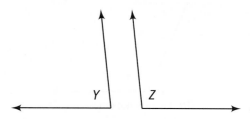

**a.** Which of the following is the correct expression for the measure of $\angle Y$?

    **A.** $(x \div 4)°$

    **B.** $(x - 4)°$

    **C.** $(4x)°$

    **D.** $(x + 4)°$

**b.** Find the value of $x$.

**c.** What is the measure of $\angle Y$?

**CCSS:** 7.G.B.5, Also 7.G.A.2

## Key Concept

**Vertical angles** are formed by two intersecting lines and are opposite each other. Vertical angles have equal measures.

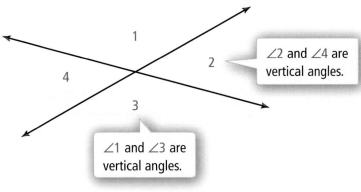

∠2 and ∠4 are vertical angles.

∠1 and ∠3 are vertical angles.

## Part 1

### Example Finding Vertical Angle Pairs

Name the angle pairs that are vertical angles.

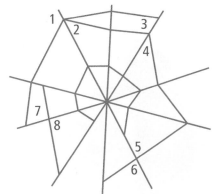

continued on next page >

## Part 1

**Example** continued

### Solution

To find vertical angles, look for angles that are formed by two intersecting lines and are opposite each other.

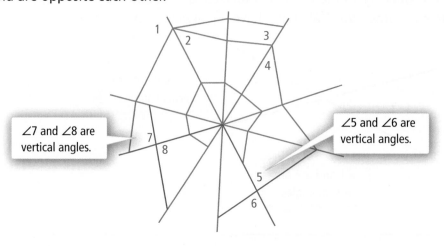

∠7 and ∠8 are vertical angles.

∠5 and ∠6 are vertical angles.

## Part 2

### Example Finding Measures of Vertical Angles Using Algebra

What is the value of $x$?

140°

$(4x + 40)°$

### Solution

Vertical angles have equal measures.

$$(4x + 40)° = 140°$$
$$4x + 40 - 40 = 140 - 40$$
$$4x = 100$$
$$\frac{4x}{4} = \frac{100}{4}$$
$$x = 25$$

The value of $x$ is 25.

**1.** Find the pair of vertical angles in the figure.

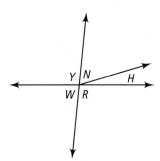

**2.** Find the angle that is vertical to ∠HJY.

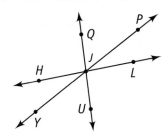

**3. Think About the Process**

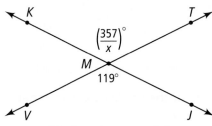

(The figure is not to scale.)

**a.** What relationship between ∠KMT and ∠VMJ should you use to find the value of x?

**b.** Find the value of x.

**4.** Find the value of x.

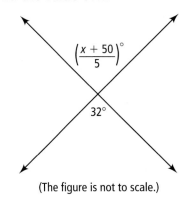

(The figure is not to scale.)

**5. Think About the Process** For the figure, ∠GKM is vertical to ∠VKX.

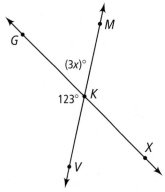

(The figure is not to scale.)

**a.** What other facts would you need in order to use this pair of angles to find the value of x? Select all that apply.

**A.** The measures of vertical angles are equal.

**B.** Adjacent angles do not share any interior points.

**C.** All right angles measure 90°.

**D.** The measures of complementary angles add up to 90°.

**E.** The measures of supplementary angles add up to 180°.

**b.** The value of x is ■.

**6.** Find the value of x.

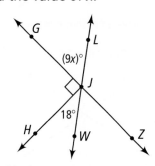

(The figure is not shown to scale.)

See your complete lesson at MyMathUniverse.com

**7. a. Reasoning** Use vertical angles to find the value of x.

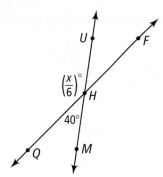

(The figure is not shown to scale.)

**b.** Is it possible to find the value of x without using vertical angles? Explain your reasoning.

**8. Intersection** While visiting your friend in the city, you see two roads that intersect as shown. Your friend tells you that the angle between the roads on the north side is 115° and the angle between the roads on the south side is (5x)°. Find the value of x.

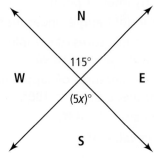

(The figure is not shown to scale.)

**9. Multiple Representations**

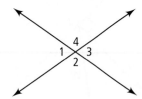

**a.** Identify the pairs of vertical angles in the figure. Select all that apply.

   **A.** ∠3 and ∠2

   **B.** ∠4 and ∠3

   **C.** ∠1 and ∠3

   **D.** ∠4 and ∠2

   **E.** ∠1 and ∠2

   **F.** ∠1 and ∠4

**b.** Draw a household item that has vertical angles. Label the vertical angles on your drawing.

**10.** Find the value of x.

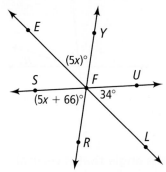

(The figure is not shown to scale.)

**11. Challenge** In the figure, ∠HSZ is vertical to ∠TSM.

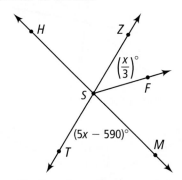

(The figure is not shown to scale.)

   **a.** Find the value of x given that m∠HSF = 130°.

   **b.** Find m∠HSZ.

   **c.** Find m∠TSM.

   **d.** Find m∠HST.

   **e.** Find m∠ZSF.

   **f.** Find m∠FSM.

CCSS: 7.G.B.5

## Part 1

**Example**  **Making Inferences About Vertical and Supplementary Angles**

Determine whether each statement about the diagram is *true* or *false*.

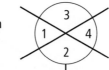

**a.** Eight angles each measure 180° or less.
**b.** If ∠4 is acute, then ∠1 is obtuse.
**c.** If $m\angle 2 = 90°$, then $m\angle 3 = m\angle 4$.
**d.** $m\angle 1 + m\angle 3 = m\angle 2 + m\angle 4$
**e.** $(m\angle 1 + m\angle 2) - (m\angle 3 + m\angle 4) = 0$

**Solution** · · · · · · · · · · · · · · · · · · · · · · · · · · · · · · · · · · · · · · · · · · · · · · · · · · ·

**a.** Angles that measure less than 180°: ∠1, ∠2, ∠3, ∠4
Angles that measure 180°: ∠1 + ∠2, ∠1 + ∠3, ∠2 + ∠4, ∠3 + ∠4
There are eight angles that measure 180° or less.
The statement is true.

**b.** ∠4 and ∠1 are vertical angles, so their measures are equal. So if ∠4 is acute, then ∠1 must also be acute.
The statement is false.

**c.** ∠3 and ∠4 are supplementary angles, so the sum of their measures is 180°. ∠2 and ∠3 are vertical angles, so their measures are equal. So $m\angle 3 = 90°$.

$$m\angle 3 + m\angle 4 = 180°$$
$$90° + m\angle 4 = 180°$$
$$90° + m\angle 4 - 90° = 180° - 90°$$
$$m\angle 4 = 90°$$

The statement is true.

**d.** ∠1 and ∠3 are supplementary angles, so the sum of their measures is 180°.
∠2 and ∠4 are supplementary angles, so the sum of their measure is also 180°.
The statement is true.

**e.** ∠1 and ∠2 are supplementary angles, so the sum of their measures is 180°. ∠3 and ∠4 are supplementary angles, so the sum of their measures is also 180°.

$$(m\angle 1 + m\angle 2) - (m\angle 3 + m\angle 4) = 0$$
$$180° - 180° = 0$$
$$0 = 0$$

The statement is true.

# Part 2

### Example Using Angle Relationships to Solve Problems

The Nazca lines are ancient lines and geoglyphs in the Nazca Desert in Peru. These lines form some vertical angles. In the diagram, $m\angle 1 = m\angle 2$. What are $m\angle 1$, $m\angle 2$, and $m\angle 3$?

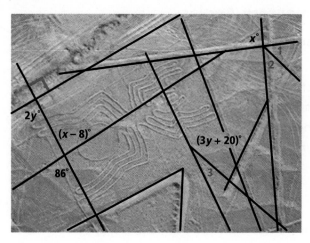

## Solution

**Step 1** Find $x$. To find $m\angle 1$ and $m\angle 2$, you need to find the value of $x$. Use the fact that the angles that measure $86°$ and $(x - 8)°$ are vertical angles.

| | |
|---|---|
| **Vertical angles have equal measures.** | $(x - 8)° = 86°$ |
| **Add 8 to each side.** | $x - 8 + 8 = 86 + 8$ |
| **Simplify.** | $x = 94$ |

The value of $x$ is 94.

**Step 2** Find $m\angle 1$ and $m\angle 2$.

| | |
|---|---|
| **Vertical angles have equal measures.** | $m\angle 1 + m\angle 2 = x°$ |
| **Substitute 94 for $x$.** | $m\angle 1 + m\angle 2 = 94$ |
| **Since $m\angle 1 = m\angle 2$, substitute $m\angle 1$ for $m\angle 2$.** | $m\angle 1 + m\angle 1 = 94$ |
| **Simplify.** | $2 \cdot m\angle 1 = 94$ |
| **Divide each side by 2.** | $\dfrac{2 \cdot m\angle 1}{2} = \dfrac{94}{2}$ |
| **Simplify.** | $m\angle 1 = 47°$ |

So $m\angle 1$ and $m\angle 2$ are $47°$.

continued on next page >

## Part 2

**Solution** continued

**Step 3** Find $y$.

| | |
|---|---|
| **Vertical angles have equal measures.** | $(2y)° = 90°$ |
| **Divide each side by 2.** | $\dfrac{2y}{2} = \dfrac{90}{2}$ |
| **Simplify.** | $y = 45$ |

The value of $y$ is 45.

**Step 4** Find $3y + 20$.

| | |
|---|---|
| **Substitute 45 for $y$.** | $3y + 20 = 3(45) + 20$ |
| **Multiply.** | $= 135 + 20$ |
| **Simplify.** | $= 155$ |

The value of $3y + 20$ is 155.

**Step 5** Find $m\angle 3$.

| | |
|---|---|
| **The sum of the measures of supplementary angles is 180°.** | $(3y + 20)° + m\angle 3 = 180°$ |
| **Substitute.** | $155° + m\angle 3 = 180°$ |
| **Simplify.** | $155° + m\angle 3 - 155° = 180° - 155°$ |
| | $m\angle 3 = 25°$ |

The measure of $\angle 1$ is 47°, the measure of $\angle 2$ is 47°, and the measure of $\angle 3$ is 25°.

**1.** Which of the conclusions about the measure of angles *w*, *x*, *y*, and *z* are true? Select all that apply.

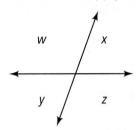

**A.** If angle *w* is obtuse then angle *z* is acute.

**B.** If angle *x* is acute then angle *y* is obtuse.

**C.** The measure of angle *w* is the same as the measure of angle *z*.

**D.** If angle *y* is acute then angle *z* is obtuse.

**2.** Which conclusion about the measure of angles *u*, *v*, *w*, *x*, *y*, and *z* in the figure shown is true?

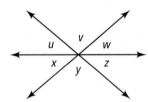

**A.** The sum of the measure of angle *x* and the measure of angle *z* is 180°.

**B.** The sum of the measure of angle *w* and the measure of angle *y* is 180°.

**C.** The sum of the measures of angles *y*, *x*, and *u* is 180°.

**D.** The sum of the measure of angle *x* and the measure of angle *y* is 180°.

**3.** A student needed to find the measure of angle *b*. He incorrectly said $m\angle b = 125°$.

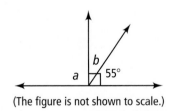

(The figure is not shown to scale.)

**a.** Find the correct measure of angle *b*.

**b.** What mistake did he likely make?

  **A.** He subtracted 55° from 90° instead of 180°.

  **B.** He subtracted 55° from 180° instead of 90°.

  **C.** He added 55° to 180° instead of 90°.

  **D.** He added 55° to 90° instead of 180°.

**4.** A dog house is at the center of a yard. The dog buried bones at each of the points. Use the geometric figure to decide which of the conclusions about the locations of the bones are true. Select all that apply.

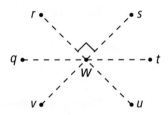

**A.** The angle from bone *s* to bone *t* is the same as the angle from bone *q* to bone *v*.

**B.** Bone *q* is 180° away from bone *s*.

**C.** The angle from bone *r* to bone *t* is the same as the angle from bone *u* to bone *r*.

**D.** Bone *r* is 90° away from bone *v*.

**5.** In the figure, $m\angle y = 22°$. Round the measure of $\angle y$ to the nearest 10° to estimate the measure of $\angle x$.

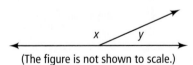

(The figure is not shown to scale.)

**a.** Estimate the measure of $\angle y$.

**b.** Estimate the measure of $\angle x$.

**c.** Find the exact measure of $\angle x$.

**6.** In the diagram, $m\angle 1 = 99°$, $m\angle 2 = (x + 54)°$, and $m\angle 3 = (y - 47)°$.

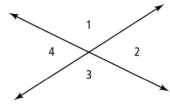

(The figure is not shown to scale.)

**a.** Find the value of $x$.

**b.** Find the value of $y$.

**7. Think About the Process** In the diagram, $m\angle 1 = (133 - y)°$, $m\angle 2 = 22°$, and $m\angle 3 = (x + 48)°$.

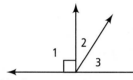

(The figure is not shown to scale.)

**a.** Write an equation to solve for $x$ and an equation to solve for $y$.

**A.** $22 + x + 48 = 90$ and
   $133 - y = 90$

**B.** $22 + x + 48 = 180$ and
   $133 - y = 90$

**C.** $x + 48 = 90$ and
   $22 + 133 - y = 90$

**D.** $22 + x + 48 = 90$ and
   $133 - y = 180$

**b.** Find the values of $x$ and $y$.

**8.** In the diagram, angle 2 is a right angle and $m\angle 1 = 30°$.

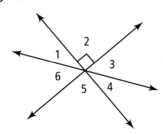

(The figure is not shown to scale.)

**a.** Find $m\angle 3$.

**b.** Find $m\angle 4$.

**c.** Find $m\angle 5$.

**d.** Find $m\angle 6$.

**9. Think About the Process**

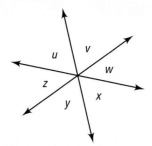

**a.** What rules can help you make a conclusion about the angles in this geometric figure?

**A.** Rules about straight angles and right angles

**B.** Rules about straight angles, supplementary angles, vertical angles, and adjacent angles

**C.** Rules about obtuse angles

**D.** Rules about supplementary and complementary angles

**b.** Use the geometric figure to make a conclusion about the angles.

**A.** The measure of angle $u$ is the same as the measure of angle $y$.

**B.** The sum of the measure of angle $y$ and angle $z$ is 180°.

**C.** The sum of the measure of angle $x$ and angle $y$ is 180°.

**D.** The sum of the measures of angles $y$, $z$, and $u$ is 180°.

**10. Challenge** In the diagram, $m\angle 1 = 64°$, $m\angle 2 = 28°$, $m\angle 3 = (w + 27)°$, $m\angle 4 = (x - 19)°$, $m\angle 5 = (7 + y)°$, and $m\angle 6 = (124 - z)°$.

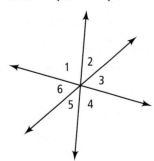

(The figure is not shown to scale.)

**a.** Find the value of $w$.

**b.** Find the value of $x$.

**c.** Find the value of $y$.

**d.** Find the value of $z$.

| # Center, Radius, and Diameter

**Vocabulary**
center of a circle, circle, diameter, radius

**CCSS:** 7.EE.B.4, 7.G.B.4, Also 7.EE.B.4a and 7.G.A.2

## Key Concept

**Parts of a Circle**

A **circle** is the set of all points in a plane that are the same distance from a given point called the center. You name a **circle** by its center. Circle *P* is shown.

A **diameter** is a segment that passes through the center of a circle and has both endpoints on the circle. The term *diameter* can also mean the length of this segment.

A **radius** is a segment that has one endpoint at the center and the other endpoint on the circle. The term *radius* can also mean the length of this segment.

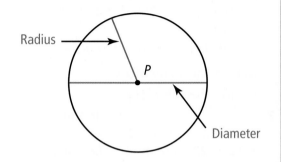

## Part 1

### Intro

You name a segment by its endpoints. Read $\overline{AB}$ as "segment *AB*." The diagram shows $\overline{AB}$, $\overline{BC}$, and $\overline{AC}$.

To refer to the length of a segment, you write the letters without the segment bar. So *AB* = 3 inches and *AC* = 3 inches.

### Example  Naming Diameters and Radii of Circles

An art class developed this logo to represent the school in an art show. Determine which segments are *radii* and which are *diameters*.

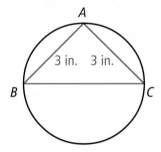

| $\overline{PC}$ | $\overline{AD}$ | $\overline{AP}$ | $\overline{AB}$ |
| --- | --- | --- | --- |
| $\overline{AC}$ | $\overline{PD}$ | $\overline{PB}$ | |

continued on next page >

## Part 1

**Example** continued

**Solution** · · · · · · · · · · · · · · · · · · · · · · · · · · · · · · · · · · · · · · · · · · · · · · · · ·

$\overline{AP}$, $\overline{PB}$, $\overline{PC}$, and $\overline{PD}$ are *radii* because each has one endpoint at the center, *P*, and the other endpoint on the circle.
$\overline{AC}$ is a diameter since both endpoints are on the circle and it passes through the center.

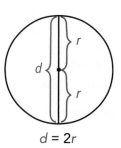

## Part 2

**Intro**

Two radii of a circle that lie on the same line form a diameter. So the length of a diameter *d* is twice the length of a radius *r*.

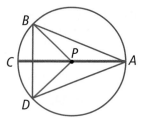

$$d = 2r$$

**Example  Using Diameters and Radii to Solve Real-World Problems**

The distance from a car to the center of the Ferris wheel is 221.5 feet. Approximately how tall is the Ferris wheel?

continued on next page >

## Example continued

### Solution · · · · · · · · · · · · · · · · · · · · · · · · · · · · · · · · · · · · · · · · · · · · · ·

The measure 221.5 feet is the length of a radius of the circle. The approximate height is the diameter of the circle.

$$d = 2r$$
$$= 2 \cdot 221.5$$
$$= 443$$

The height of the Ferris wheel is about 443 ft.

## Part 3

### Example Using Diameters and Radii to Solve Equations

The expression $3x - 1$ represents the diameter of the orange slice.

What is the value of $x$?

2.5 in.

### Solution · · · · · · · · · · · · · · · · · · · · · · · · · · · · · · · · · · · · · · · · · · · · · ·

| Know | Need | Plan |
|------|------|------|
| • The radius<br>• An expression that represents the diameter<br>• $d = 2r$ | The value of $x$ | Substitute the radius into $d = 2r$ to find the value of $d$. Then write and solve an equation involving the value of $d$ and the expression $3x - 1$. |

$3x - 1$ represents a diameter.
2.5 is the length of the radius.

continued on next page >

# Part 3

**Solution** continued

**Step 1** Find the diameter.

$$d = 2r$$
$$d = 2 \cdot 2.5$$
$$d = 5$$

The diameter of the orange slice is 5 in.

**Step 2** Write an equation and solve for $x$.

| | |
|---|---|
| **Use the expression for the diameter to write an equation.** | $3x - 1 = d$ |
| **Substitute 5 for $d$.** | $3x - 1 = 5$ |
| **Add 1 to each side.** | $3x - 1 + 1 = 5 + 1$ |
| **Simplify.** | $3x = 6$ |
| **Divide each side by 3.** | $\dfrac{3x}{3} = \dfrac{6}{3}$ |
| **Simplify.** | $x = 2$ |

The value of $x$ is 2.

**1.** What are the radii of the circle shown with *O* as the center?

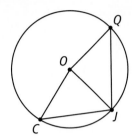

**A.** $\overline{JC}$, $\overline{QO}$, and $\overline{QJ}$

**B.** $\overline{JO}$, $\overline{QO}$, and $\overline{CO}$

**C.** $\overline{JO}$, $\overline{QC}$, and $\overline{CJ}$

**D.** $\overline{JQ}$, $\overline{QC}$, and $\overline{CJ}$

**2.** Which is the diameter of the circle shown?

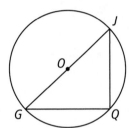

**A.** $\overline{GO}$      **B.** $\overline{QG}$

**C.** $\overline{JO}$      **D.** $\overline{JG}$

**3.** Find the length of the diameter of the circle.

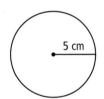

5 cm

**4. Think About the Process**

**a.** How do you find the radius of a circle when given the diameter?

**A.** To find the radius, you need to add 2 to the diameter.

**B.** To find the radius, you need to divide the diameter by 2.

**C.** To find the radius, you need to subtract 2 from the diameter.

**D.** To find the radius, you need to multiply the diameter by 2.

**b.** Find the radius of a circle with a 8 cm diameter.

**5.** Find the length of the radius of the circle shown.

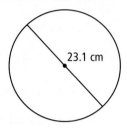

23.1 cm

**6. Think About the Process** The radius of a pumpkin is 24 cm. The expression $5x + 38$ represents the diameter.

**a.** What must you do before you can write an equation to solve for *x*?

**A.** Subtract 2 from the radius to find the diameter.

**B.** Divide the radius by 2 to find the diameter.

**C.** Multiply the radius by 2 to find the diameter.

**D.** Add 2 to the radius to find the diameter.

**b.** Write an equation to solve for *x*. Choose the correct answer below.

**A.** $5x + 38 = 22$

**B.** $5x + 38 = 12$

**C.** $5x + 38 = 26$

**D.** $5x + 38 = 48$

**c.** Find the value of *x*.

**7.**

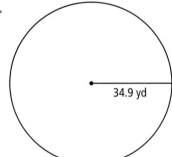

34.9 yd

**a. Writing** Find the diameter of the circle.

**b.** Describe the relationships among the center, radius, and diameter of a circle.

See your complete lesson at MyMathUniverse.com

**8.**

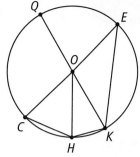

**a. Reasoning** Which segment(s) of the circle are diameters? Select all that apply.

   **A.** $\overline{EC}$          **B.** $\overline{KC}$

   **C.** $\overline{EO}$          **D.** $\overline{CO}$

   **E.** $\overline{EQ}$          **F.** $\overline{KQ}$

**b.** Explain the difference between segments that are diameters and segments that are not diameters.

**9. Multiple Representations** The diameter of a circle is 10 in. $2x + 3$ represents the radius.

**a.** Which two equations can you use to solve for $x$?

   **A.** $2x + 3 = 10$

   **B.** $2x + 3 = 5$

   **C.** $2(2x + 3) = 5$

   **D.** $2(2x + 3) = 10$

**b.** Find the value of $x$.

**10.** $\overline{AB}$ has length 19 cm, $\overline{BC}$ has length 23 cm, and $\overline{CD}$ has length 17 cm. What is the length of the diameter, $\overline{ED}$, if the radius is $\overline{AD}$?

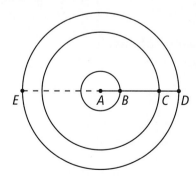

**11.** The design for a T-shirt logo is shown. The points $L$, $M$, $N$, and $O$ are centers of the circles. The radius of each circle is 9 cm. The perimeter of the square is represented by $4(6x - 36)$.

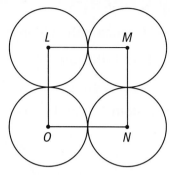

**a.** Which is an equation for $x$?

   **A.** $4(6x - 36) = 18$

   **B.** $(6x - 36) = 9$

   **C.** $4(6x - 36) = 72$

   **D.** $4(6x - 36) = 9$

**b.** Find the value of $x$.

**12. Challenge** Tennis balls are sold in packages of three. The length of the package is 20.1 cm. $4x - 20.65$ represents the radius of one tennis ball.

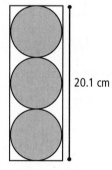

20.1 cm

**a.** Which equation can you use to find the value of $x$?

   **A.** $4x - 20.65 = 6.7$

   **B.** $4x - 20.65 = 20.1$

   **C.** $4x - 20.65 = 10.05$

   **D.** $4x - 20.65 = 3.35$

**b.** Find the value of $x$.

CCSS: 7.G.A.2, 7.G.B.4

## Key Concept

**Circumference** is the distance around a circle.

**Pi (π)** **Pi (π)** is the ratio of a circle's circumference $C$ to its diameter $d$.

**Approximations for pi (π)** $π$ is a nonterminating and nonrepeating decimal. Both 3.14 and $\frac{22}{7}$ are good approximations for $π$.

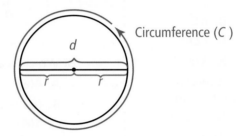

Circumference $(C)$

**Formula** The circumference of a circle is $π$ times the diameter $d$.

$$π = \frac{C}{d}$$

$$C = πd, \text{ or } C = 2πr$$

## Part 1

### Example  Understanding the Circumference Formula

Which equations describe a circle with a circumference of $3π$ m or $4π$ m?

$d = 4$ m    $r = 2$ m    $r = 1.5$ m    $d = 2$ m    $r = 3$ m    $d = 3$ m

### Solution

Use the formulas $C = 2πr$ and $C = πd$ to find which values of $r$ and $d$ describe a circle with a circumference of $3π$ m or $4π$ m.

Correct Answers:

$C = 3π$ m

$C = 4π$ m

If $r = 1.5$ m: $C = 2 \cdot π \cdot 1.5$
$\qquad\qquad\quad C = 3π$
If $d = 3$ m:  $C = π \cdot 3$
$\qquad\qquad\quad C = 3π$

If $r = 2$ m:  $C = 2 \cdot π \cdot 2$
$\qquad\qquad\quad C = 4π$
If $d = 4$ m:  $C = π \cdot 4$
$\qquad\qquad\quad C = 4π$

continued on next page >

## Part 1

### Solution continued

Incorrect Answers:

If $r = 3$ m:  $C = 2 \cdot \pi \cdot 3$
              $C = 6\pi$

If $d = 2$ m:  $C = \pi \cdot 2$
              $C = 2\pi$

## Part 2

### Intro

A measuring wheel rolls along a field. The distance it travels in one complete turn is the same as the distance around the edge of the wheel. This distance is the wheel's circumference.

### Example  Calculating Circumferences

What is the length of the tire track made by one rotation of the 20-inch wheel? Use 3.14 for $\pi$. Round to the nearest tenth.

20 in.

### Solution

The length of the tire track after one rotation is the circumference of the wheel. You know that the wheel has a diameter of 20 in.

$C = \pi d$

> Use 3.14 for $\pi$

$C \approx 3.14 \cdot 20$

$\phantom{C} = 62.8$

The length of the tire track is about 62.8 in.

# Part 3

### Example Finding Diameters of Circles Given the Circumference

The circumference for each coin is given. Find the diameter of each coin. Use 3.14 for $\pi$.

**a.**

C = 62.05 mm

**b.**

C = 69.90 mm

**c.**

C = 76.18 mm

**d.**

C = 73.04 mm

**e.**

C = 80.90 mm

## Solution

You can substitute the circumference of each coin into the formula for circumference. Then solve the equation to find the diameter of the coin.

**a.** The 10-cent euro coin has C = 62.05 mm.

| | |
|---|---|
| **Write the circumference formula that uses *d*.** | $C = \pi d$ |
| **Substitute 62.05 for C and 3.14 for $\pi$.** | $62.05 \approx 3.14 \cdot d$ |
| **Divide each side by 3.14.** | $\dfrac{62.05}{3.14} = \dfrac{3.14d}{3.14}$ |
| **Simplify.** | $19.8 \approx d$ |

The diameter is about 19.8 mm.

continued on next page >

# Part 3

**Solution** continued

Calculate the diameters of the other coins the same way.

**b.** The 20-cent euro coin has
$C = 69.90$ mm.

$$C = \pi d$$

$$69.90 \approx 3.14 \cdot d$$

$$\frac{69.90}{3.14} = \frac{3.14d}{3.14}$$

$$22.3 \approx d$$

The diameter is about 22.3 mm.

**c.** The 50-cent euro coin has
$C = 76.18$ mm.

$$C = \pi d$$

$$76.18 \approx 3.14 \cdot d$$

$$\frac{76.18}{3.14} = \frac{3.14d}{3.14}$$

$$24.3 \approx d$$

The diameter is about 24.3 mm.

**d.** The one-euro coin has
$C = 73.04$ mm.

$$C = \pi d$$

$$73.04 \approx 3.14 \cdot d$$

$$\frac{73.04}{3.14} = \frac{3.14d}{3.14}$$

$$23.3 \approx d$$

The diameter is about 23.3 mm.

**e.** The two-euro coin
$C = 80.90$ mm.

$$C = \pi d$$

$$80.90 \approx 3.14 \cdot d$$

$$\frac{80.90}{3.14} = \frac{3.14d}{3.14}$$

$$25.8 \approx d$$

The diameter is about 25.8 mm.

**1.** Find the circumference of the circle. Write an exact answer in terms of π.

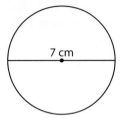

7 cm

**2.** Find the circumference of the circle. Write an exact answer in terms of π.

12 mi

**3.** Find the circumference of the circle. Use 3.14 for π. Write an integer or decimal rounded to the nearest hundredth as needed.

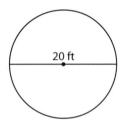

20 ft

**4.** Find the circumference of the circle. Use 3.14 for π. Round to the nearest hundredth as needed.

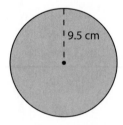

9.5 cm

**5.** Find the diameter of the circle with the circumference C = 27cm. Use 3.14 for π. Round to the nearest tenth as needed.

**6.** Find, in centimeters, the circumference of a circle with a diameter of 0.15 m. Give an exact answer in terms of π.

**7.** The distance around a meteor crater is 9,687 ft. Find the diameter of the crater. Use $\frac{22}{7}$ for π. Write an integer or decimal rounded to the nearest tenth as needed.

**8. Estimation** To protect an elm tree in your backyard, you need to put gypsy moth caterpillar tape around the trunk. The diameter of the tree is 2.7 ft. Round the diameter to the nearest foot in order to estimate the length of tape needed. Use 3.14 for π.

**9. a. Writing** What is the diameter of a circle with a circumference of 29.6 ft? Use 3.14 for π. Round to the nearest tenth as needed.

**b.** How does tripling the circumference of the circle affect the diameter of the circle? Give at least three examples to support your answer.

**10. Reasoning** Circle I has a radius of 21 meters and Circle II has a radius of 28 meters.

**a.** Find the circumference of the two circles. Write an exact answer in terms of π.

**b.** Is the relationship between the radius of a circle and the distance around the circle the same for all circles? Explain.

**11. Think About the Process** Circle I has a radius of 22 meters and Circle II has a radius of 27 meters.

**a.** Find the circumferences of each circle. Give exact answers in terms of π.

The circumference of Circle I is ■ meters.

The circumference of Circle II is ■ meters.

**b.** The circumference of Circle II is ■ meters greater than the circumference of Circle I.

See your complete lesson at MyMathUniverse.com

**12. Error Analysis** The diameter of the circle is 18 m. Tim incorrectly says that the circumference of the circle is about 28.26 m.

   **a.** What is the circumference of the circle? Use 3.14 for $\pi$.

   **b.** What mistake did Tim make?

      **A.** Tim did not multiply by 3.14.

      **B.** Tim squared the diameter.

      **C.** Tim used 9 instead of 18 for diameter.

      **D.** Tim used 36 instead of 18 for diameter.

**13. Fencing** How much fencing is required to enclose a circular garden whose radius is 22 m? Use 3.14 for $\pi$.

**14. Mental Math** What is the diameter of a circle with a circumference of 132 ft? Use $\frac{22}{7}$ for $\pi$.

**15. Estimation** Wheel I has diameter 25.4 in. Wheel II has diameter 22.5 in. Round the diameter of each wheel to the nearest inch. About how much farther will Wheel I travel in one rotation? Use 3.14 for $\pi$.

**16. Think About the Process** The circumference of one coin is 7.14 cm. The circumference of another coin is 0.33 cm smaller. Use 3.14 for $\pi$.

   **a.** What is the first step to find the diameter of the smaller coin?

      **A.** Find the radius of the smaller coin.

      **B.** Find the diameter of the larger coin.

      **C.** Find the circumference of the larger coin.

      **D.** Find the circumference of the smaller coin.

   **b.** The diameter of the smaller coin is about ■ cm.

**17.** The circumference of the inner circle is 44 ft. The distance between the inner circle and the outer circle is 2 ft. By how many feet is the circumference of the outer circle greater than the circumference for the inner circle? Use $\frac{22}{7}$ for $\pi$.

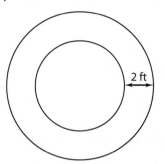

**18. Challenge** How many flowers, spaced every 4 in., are needed to surround a circular garden with a 200-ft radius? Use 3.14 for $\pi$.

**19. Challenge** A bicycle wheel makes five rotations. The bicycle travels 37.94 ft. Find the diameter of the wheel in inches. Use 3.14 for $\pi$.

CCSS: 7.G.B.4, Also 7.G.A.2

## Key Concept

The formula for area of a circle is $A = \pi r^2$.

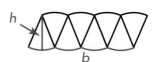

## Part 1

### Example Finding Areas of Circles

The distance of intense shaking from the epicenter of a particular earthquake to the outer edge was about 134 miles. To the nearest square mile, what was the area of intense shaking?

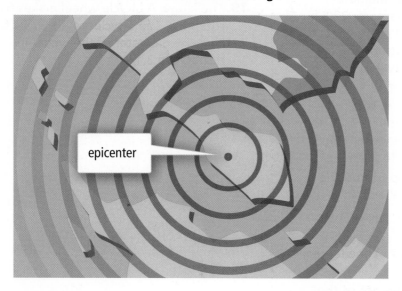

epicenter

Use 3.14 for $\pi$.

**Solution** · · · · · · · · · · · · · · · · · · · · · · · · · · · · · · · · · · · · · · · · · · · · · · · · · · · · · · · · · · · · ·

The distance from the epicenter of the earthquake to the outer edge is about 134 miles. This is the radius of a circle.

$$A = \pi r^2$$
$$\approx 3.14 \cdot 134^2$$
$$= 3.14 \cdot 17{,}956$$
$$= 56{,}381.84$$

The area of intense shaking was about 56,382 mi².

See your complete lesson at MyMathUniverse.com

# Part 2

> ## Example Finding Areas of Circles to Solve Real World Problems

The diameter of the eye of a certain hurricane was 30 miles. To the nearest square mile, what was the area of the eye? Use 3.14 for $\pi$.

Hurricane eye

## Solution ·······················································

You know the diameter of the circular eye was 30 miles.

**Step 1** Find the radius of the eye.

| | |
|---|---|
| **Diameter is two times the radius.** | $d = 2r$ |
| **Substitute 30 for d.** | $30 = 2r$ |
| **Divide each side by 2.** | $\frac{30}{2} = \frac{2r}{2}$ |
| **Simplify.** | $15 = r$ |

The radius of the eye was 15 miles.

**Step 2** Find the area of the eye.

$$A = \pi r^2$$
$$= \pi \cdot 15^2$$

*Use 3.14 for $\pi$.*

$$\approx 3.14 \cdot 225$$
$$= 706.5$$

The area of the eye of the hurricane was 707 mi$^2$.

# Part 3

## Example  Comparing Areas of Circles

One crop circle has a diameter of 40 feet and another has a diameter of 80 feet. Is the area of the larger crop circle twice that of the smaller circle? Justify your answer.

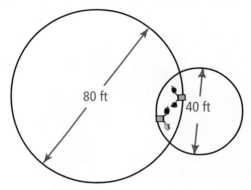

### Solution

**Step 1** Find the radius of the smaller circle.

$$d = 2r$$
$$40 = 2r$$
$$\frac{40}{2} = \frac{2r}{2}$$
$$20 = r$$

> The diameter of the smaller circle is 40 feet.

The radius of the smaller circle is 20 ft.

**Step 2** Find the area of the smaller circle.

$$A = \pi r^2$$
$$= \pi \cdot 20^2$$
$$= \pi \cdot 400$$
$$= 400\pi$$

The area of the smaller circle is $400\pi$ ft$^2$.

**Step 3** Find the radius of the larger circle.

$$d = 2r$$
$$80 = 2r$$
$$\frac{80}{2} = \frac{2r}{2}$$
$$40 = r$$

> The diameter of the larger circle is 80 feet.

The radius of the larger circle is 40 ft.

continued on next page >

## Part 3

**Solution** continued

> **Step 4** Find the area of the larger circle.
>
> $$A = \pi r^2$$
> $$= \pi \cdot 40^2$$
> $$= \pi \cdot 1{,}600$$
> $$= 1{,}600\pi$$
>
> The area of the larger circle is $1{,}600\pi$ ft$^2$.

> **Step 5** Compare the areas.
>
> Find the ratio of the area of the larger circle to the area of the smaller circle.
>
> $$\frac{1{,}600\pi}{400\pi} = \frac{4}{1}$$

The area of the larger circle is not twice that of the smaller circle. The larger circle has an area of $1{,}600\pi$ ft$^2$ while the area of the smaller circle is $400\pi$ ft$^2$.

So the area of the larger circle is 4 times that of the smaller circle.

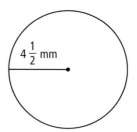
**1.** Find the area of the circle. Use 3.14 for $\pi$. Round to the nearest hundredth as needed.

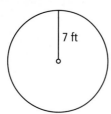

7 ft

**2.** A water sprinkler sends water out in a circular pattern. How large is the watered area if the radius of the watering pattern is 18 ft? Write an exact answer in terms of $\pi$. Simplify your answer.

**3.** Find the area of the circle. Use 3.14 for $\pi$. Round to the nearest hundredth as needed.

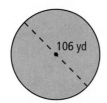

106 yd

**4. Think About the Process**

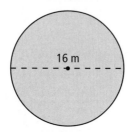

16 m

**a.** What is the first step in finding the exact area of this circle?

**A.** Multiply the diameter by $\pi$ to find the circumference.

**B.** Divide the diameter by $\pi$ to find the circumference.

**C.** Divide the diameter by 2 to find the radius.

**D.** Multiply the diameter by 2 to find the radius.

**b.** The exact area of the circle is ■ m².

**5.** A certain coin is a circle with diameter 18 mm. What is the exact area of each side of the coin? Simplify your answer.

**6.** Find the area of the circle. Use 3.14 for $\pi$.

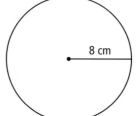

$4\frac{1}{2}$ mm

**7.** The radius of a circular sign is 12 inches. Equal parts of the sign are painted red and yellow. How many square inches are painted each color? Use 3.14 for $\pi$. Round to the nearest hundredth as needed.

**8. a. Writing** The diameter of Circle X is 18 cm. The diameter of Circle Y is 31 cm. Which circle has the greater area and by how much? Use 3.14 for $\pi$.

**b.** Describe two ways you can compare the areas of two circles. Explain when you might prefer to use each.

**9.**

8 cm

**a. Reasoning** Find the exact area of the circle in terms of $\pi$. Simplify your answer.

**b.** Explain how you could use the area of a parallelogram to estimate the area of the circle.

**10.** Circle 1          Circle 2

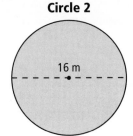

a. Find the areas of Circle 1 and Circle 2. Give exact answers in terms of $\pi$.

b. How many copies of Circle 1 would you need to equal the area of Circle 2?

c. If the diameters of both circles were given in feet instead of meters, would you need a different number of copies of Circle 1 to equal the area of Circle 2? Explain.

**11.** **Gardening** Sandra just finished planting celery, carrots, radishes, cabbage, and spinach in her new garden. The garden is a circle whose diameter is 50 yards. If she planted equal regions of each vegetable, what is the area of Sandra's garden that has carrots? Use 3.14 for $\pi$. Round to the nearest hundredth as needed.

**12.** **Estimation** A machine drills a hole into a sheet of aluminum. The radius of the hole is exactly 2.34 in.

a. Round the radius to the nearest inch to estimate the area of the hole. Use 3.14 for $\pi$. Round to the nearest hundredth as needed.

b. Find the area of the hole using the exact radius.

**13.** A radio station broadcasts from the top of a mountain. The signal can be heard up to 112 miles away in every direction.

a. How many square miles are in the receiving range of the radio station? Simplify your answer.

b. Explain two ways to find this area in square kilometers.

**14.** The diameter of a circular stained glass window is 10 feet and 6 inches.

a. What is the area of the window in square feet? Use 3.14 for $\pi$. Round to the nearest hundredth as needed.

b. What is the area of the window in square inches?

**15.** **Think About the Process** The floor of a new planetarium will be a circle with a 35-foot diameter. The material for the floor will cost $3.95 per square foot.

a. If no material is wasted when making the floor, how could you find how much the floor will cost?

   **A.** Find the circumference of the floor. Then divide the circumference by 3.95.

   **B.** Find the circumference of the floor. Then multiply the circumference by 3.95.

   **C.** Find the area of the floor. Then multiply the area by 3.95.

   **D.** Find the area of the floor. Then divide the area by 3.95.

b. How much will the floor cost? Use 3.14 for $\pi$.

**16.** **Challenge** Sarah bought a circular marble tabletop to use as her dining room table. It is 6 feet in diameter and costs $81 per square yard.

a. Find the cost of the tabletop. Use 3.14 for $\pi$. Round to the nearest cent as needed.

b. What is the area of the smallest square tablecloth that would completely cover the table?

# Relating Circumference and Area of a Circle

CCSS: 7.G.B.4

## Part 1

### Example  Approximating Area from Circumference

The world's largest coin is a giant gold coin minted in Canada. It has a circumference of about 61.9 in. and weighs about 220 lb. What is the area, to the nearest square inch, of a face of this coin? Use 3.14 for $\pi$.

**Solution** · · · · · · · · · · · · · · · · · · · · · · · · · · · · · · · · · · · · · · · · · · · · · · · · ·

**Step 1** Find the radius of the coin.

| | |
|---|---|
| **Write the formula for circumference.** | $C = 2\pi r$ |
| **Substitute 61.9 for C and 3.14 for $\pi$.** | $61.9 \approx 2 \cdot 3.14 \cdot r$ |
| **Multiply.** | $61.9 = 6.28r$ |
| **Divide each side by 6.28.** | $\dfrac{61.9}{6.28} = \dfrac{6.28r}{6.28}$ |
| **Simplify.** | $9.9 \approx r$ |

The radius of the coin is about 9.9 in.

**Step 2** Find the area of the coin.

| | |
|---|---|
| **Write the formula for the area.** | $A = \pi r^2$ |
| **Substitute 3.14 for $\pi$ and 9.9 for r.** | $\approx 3.14 \cdot 9.9^2$ |
| **Simplify.** | $= 3.14 \cdot 98.01$ |
| **Multiply.** | $\approx 307.8$ |

The area of the coin is about 308 in.$^2$.

**Example** Describing a Pattern for the Ratio of Area to Circumference and the Radius

Complete the table.

| Radius (cm) | Area (A) (cm²) | Circumference (C) (cm) | $\frac{A}{C}$ | $\frac{A}{C}$ in simplest form |
|---|---|---|---|---|
| 4 | $16\pi$ | $8\pi$ | $\frac{16\pi}{8\pi}$ | $\frac{2}{1}$ |
| 6 | ▪ | ▪ | ▪ | ▪ |
| 8 | ▪ | ▪ | ▪ | ▪ |
| 10 | ▪ | ▪ | ▪ | ▪ |

Describe a pattern in the relationship between the ratio $\frac{A}{C}$ and the radius. Then use your pattern to predict the ratio $\frac{A}{C}$ of a circle with a radius of 32 cm.

**Solution**

$A = \pi r^2$    $C = 2\pi r$

| Radius (cm) | Area (A) (cm²) | Circumference (C) (cm) | $\frac{A}{C}$ | $\frac{A}{C}$ in simplest form |
|---|---|---|---|---|
| 4 | $16\pi$ | $8\pi$ | $\frac{16\pi}{8\pi}$ | $\frac{2}{1}$ |
| 6 | $36\pi$ | $12\pi$ | $\frac{36\pi}{12\pi}$ | $\frac{3}{1}$ |
| 8 | $64\pi$ | $16\pi$ | $\frac{64\pi}{16\pi}$ | $\frac{4}{1}$ |
| 10 | $100\pi$ | $20\pi$ | $\frac{100\pi}{20\pi}$ | $\frac{5}{1}$ |

The ratio $\frac{2}{1}$ is equivalent to 2, which is half the length of the radius.

The pattern shows that the ratio $\frac{A}{C}$ for any circle is one-half the radius of that circle to one.

So if the radius of a circle is 32 cm, the ratio $\frac{A}{C}$ of the circle is $\frac{16}{1}$.

1. A circular plate has circumference 16.3 inches. What is the area of this plate? Use 3.14 for $\pi$. Round to the nearest whole number as needed.

2. A circle has circumference 18.2 cm. What is the area of the circle? Use 3.14 for $\pi$. Round to the nearest whole number as needed.

3. The circumference of a circular table top is 272.61 inches. Find the area of this table top. Use 3.14 for $\pi$.

4. The ratio of the area of a circle to the circumference of a circle, $\frac{A}{C}$, is $\frac{13}{1}$. Find the circumference of the circle.

5. The face of a clock is a circle. The ratio of the area, in square centimeters, of the face of the clock to the circumference, in centimeters, of the face of a clock, $\frac{A}{C}$, is $\frac{26}{1}$. Find the circumference of the face of the clock. Use 3.14 for $\pi$. Round to the nearest hundredth as needed.

6. **Writing** The circumference of a circle is 285.17 m.

   **a.** What is the approximate area of the circle? Use 3.14 for $\pi$. Round to the nearest whole number as needed.

   **b.** Explain how the area of a circle changes when the circumference of a circle changes.

7. **Reasoning** The ratio of the area of a circle to the circumference of a circle, $\frac{A}{C}$, is $\frac{18}{1}$.

   **a.** Find the circumference of a circle with four times the radius of the given circle.

   **b.** How do the area and the radius of a circle four times the size differ from the original circle? Explain.

8. **Mental Math** The ratio of the area of a circle to the circumference of a circle, $\frac{A}{C}$, is $\frac{50}{1}$. Find the radius and circumference of a circle with three times the radius of the original circle. Give an exact answer in terms of $\pi$.

9. **Error Analysis** The circumference of a circle is 84.65 cm. A student was asked to approximate the area of the circle. He incorrectly said the area of the circle is about 1,141 cm$^2$.

   **a.** What is the approximate area of the circle? Use 3.14 for $\pi$.

   **b.** What mistake might the student have made?

   **A.** He found the radius of the circle.

   **B.** He found the diameter of the circle.

   **C.** He used the formula $A = 2\pi r^2$.

   **D.** He used the diameter of the circle to calculate the area.

10. **Coin Collecting** You have a coin jar and the opening at the top has a circumference of 200.96 cm. You have a unique coin and the ratio of the area, in square centimeters, of the coin to the circumference, in centimeters, of the coin, $\frac{A}{C}$, is $\frac{14}{1}$.

    **a.** Find the circumference of the coin. Use 3.14 for $\pi$. Round to the nearest hundredth as needed.

    **b.** Will your unique coin fit in your coin jar?

11. The circumference of the hub cap of a tire is 81.58 centimeters.

    **a.** Find the area of this hub cap. Use 3.14 for $\pi$.

    **b.** If the circumference of the hub cap were smaller, explain how this would change the area of the hub cap.

**12. Mental Math** You purchased a circular table and you have to find out if it will fit through a doorway that is 24 in. wide. If the table will not fit, you can remove the legs from the table and turn it sideways to get it through the door. The table is measured in inches. The ratio of the area of the table to the circumference of the table, $\frac{A}{C}$, is $\frac{5}{1}$.

  **a.** Find the diameter of the table.

  **b.** Will your table fit through your doorway or do you need to take the legs off and turn it sideways?

    **A.** You need to remove the legs from the table and turn it sideways.

    **B.** The table will fit through the doorway.

**13. Think About the Process** The circumference of a circle is about 14.51 in.

  **a.** What is the first step to find the approximate area of the circle?

    **A.** Use the formula $C = \pi d$ to find the diameter of the circle.

    **B.** Use the formula $C = \pi r$ to find the radius of the circle.

    **C.** Use the formula $C = 2\pi r$ to find the radius of the circle.

    **D.** Use the formula $C = 2\pi d$ to find the diameter of the circle.

  **b.** Find the approximate area of the circle. Use 3.14 for $\pi$.

**14. Think About the Process** The ratio of the area of a circle to the circumference of a circle, $\frac{A}{C}$, is $\frac{16}{1}$.

  **a.** What is the first step to find the circumference of the circle?

    **A.** Use the formula $\frac{A}{C} = \frac{1}{2}r$ to find the radius.

    **B.** Use the formula $\frac{A}{C} = \frac{1}{2}d$ to find the diameter.

    **C.** Use the formula $\frac{A}{C} = 2d$ to find the diameter.

    **D.** Use the formula $\frac{A}{C} = 2r$ to find the radius.

  **b.** The circumference of the circle is ■ units. Give an exact answer in terms of $\pi$.

**15. Challenge** You are running a campaign and want to purchase the larger campaign pin. The circumference of Pin A is 4.46 cm. The radius of Pin B is 0.46 cm.

  **a.** Find the area of each campaign pin. Use 3.14 for $\pi$. Round to the nearest hundredth as needed.

  **b.** Which pin should you buy?

**16. Challenge** You own a pizza shop and you have a new circular box. You want to determine if your largest pizza will fit in the circular box. Both the boxes and the pizza are measured in inches. The diameter of the base of the box is 12 inches. The ratio of the area of the pizza to the circumference of the pizza, $\frac{A}{C}$, is $\frac{6}{1}$.

  **a.** Find the diameter of the pizza.

  **b.** Will the pizza fit in the circular box?

CCSS: 7.G.B.4

## Part 1

### Example  Finding Areas of Composite Shapes

Your school has a new running track. The interior will be planted with grass. To the nearest square meter, how much grass seed is needed to cover the interior of the track? Use 3.14 for $\pi$.

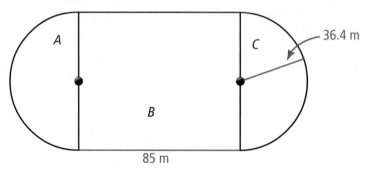

### Solution

**Step 1** Section $A$ and section $C$ are each half a circle. Combine them and find the area of one circle.

$$A = \pi r^2$$ ⟵ Formula for the area of a circle.

$$\approx 3.14 \cdot 36.4^2$$

$$= 3.14 \cdot 1,324.96$$

$$= 4,160.3744$$ ⟵ The combined area of sections $A$ and $C$.

The area of the circle is about 4,160.3744 m$^2$.

**Step 2** Section B is a rectangle with length 85 m. The width of the rectangle is the diameter of the circle. Find the area of the rectangle.

$$d = 2r$$ ⟵ Formula for diameter given radius.

$$= 2 \cdot 36.4$$

$$= 72.8$$

The width of the rectangle is 72.8 m.

$$A = \ell \cdot w \text{ or } b \cdot h$$ ⟵ Formula for the area of a rectangle.

$$= 85 \cdot 72.8$$

$$= 6,188$$

The area of the rectangle is 6,188 m$^2$.

continued on next page >

## Part 1

**Solution** continued

> **Step 3** Find the total area by adding the areas of the circle and rectangle.
>
> $$\text{Total Area} = \text{Area of Circle} + \text{Area of Rectangle}$$
>
> $$\approx 4{,}160.3744 + 6{,}188$$
>
> $$= 10{,}348.3744$$
>
> About 10,348 $m^2$ of grass seed will cover the interior of the track.

## Part 2

### Example  Finding Areas Formed by Circles

An archery target has colored scoring zones formed by five circles that share a center. The radius of the yellow zone is 12.2 cm. The width of each of the other zones is also 12.2 cm. What percent of the area of the blue zone is the area of the red zone?

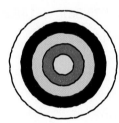

**Solution** · · · · · · · · · · · · · · · · · · · · · · · · · · · · · · · · · · · · · · · · · · · · · · · ·

> **Step 1** Find the area that includes the red zone and the yellow circle.
>
> Find the area of the circle with an outer border of red. This includes the red zone and the yellow circle in the center.
>
> $$r = 12.2 + 12.2$$
>
> $$r = 24.4$$
>
>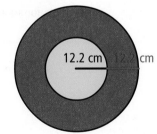
>
> 12.2 cm   12.2 cm
>
> The radius of the large circle is 24.4 cm.
>
> Formula for area of a circle ⟶ $A = \pi r^2$
>
> $$= \pi \cdot 24.4^2$$
>
> $$= 596.36\pi$$
>
> The area of the circle with an outer border of red is 595.36$\pi$ $cm^2$.

continued on next page >

**Solution** continued

> **Step 2** Find the area of the red zone.
>
> The red zone is the area of the entire red circle minus the area of the yellow circle. Find the area of the yellow circle.
>
> Formula for area of a circle → $A = \pi r^2$
>
> $$= \pi \cdot 12.2^2$$
> $$= 148.84\pi$$
>
> The area of the yellow circle is $148.84\pi$ cm$^2$.
>
> Red zone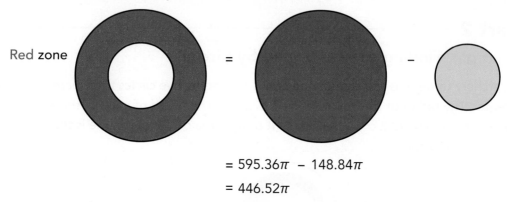
>
> $$= 595.36\pi - 148.84\pi$$
> $$= 446.52\pi$$
>
> The area of the red zone is $446.52\pi$ cm$^2$.

> **Step 3** Find the area of the blue zone.
>
> First find the area of the circle with an outer border of blue.
>
> $$r = 12.2 + 12.2 + 12.2$$
> $$r = 36.6$$
>
> The radius of the large circle is 36.6 cm.
>
>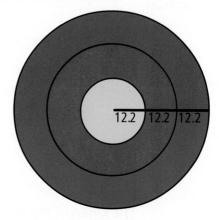
>
> Formula for area of a circle → $A = \pi r^2$
>
> $$= \pi \cdot 36.6^2$$
> $$= 1{,}339.56\pi$$
>
> The area of the circle with an outer border of blue is $1{,}339.56\pi$ cm$^2$.

continued on next page >

**Solution** continued

The blue zone is the area of the entire blue circle minus the area of the red zone and yellow circle.

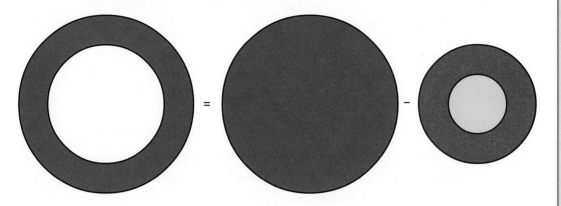

Area of the blue zone $= 1{,}339.56\pi - 595.36\pi$

$$= 744.2\pi$$

The area of the blue zone is $744.2\pi$ cm$^2$.

**Step 4** Use a ratio to calculate the percent.

$$\frac{\text{Area of Red Zone}}{\text{Area of Blue Zone}} = \frac{446.52\pi}{744.2\pi}$$

$$= \frac{446.52}{744.2}$$

Divide out the common factor $\pi$.

$$= 0.6$$

0.6 is equivalent to 60%.

The area of the red zone is 60% of the area of the blue zone.

# Part 3

### Example Comparing Areas of Shapes

You have 44 feet of fencing to make a pen for your pet rabbit. Sketch a rectangle, a square, and a circle. Label each with dimensions that use all of your fencing. Which figure gives your rabbit the least room for hopping? The most room? Justify your answers.

**Solution** · · · · · · · · · · · · · · · · · · · · · · · · · · · · · · · · · · · · · · · · · · · · · · · · ·

Rectangle

**Step 1** Find the dimensions of a rectangle with a perimeter of 44 ft.

The dimensions of the rectangle may be any two measurements that add up to 22 ft, since adding the length and the width will give half the perimeter.

The rectangle that will be used for the solution has dimensions 8 ft by 14 ft. There are many other possibilities.

**Step 2** Find the area of the rectangle.

$$A = l \cdot w \text{ or } b \cdot h$$

$$= 14 \cdot 8$$

$$= 112$$

**Rectangle (sample)**

8 ft    $A = 112 \text{ ft}^2$

14 ft

The area of this rectangle is 112 ft².

Square

**Step 1** Find the dimensions of a square with a perimeter of 44 ft.

$$p = 4s \quad \longleftarrow \boxed{\text{Formula for the perimeter of square}}$$

$$44 = 4s$$

$$\frac{44}{4} = \frac{4s}{4}$$

$$11 = s$$

The square has dimensions 11 feet by 11 feet.

continued on next page >

**Solution** continued

Step 2 Find the area of the square.

$$A = s^2$$

$$= 11^2$$

$$= 121$$

The area of the square is 121 ft².

**Square**

11 ft | $A = 121$ ft²

11 ft

Circle

Step 1 Find the radius of the circle with a circumference of 44 ft.

$$C = 2\pi r$$

Formula for circumference of a circle.

$$44 \approx 2 \cdot 3.14 \cdot r$$

$$44 = 6.28r$$

$$\frac{44}{6.28} = \frac{6.28r}{6.28}$$

$$7.0 \approx r$$

**Circle**

7 ft

$A = 153.86$ ft²

The radius of the circle is about 7.0 ft.

Step 2 Find the area of the circle.

$$A = \pi r^2$$

$$\approx 3.14 \cdot 7^2$$

$$= 3.14 \cdot 49$$

$$= 153.86$$

The area of the circle is about 153.86 ft².

continued on next page >

# Part 3

**Solution** continued

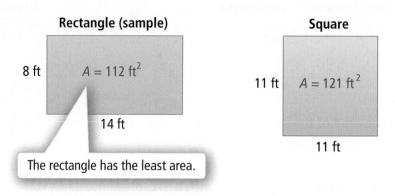

**Rectangle (sample)**

8 ft | $A = 112\ \text{ft}^2$

14 ft

The rectangle has the least area.

**Square**

11 ft | $A = 121\ \text{ft}^2$

11 ft

**Circle**

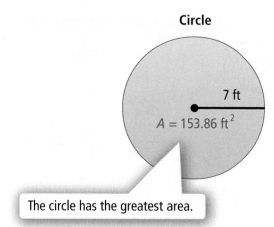

7 ft

$A = 153.86\ \text{ft}^2$

The circle has the greatest area.

A rectangle is the shape that gives the rabbit the least room for hopping. A circle is the shape that gives the rabbit the most room for hopping.

1. An oval track is made by enclosing semicircles on each end of a 42 m by 84 m rectangle. Find the area enclosed by the track. Use 3.14 for $\pi$. Round to the nearest hundredth as needed.

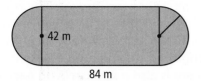

42 m

84 m

2. Find the area inside the square and outside the circle. Use 3.14 for $\pi$. Round to the nearest hundredth as needed.

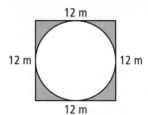

12 m

12 m        12 m

12 m

3. A farmer is putting up a fence for her animals. She originally had the fence enclosing a square area. The square was 19 ft by 19 ft. Suppose she uses the same amount of fencing to enclose a circular area. What is the area of the circle? Use 3.14 for $\pi$. Round to the nearest whole number as needed.

4. a. Find the area of the shaded region. Use 3.14 for $\pi$. Round to the nearest hundredth as needed.

   b. What would happen to the area if one of the dimensions were changed? Explain your reasoning.

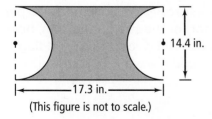

14.4 in.

17.3 in.

(This figure is not to scale.)

5. Frank needs to find the area enclosed by the figure. The figure is made by attaching semicircles to each side of a 40-m-by-40-m square. Frank says the area is 912.00 m².

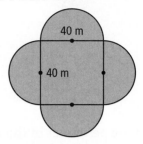

40 m

40 m

a. Find the area enclosed by the figure. Use 3.14 for $\pi$. Round to the nearest hundredth as needed.

b. What error might Frank have made?

   A. Frank only found the area of two of the semicircles.

   B. Frank did not find the areas of the semicircles.

   C. Frank subtracted the square's area from the area of the semicircles when he should have added it to it.

   D. Frank did not find the area of the square.

6. A square is 34 ft by 34 ft. There is a semicircle on three sides of the square. Find the area of the described figure. Use 3.14 for $\pi$.

7. A circular flower bed is 20 m in diameter and has a circular sidewalk around it that is 3 m wide. Find the area of the sidewalk in square meters. Use 3.14 for $\pi$. Round to the nearest whole number as needed.

**8.** The figure shows the outline of a new pier that is going to be built at the ocean. What is the area of the pier? Use 3.14 for $\pi$. Round to the nearest hundredth as needed.

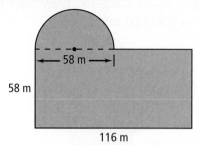

**9. a.** Find the perimeter of the figure a student has drawn in art class. Use 3.14 for $\pi$. Round to the nearest hundredth as needed.

**b.** Draw another figure that has the same perimeter as the given figure.

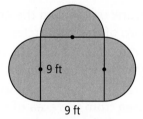

**10.** Find the area of the figure.

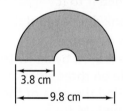

(This figure is not to scale.)

**11. Think About the Process**

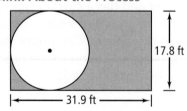

**a.** What values do you need in order to find the area of the shaded region?

**A.** The circumference of the circle and the area of the rectangle

**B.** The circumference of the circle and the perimeter of the rectangle

**C.** The area of the circle and the perimeter of the rectangle

**D.** The area of the circle and the area of the rectangle

**b.** Find the area of the shaded region. Use 3.14 for $\pi$.

**12. Think About the Process** The figure shows a picture of a track. The track consists of a rectangle which has length 120 m and area 7,200 m². There is also a semicircle on each end of the rectangle.

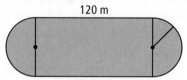

**a.** What should be the first step for finding the perimeter of the track?

**A.** Find the area of the semicircles.

**B.** Find the circumference of the semicircles.

**C.** Find the width of the rectangle.

**D.** Find the perimeter of the rectangle.

**b.** What is the perimeter of the track? Use 3.14 for $\pi$.

**13. Challenge** Jim created this stained glass window. Find the area of the window.

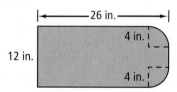

(This figure is not to scale.)

**14. Challenge** At $10.59 per foot for the semicircular portion and $2.58 per foot for the straight portion, how much will it cost to put molding around the window pictured?

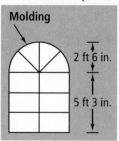

(This figure is not to scale.)

CCSS: 7.G.A.2

## Part 1

### Intro

You can draw geometric figures freehand. How would you draw a rectangle?

You know that a rectangle has two pairs of parallel segments, and each pair has the same length. Draw the first pair of parallel segments of equal length and the same distance apart. To indicate that your segments are parallel, you can draw arrows on them.

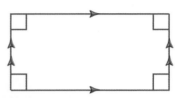

You also know that each corner of a rectangle is a right angle. Draw the second pair of segments perpendicular to the first pair. To indicate right angles, draw a small box in each corner.

Finally, to indicate that the two shorter segments are parallel, you can draw double arrows on them.

Freehand drawings are meant to show the general shape of a figure. The measurements might not be exact.

### Example  Drawing Quadrilaterals Freehand

Draw a quadrilateral for each given description:

   **a.** Exactly one pair of perpendicular sides

   **b.** Two pairs of parallel sides and no right angles

### Solution · · · · · · · · · · · · · · · · · · · · · · · · · · · · · · · · · · · · · · · · · · · · · ·

   **a.** Sample

   **b.** Sample

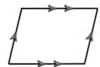

You can draw more precise geometric figures with a ruler and protractor. Draw a parallelogram with two 3-in. sides, two 4-in. sides, two 60° angles, and two 120° angles.

To draw a parallelogram, begin by drawing one of its sides. Use the ruler to measure and draw a 4-inch segment. Label the length.

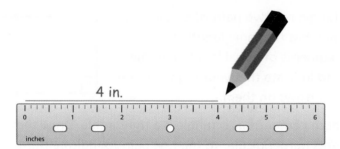

Next, measure an angle so you can draw a connecting side. Center the protractor on one endpoint of the segment and align the segment with the 0 on the protractor. Find 60° on the scale that starts with zero and make a mark to show the measurement.

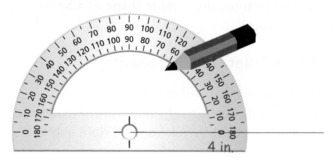

Align the ruler to connect the endpoint with the mark. Then use the ruler to measure a 3-inch segment.

Draw another 3-inch segment parallel to the first 3-inch segment. Use the endpoint of the base segment to start the new segment. Center the protractor on the endpoint and align segment with the 0 on the protractor.

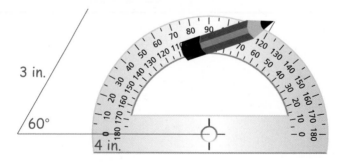

continued on next page >

See your complete lesson at MyMathUniverse.com

**Intro** continued

Find 120° on the scale and make a mark to show the measurement. Align the ruler to connect the endpoint with the mark. Then use the ruler to measure a 3-inch segment.

Use the ruler to draw and measure the top segment of the parallelogram. The opposite angles of a parallelogram are equal. Use arrows to show that the sides are parallel.

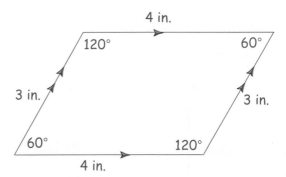

## Example Drawing with a Ruler and Protractor

Use a ruler and protractor to sketch the figure. If the figure is not possible, explain why.

**a.** A rectangle with two sides 4 in. and two sides 2 in.

**b.** A triangle with two 100° angles

**Solution** · · · · · · · · · · · · · · · · · · · · · · · · · · · · · · · · · · · · · · · · · · · · · · · · · · · ·

**a.** Use the ruler to measure and draw the sides. Use the protractor to measure and draw the right angles of the rectangle.

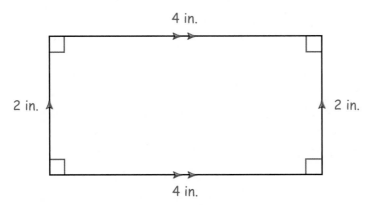

**b.** It is not possible to draw this triangle. The rays forming 100° angles will be headed in opposite directions and can never meet.

See your complete lesson at MyMathUniverse.com

### Example Drawing with the 2-D Geometry Tool

Draw the following figures.

**a.** A square with side lengths of 10 units.

**b.** A quadrilateral with one angle measure of 50° and one side length of 4 units.

**Solution** · · · · · · · · · · · · · · · · · · · · · · · · · · · · · · · · · · · · · · · · · · · · · · · · · · ·

**a.** Sample

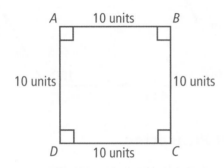

**b.** Sample

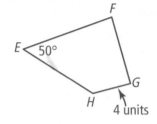

**1.** What geometric shapes can you draw that have exactly four pairs of perpendicular sides? Select all that apply.

   **A.** square      **B.** trapezoid

   **C.** rectangle      **D.** regular octagon

**2.** What geometric shapes can you draw that have exactly one pair of parallel sides? Select all that apply.

   **A.** regular pentagon

   **B.** trapezoid

   **C.** regular octagon

   **D.** parallelogram

**3.** What quadrilaterals can you draw that have two sides with length 9 cm and two sides with length 4 cm? Select all that apply.

   **A.** parallelogram

   **B.** kite

   **C.** trapezoid

   **D.** square

**4.** A four-sided sandbox has more than two right angles, two side lengths 2 ft, and two side lengths 5 ft. What geometric shape best describes the shape of the sandbox?

   **A.** parallelogram

   **B.** kite

   **C.** rectangle

   **D.** trapezoid

**5.** A friend is building a garden with two side lengths 19 ft and exactly one right angle. What geometric figures could describe how the garden might look? Select all that apply.

   **A.** isosceles right triangle

   **B.** kite

   **C.** quadrilateral

   **D.** parallelogram

**6. a.** Which quadrilaterals have exactly two pairs of perpendicular sides? Select all that apply.

   **A.**

   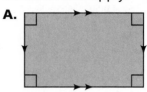

   **B.**

   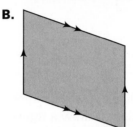

   **C.**

   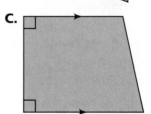

   **D.**

   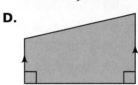

   **b.** Are quadrilaterals with exactly two pairs of perpendicular sides unique?

**7.** You are planning to build a flower box. You have two 6-ft boards and two 7-ft boards.

   **a.** Select the two different possible flower box designs.

   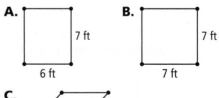

   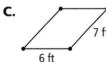

   **b.** Find the perimeter of each flower box.

   **c.** Explain why the perimeter for each flower box is the same.

**8. Multiple Representations** Which quadrilateral has one angle measure of 20° and exactly one side length of 4 units?

**A.**

4 units

20°

**B.**

20°
4 units

**C.**

20°    4 units

**9.** A triangle has two 110° angles. Why is it not possible to draw a figure with the given conditions?

**A.** It is not possible because the rays forming the angles will never meet.

**B.** It is not possible because the sum of the angles is 180°.

**C.** It is not possible because the sum of the angles is less than 180°.

**D.** It is not possible because a triangle must have a right angle.

**10. Think About the Process**

**a.** What step should you do first to draw a triangle with angles 30° and 105°?

**A.** Use a protractor to draw two sides with an angle of 135°.

**B.** Use a ruler to draw two parallel lines.

**C.** Use a protractor to draw two sides with an angle of 30°.

**D.** Use a protractor to draw two sides with an angle of 180°.

**b.** Which figure meets the given conditions?

**A.**

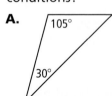

105°

30°

**B.**

30°

105°

**C.**

105°

30°

**11. Think About the Process**

**a.** How can you make different trapezoids given two sides and an angle?

**A.** You can make all four angles of each trapezoid different.

**B.** You can make all four sides of each trapezoid different.

**C.** You can make the parallel sides of each trapezoid different.

**D.** All trapezoids will be the same given two sides and an angle.

**b.** Which trapezoids have side lengths 7 in. and 5 in. and an angle of 90°? Select all that apply.

**A.**

7 in.          5 in.
     90°

**B.**

5 in.
90°
7 in.

**C.**

5 in.
7 in.
          90°

**D.**

5 in.
7 in.
          90°

CCSS: 7.G.A.2

## Part 1

**Example** **Drawing Triangles with Given Side Lengths**

The theater club at your school has three pieces of wood to make a triangle-shaped prop. The pieces of wood are 4 ft, 6 ft, and 7 ft. Three people from the set crew sketched plans for the prop. Would they all build the same prop? Explain.

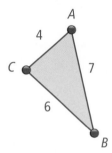 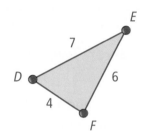 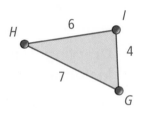

**Solution** · · · · · · · · · · · · · · · · · · · · · · · · · · · · · · · · · · · · · · · · · · · · ·

The three triangles represent the three props the crew members sketched. You can rotate and drag the triangles to lie on top of each other to see that they have the same shape and size.

First, rotate △DEF and △GHI so they are oriented the same as △ABC. Then slide △DEF and △GHI to lie on top of △ABC. △DEF, △GHI, and △ABC have the same shape and size.

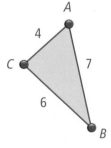 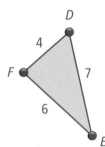 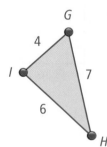

Yes, the three people will all build the same prop.

# Part 2

## Intro

Sometimes it is helpful to talk about the positions of angles and sides of a triangle in relation to each other. An **included side** is a side that is between two angles. An **included angle** is an angle that is between two sides.

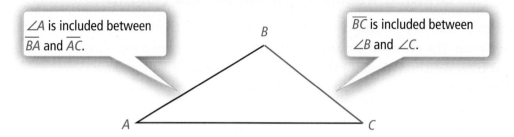

$\angle A$ is included between $\overline{BA}$ and $\overline{AC}$.

$\overline{BC}$ is included between $\angle B$ and $\angle C$.

## Example Drawing Triangles Given Two Sides and an Included Angle

Suppose a triangle has sides of lengths 3 in. and 4 in. that have an included 90° angle. Is this enough information to form the triangle? If so, is the triangle unique? Explain.

### Solution

Yes, this is enough information to form the triangle, and the triangle is unique. You can form the triangle many ways, but if you flip and turn the triangle you can see that it is always the same shape and size.

One way:

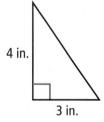

4 in.

3 in.

Another way:

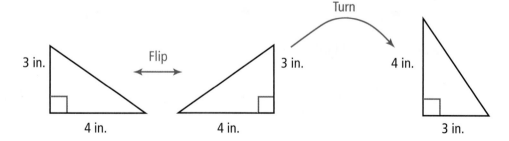

3 in.    Flip    3 in.    Turn    4 in.

4 in.    4 in.    3 in.

# Part 3

Example **Drawing Triangles Given Two Sides and a Non-Included Angle**

For triangle *ABC* with the given conditions, can you draw a unique triangle, more than one triangle, or no triangle? Explain.

$AB$ = 6 units
$CA$ = 8 units
$m\angle ACB$ = 44°

## Solution

You can draw more than one triangle with the given information. One triangle is acute, and the other is obtuse.

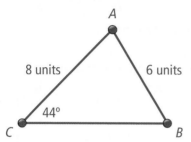
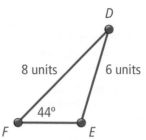

# Key Concept

The sum of the lengths of any two sides of a triangle must be greater than the length of the third side. If you can form a triangle, certain side length and angle measure conditions determine whether you can draw a unique triangle or more than one triangle.

Unique triangle:

- Three side lengths
- Two side lengths and the included angle measure

More than one triangle:

- Two side lengths and a nonincluded angle measure (except in certain cases, such as when the given sides are the same length)

**1.** Which triangle has side lengths of 4 units, 5 units, and 7 units?

**A.** 4 units

**B.** 4 units

**C.** 4 units

**B.**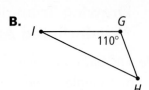

5 units

**C.** 5 units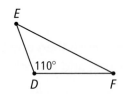

**b.** Are the triangles the same?

**2. a.** Which two triangles have side lengths of 3 units, 4 units, and 6 units?

**A.** 3 units

**B.** 3 units

**C.** 3 units

**b.** Are the triangles the same?

**3. a.** Which triangle has side lengths of 9 units and 5 units and an included angle of 110°?

**A.** 5 units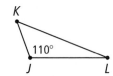

**4. a. Mental Math** Which triangle has side lengths 4 m, 5 m, and 8 m?

**A.** 4 m

**B.** 4 m

**5. a.** Which triangle has side lengths 13 cm, 12 cm, and 5 cm?

**A.** 5 cm

**B.** 5 cm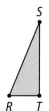

**C.** 5 cm

**b.** Draw a different triangle if possible.

**6. Think About the Process** The triangle shown has side lengths 20 in., 50 in., and 60 in.

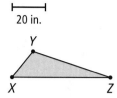

**a.** Select each process you could use to draw a triangle with the same side lengths.

  **A.** Slide the triangle down 15 in.

  **B.** Add 2 in. to each side length.

  **C.** Rotate the triangle.

  **D.** Subtract 2 in. from each side length.

  **E.** Multiply each side length by 2.

  **F.** Flip the triangle.

**b.** Which two triangles have side lengths 20 in., 50 in., and 60 in.? Select all that apply.

  **A.**

  **B.** 

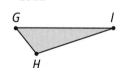

  **C.** 

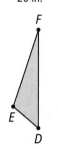

**c.** Are the triangles the same as the original?

**7. Think About the Process**

**a.** Which of these descriptions would produce a triangle with two given side lengths and a given measure of a non-included angle? Select all that apply.

  **A.** Draw one side with a given length. Use this side to form an angle with the given measure. Then draw the opposite side with the given length.

  **B.** Form an angle with the given measure. Make each of the sides of the angle have a given length. Then draw the side opposite the angle.

  **C.** Form an angle with the given measure. Make one of the sides of the angle have a given length. Then draw the side opposite the angle with the given length.

**b.** Which of these triangles have side lengths 11 cm and 13 cm and a non-included angle of 55°? Select all that apply.

  **A.**

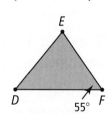

  **B.**

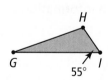

  **C.**

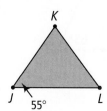

**c.** Are the triangles the same?

See your complete lesson at MyMathUniverse.com

# Drawing Triangles with Given Conditions 2

CCSS: 7.G.A.2

## Part 1

### Example  Drawing Triangles with Given Angle Measures

Form a triangle with angle measures 60°, 60°, and 60°. Is the triangle unique? If so, explain why. If not, provide a counterexample.

#### Solution

The triangle is not unique. You can form more than one triangle that has the angle measures 60°, 60°, and 60°. The side lengths can vary.

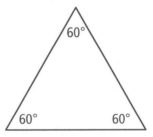

## Part 2

### Example  Drawing Triangles Given Two Angles and an Included Side

A company sells triangle-shaped pennants for school sports teams. They provide the manufacturer with the following information for making the pennants. Two angles measure 65° and their included side is 12 in.

Is this enough information to be sure all pennants are the same? Explain.

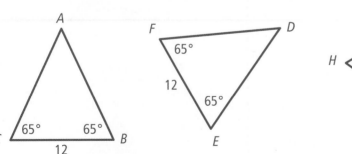

continued on next page >

See your complete lesson at MyMathUniverse.com

## Part 2

**Example** continued

**Solution** · · · · · · · · · · · · · · · · · · · · · · · · · · · · · · · · · · · · · · · · · · · · · · · · · · · · · · · · ·

The three triangles represent three pennants, each having two angles
measuring 65° and an included side measuring 12 in. You can rotate
△DEF and △GHI so that they are oriented the same as △ABC. You can
rotate △DEF and △GHI so they are oriented the same as △ABC.

△DEF, △GHI, △ABC and have the same shape and size.

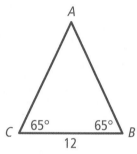 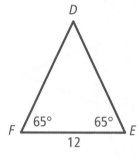 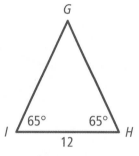

Yes, the given information is enough to make sure the pennants are all the
same size.

## Part 3

**Example** **Drawing Triangles Given Two Angles and a
Non-Included Side**

You are assembling a cardboard net
to fold up into a box that has the
shape of a square pyramid. You start
with the parts shown at the right.
Using the given information, can you
be sure that you can make all of the
other triangle pieces the same size as
the given triangle? Explain.

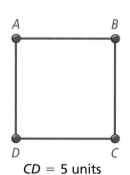 

**Solution** · · · · · · · · · · · · · · · · · · · · · · · · · · · · · · · · · · · · · · · · · · · · · · · · · · · · · · · · ·

To make a net of a square pyramid, you need to attach a base of the
triangle to the square. You are given two angle measures of the triangle.
Since the square has side length 5 units, the triangle base length will also be
5 units. So, you know the measures of two angles and a non-included side.

continued on next page >

### Solution continued

Any triangle you try to form with these measurements is exactly the same (unique), as long as the position of the known side is the same in relation to the known angles. So, based on what you know about the given triangle, you can make sure that you make all the other triangle pieces the same.

A net of a square pyramid is a square with four triangles as shown.

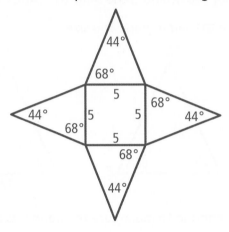

## Key Concept

The angle measures of a triangle must add up to 180°. If you can form a triangle, certain angle measure and side length conditions determine whether you can draw a unique triangle or more than one triangle.

Unique triangle:

- Two angle measures and the included side length
- Two angle measures and a nonincluded side length

More than one triangle:

- Three angle measures

**1.** Which different triangles have angle measures of 90°, 25°, and 65°? Select all that apply.

**A.**     **B.**

**C.**     **D.**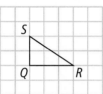

**2. a.** Form triangles named *QRS* where $m\angle QSR = 85°$, $m\angle SQR = 60°$, and $QR = 3$ units. Select all that apply.

**A.**

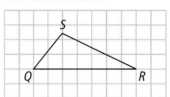

**B.**

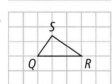

**C.**

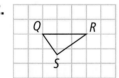

**D.**

**b.** Are these triangles unique? Why or why not?

**3. a.** For a project, you need to make a triangular flag using the given information about triangle *DEF*. In triangle *DEF*, $m\angle FDE = 60°$, $m\angle FED = 40°$, and $DE = 6$ inches. Each square on the grid is equal to 1 square inch.

**A.**

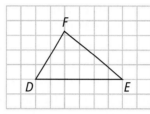

**B.**

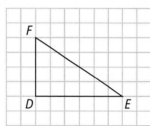

**C.**

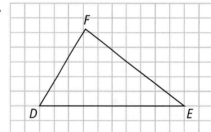

**b.** Is this triangle unique? Why or why not?

**4. Think About the Process**

**a.** How can you make different triangles with the same angle measures?

 **A.** You can make triangles with the same angle measures but different side lengths.

 **B.** It is not possible to make different triangles with the same angle measures.

 **C.** You can make triangles with the same angle measures and the same side lengths.

 **D.** You can make triangles with the same side lengths but different angle measures.

**b.** Which triangles have angle measures 90°, 30°, and 60°? Select all that apply.

 **A.**

 **B.**

 **C.**

 **D.** ◹

**5. Think About the Process**

**a.** How can you make triangles with two of the angle measures and one side length the same?

 **A.** You can make the two other side lengths unique in each triangle.

 **B.** You cannot make more than one triangle with two of the angle measures and one side length the same.

 **C.** You can make the third angle unique in each triangle.

 **D.** You can draw more than one orientation of the triangle by rotating the triangle.

**b.** Form triangles named *XYZ* where $m\angle XZY = 85°$, $m\angle ZXY = 45°$, and $XY = 5$ units. Select all that apply.

**A.**
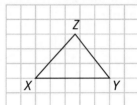

**B.**
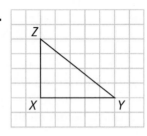

**C.**
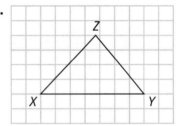

**D.**
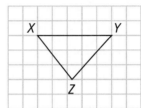

**6. a.** **Challenge** Draw triangles *QRS* where $m\angle QSR = 100°$, $m\angle SQR = 60°$, and $QR = 8$ units.

**b.** Are the triangles you drew the same?

**c.** If the triangles are the same, explain one way that two triangles can look different but be the same. If the triangles are not the same, draw another different triangle with the same measurements as *QRS*.

CCSS: 7.G.A.3

## Key Concept

A **cross section** is the intersection of a three-dimensional figure and a plane. You can think of a cross section as a two-dimensional slice of the figure.

**Vertical Slice I**  A vertical slice can be parallel to the left and right faces. The cross section always has the same shape and dimensions as these faces.

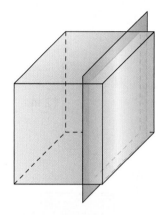

**Vertical Slice II**  A vertical slice can also be parallel to the front and back faces. The cross section always has the same shape and dimensions as these faces.

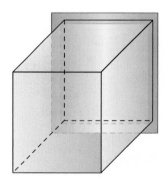

**Horizontal Slice**  A horizontal slice is parallel to the bases. The cross section always has the same shape and dimensions as the bases.

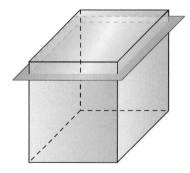

## Example Identifying Cross Sections of Rectangular Prisms

Match each cross section below with its corresponding rectangular prism and slicing plane. (Figures are not drawn to scale.)

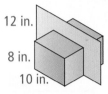

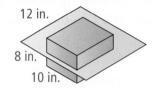

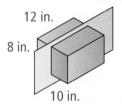

**a.**

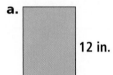

**b.**

**c.**

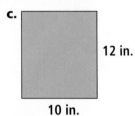

## Solution

**a.** Slice the rightmost prism at the vertical intersecting plane and pull the two halves apart. The cross section is a rectangle with dimensions 12 in. by 8 in.

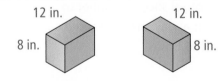

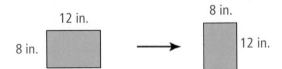

continued on next page >

**Solution** continued

**b.** Slice the leftmost prism at the vertical intersecting plane and pull the two halves apart. The cross section is a rectangle with dimensions 8 in. by 10 in.

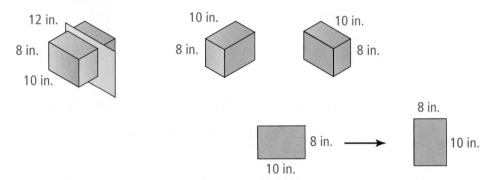

**c.** Slice the middle prism at the horizontal intersecting plane and pull the two halves apart. The cross section is a rectangle with dimensions 12 in. by 10 in.

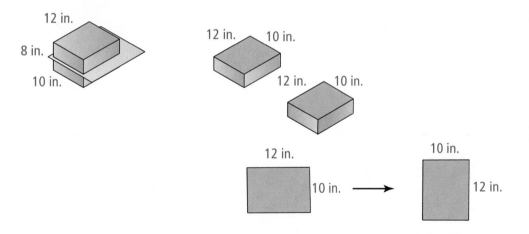

# Part 2

## Intro

How do you draw cross sections?

Horizontal Cross Section

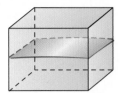

Vertical Cross Section

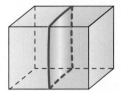

## Example  Identifying Cross Sections of Rectangular Prisms

Draw and describe a cross section formed by a plane that slices a cube as follows.

**a.** The plane is vertical and intersects the right and left faces.

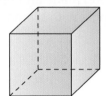

**b.** The plane is horizontal and intersects the front and back faces.

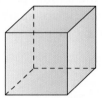

## Solution

**a.** Sample

The cross section is a vertical square that has the same shape and side lengths as the front and back faces of the cube.

**b.** Sample

The cross section is a horizontal square that has the same shape and side lengths as the top and bottom faces of the cube.

**1.** What are the dimensions of the vertical cross section of the right rectangular prism? Note that the figure is not drawn to scale.

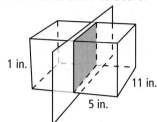

1 in.
11 in.
5 in.

**A.**
11 in.
1 in.

**B.**
11 in.
5 in.

**C.**
5 in.
1 in.

**2.** What are the dimensions of the horizontal cross section of the right rectangular prism? Note that the figure is not drawn to scale.

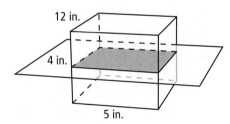

12 in.
4 in.
5 in.

**A.**
5 in.
4 in.

**B.**
12 in.
5 in.

**C.**
12 in.
5 in.

**3.** What are the dimensions of the vertical cross section formed when slicing the right rectangular prism with the plane? Note that the figure is not drawn to scale.

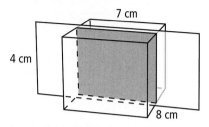

7 cm
4 cm
8 cm

**A.** 7 cm × 8 cm

**B.** 4 cm × 7 cm

**C.** 4 cm × 8 cm

**4.** Which is the best description of the vertical cross section of the rectangular prism? Note that the figure is not drawn to scale.

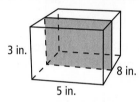

3 in.
8 in.
5 in.

**A.** The vertical cross section is a right rectangular prism.

**B.** The vertical cross section is a rectangle.

**C.** The vertical cross section is a square.

**5. a.** Estimation Which of the following are the correct dimensions of the horizontal cross section? Note that the figure is not drawn to scale.

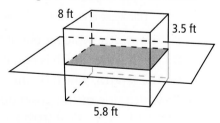

8 ft
3.5 ft
5.8 ft

**A.** 5.8 ft × 8 ft

**B.** 3.5 ft × 8 ft

**C.** 3.5 ft × 5.8 ft

**b.** Estimate the area of the cross section.

**6. Estimation**

**a.** Which of the following two-dimensional figures shows the dimensions of the vertical cross section of the right rectangular prism shown?

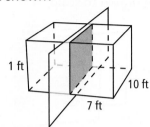

(The figure is not drawn to scale.)

**A.**

10 ft / 1 ft

**B.**

7 ft / 1 ft

**C.**
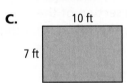
10 ft / 7 ft

**b.** How many entire cross sections do you need to cover an area of 25 ft²?

**7. Think About the Process**

**a.** To which side of the prism does side *x* of the vertical cross section correspond?

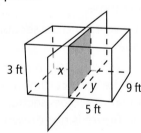

(The figure is not drawn to scale.)

**A.** The width, which is equal to 5 ft
**B.** The height, which is equal to 3 ft
**C.** The length, which is equal to 9 ft

**b.** To which side of the prism does side *y* of the vertical cross section correspond?

**A.** The length, which is equal to 9 ft
**B.** The width, which is equal to 5 ft
**C.** The height, which is equal to 3 ft

**c.** What are the dimensions of the vertical cross section?

**A.** 3 ft × 5 ft
**B.** 3 ft × 9 ft
**C.** 5 ft × 9 ft

**8. Think About the Process**

**a.** The horizontal cross section has the same shape and dimensions as which sides of the right rectangular prism? Select all that apply.

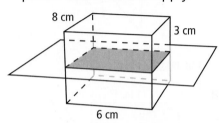

(The figure is not drawn to scale.)

**A.** Top face
**B.** Left face
**C.** Back face
**D.** Bottom face
**E.** Front face
**F.** Right face

**b.** What are the dimensions?

**A.** 6 cm × 3 cm
**B.** 8 cm × 3 cm
**C.** 6 cm × 8 cm

**9. Challenge** A right rectangular prism has length 104 in. and width 66 in. The prism is 54 in. tall.

**a.** What are the dimensions of a horizontal cross section of the prism?

**A.** 54 in. × 104 in.
**B.** 66 in. × 104 in.
**C.** 54 in. × 66 in.

**b.** How could the dimension of a horizontal cross section change? Explain.

# 2-D Slices of Right Rectangular Pyramids

CCSS: 7.G.A.3

## Key Concept

If you make any horizontal slice, or a vertical slice through the vertex of a rectangular pyramid, the resulting cross section is a rectangle or a triangle.

**Horizontal Slice** If you make any horizontal slice of a rectangular pyramid, the resulting cross section, or slice, is a rectangle. The size of the rectangle depends on the distance of the slice from the base.

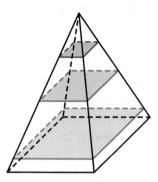

Note that these rectangles all have the same shape, but are different sizes.

**Vertical Slice** If you make a vertical slice of a rectangular pyramid through the vertex, the resulting cross section, or slice, is an isosceles triangle. The base of the triangle is equal in length to an edge of the rectangular base. The height of the triangle is equal to the height of the pyramid.

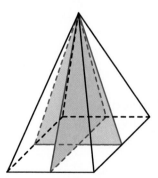
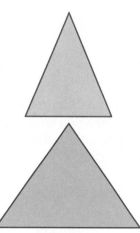

Note that these triangles have the same height, but are different lengths of bases.

## Example  Identifying Cross Sections of Square Pyramids

Match the cross section with the rectangular pyramid and the plane slicing it.

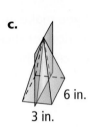

2 in.
1 in.

6 in.

3 in.

**a.** 6 in.
3 in.

**b.** 6 in.
3 in.

**c.** 6 in.
3 in.

### Solution

**a.** The first slice is a vertical slice through the vertex of the pyramid. The resulting cross section is an isosceles triangle with a base equal in length to the edge of the rectangular base that it is parallel to, 3 inches.

6 in.
3 in.

3 in.

**b.** The second slice is a horizontal slice about one-third of the way down from the vertex of the pyramid. The resulting cross section is a rectangle that is the same shape as the rectangular base of the pyramid, but smaller in size.

6 in.
3 in.

2 in.
1 in.

**c.** The third slice is a different vertical slice through the vertex of the pyramid. The resulting cross section is an isosceles triangle with a base equal in length to the edge of the rectangular base that it is parallel to, 6 inches.

6 in.
3 in.

6 in.

# Part 2

**Example** Drawing Cross Sections of Square Pyramids

Draw and describe a cross section formed by a plane that slices a rectangular pyramid as follows.

**a.** The plane is vertical and intersects the front face and the vertex of the pyramid.

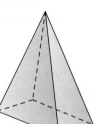

**b.** The plane is horizontal and halfway up the pyramid.

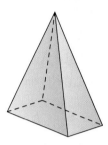

**Solution**

**a.** Answers may vary. Sample is shown.

The vertical cross section is an isosceles triangle that has a base length equal to the width of the rectangular base and a height that is the same as the height of the pyramid.

**b.**

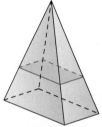

The horizontal cross section is a rectangle that has dimensions that are less than the dimensions of the rectangular base of the pyramid.

1. Which figure shows the cross section of the figure below? Note the figure is not drawn to scale.

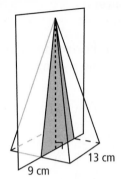

13 cm

9 cm

**A.**

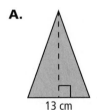

13 cm

**B.**

9 cm

2. The base of a right rectangular pyramid has length 12 cm, width 6 cm, and height 14 cm. Which statement best describes the cross section formed by a horizontal plane that intersects the faces of the pyramid above the base?

**A.** a rectangle with length greater than 12 cm and width greater than 6 cm

**B.** an equilateral triangle with base length less than 12 cm and height less than 14 cm

**C.** an isosceles triangle with base length less than 6 cm and height less than 14 cm

**D.** a rectangle with length less than 12 cm and width less than 6 cm

3. Describe a cross section formed by a vertical plane that intersects the edge of the front and right faces, but not the vertex, of the pyramid shown. The figure is not drawn to scale.

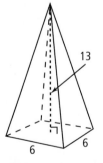

13

6     6

**A.** An isosceles triangle with height less than the height of the pyramid

**B.** A square with side length less than the side length of the base of the pyramid

**C.** An isosceles triangle with height greater than the height of the pyramid

**D.** A square with side length equal to the side length of the base of the pyramid

4. **a.** Writing  Which figure could show the cross section of the figure below? Note the figure is not drawn to scale.

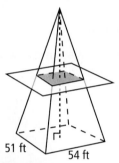

51 ft     54 ft

**A.**

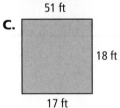

72 ft

68 ft

**B.**

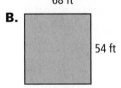

54 ft

51 ft

**C.**

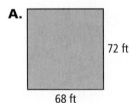

18 ft

17 ft

**b.** Write a situation that could be modeled using this figure. Interpret the cross section in the context of your situation.

**5. Mental Math** The area of the cross section shown is 52 yd². What is the length of the unknown side? The figure is not drawn to scale.

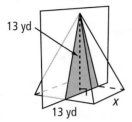

**6. Think About the Process**

**a.** What is always true about the dimensions of a horizontal cross section of a rectangular pyramid?

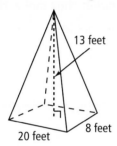

(The figure is not drawn to scale.)

**A.** The length and width are equal to the length and the width of the base.

**B.** The length and width are less than the length and width of the base.

**C.** The width is less than the width of the base and the length is equal to the length of the base.

**D.** The length is less than the length of the base and the width is equal to the width of the base.

**b.** Which figure below could describe the cross section formed by a horizontal plane that intersects the faces of the pyramid shown?

**A.** A rectangle with area 40 square feet

**B.** A rectangle with area 360 square feet

**C.** A rectangle with area 160 square feet

**7. Think About the Process** The figure is not drawn to scale.

**a.** Which statement could describe a cross section formed by a vertical plane that intersects the edge of the right and front faces but not the vertex of the rectangular pyramid shown?

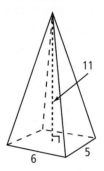

**A.** An isosceles triangle with base length less than the length of the pyramid and height equal to the height of the pyramid

**B.** A scalene triangle with side lengths less than the length and width of the base of the pyramid

**C.** An isosceles triangle with height less than the height of the pyramid and base length that can be less than, greater than, or equal to the length of the pyramid

**b.** How does the cross section described in part (a) compare to the cross section formed by a vertical plane that intersects the vertex of the pyramid and a diagonal of the base?

**A.** The cross section that does not intersect the vertex is smaller than the cross section that intersects the vertex.

**B.** The cross section that does not intersect the vertex is larger than the cross section that intersects the vertex.

**C.** The cross sections have the same dimensions.

CCSS: 7.G.A.2, 7.G.A.3, 7.G.B.6

## Part 1

### Example  Sketching Shapes from Descriptions

A jeweler left instructions for an assistant. Sketch two possible frames the assistant could make. Then choose one and describe any extra information the jeweler would need to provide to guarantee that the assistant makes that exact shape.

Frame for gemstone necklace

Cut a frame with five sides. The top of the frame where the chain passes through should have a 108° angle.

The two sides that make the 108° angle should be $\frac{1}{2}$ inch long.

### Solution · · · · · · · · · · · · · · · · · · · · · · · · · · · · · · · · · · · · · · · · · · · · · · · ·

Sample Answer:

Frame 1

The jeweler would add that all angles equal 108° and all sides are $\frac{1}{2}$ inch in length.

Frame 2

The jeweler left out the remaining angles of the frame. The base of the figure has a pair of 90° angles and the remaining angles are a pair of 126° angles.

# Part 2

### Example Using Slices to Solve Problems

A carpenter wants to cut the wood box shown into a smaller box, one with dimensions 12 in. × 8 in. × 4 in. About how many square inches of wood does the carpenter need to close the side of the new box?

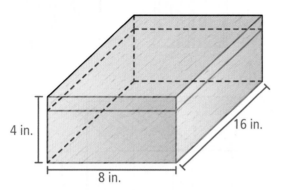

4 in.

16 in.

8 in.

**Solution** · · · · · · · · · · · · · · · · · · · · · · · · · · · · · · · · · · · · · · · · · · · ·

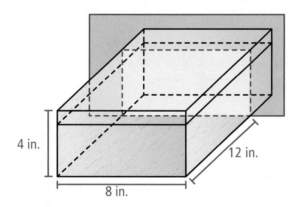

4 in.

12 in.

8 in.

A slice is reducing the length of this rectangular prism. In this case, the slice is parallel to the faces that have dimensions 4 in. by 8 in. So, the area of the new side is equal to the area of the original side.

$$\text{Area} = bh$$

$$= 8 \cdot 4$$

$$= 32$$

The carpenter will need about 32 square inches of wood to close the side of the new box.

# Part 3

### Example Identifying Slices of Complex Figures

Match each cross section with the horizontal plane that produces it.

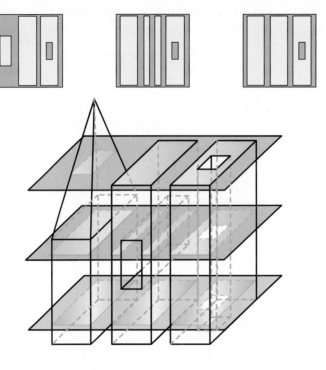

## Solution

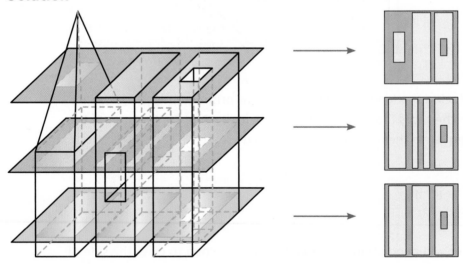

**1.** A graphic designer is asked to sketch a pendant of a dark gray isosceles triangle on top of a light gray square. The base of the triangle and the side of the square are 10 units in length. Note that the figures are not drawn to scale. Which figures represent possible sketches of the pendant? Select all that apply.

**A.**  **B.**

**C.** 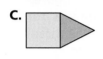 **D.**

**E.** 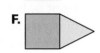 **F.**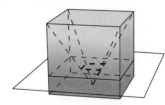

**2.** The figure shown is a design for a trash barrel. Before the trash barrel can be made, the designer first has to submit a sketch of a cross section. Which figure is the sketch of the cross section shown?

**A.**  **B.**

**C.**

**3.** A 0.75-in.-thick slice is cut from a stick of butter as shown. Note that the figure is not drawn to scale.

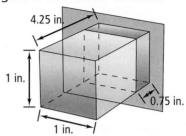

4.25 in.

1 in.

0.75 in.

1 in.

**a.** Which figure represents the cross section?

**A.** 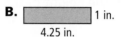 0.75 in.
4.25 in.

**B.** 1 in.
4.25 in.

**C.** 1 in.
1 in.

**b.** What is the area of the cross section?

**4.** A kite maker receives an order. The customer asks that the kite have a gray isosceles triangle that points upward and a black isosceles triangle below it that points downward. Both triangles have the same base, 12 units. The gray triangle has height 11 units and the black triangle has height 33 units. Make a figure that represents the design of the kite. Note that the figures are not drawn to scale.

**A.** **B.**

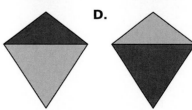

**C.** **D.**

**5. Think About the Process**

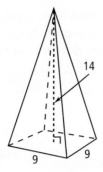

(The figure is not drawn to scale).

**a.** What is the best way to slice the figure shown so that you have two identical pieces?

  **A.** Cut a horizontal slice at the center of the height of the pyramid. This will give a square cross section.

  **B.** Cut a vertical slice from the top of the pyramid. This will give a triangular cross section.

**b.** Which figure represents the cross section of the pyramid cut into two identical pieces?

  **A.**

  **B.**

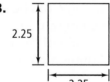

**c.** The area of the cross section is ■ square units.

**6. Think About the Process**

   **Horizontal Slice**   **Vertical Slice**

**a.** How can you use a horizontal and a vertical slice to draw a three-dimensional figure? What information do they give?

  **A.** The horizontal slice gives a top or bottom view of the three-dimensional figure. A vertical slice gives a front or back view of the three-dimensional figure.

  **B.** The horizontal slice gives a front or back view of the three-dimensional figure. A vertical slice gives a top or bottom view of the three-dimensional figure.

**b.** Which figure is represented by the horizontal and vertical slices shown?

  **A.**

  **B.**

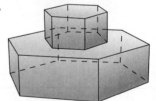

  **C.**

CCSS: 7.G.B.6

**Vocabulary**
lateral area of a prism, surface area of a cube, surface area of a prism

## Key Concept

The **lateral area of a prism** is the sum of the areas of the lateral faces.

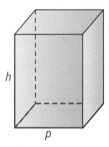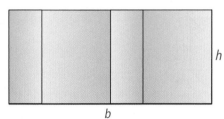

Lateral Area = perimeter of base · height of prism

$$\text{L. A.} = ph$$

The **surface area of a prism** is the sum of the lateral area and the areas of its bases.

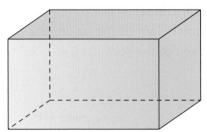

Surface Area = Lateral Area + 2 · area of a base

$$\text{S. A.} = \text{L. A.} + 2B$$

The **surface area of a cube** is the sum of the areas of the faces of the cube.

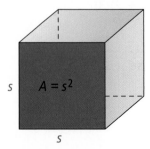

$A = s^2$

Surface Area = 6 · area of a face

$$\text{S. A.} = 6s^2$$

# Part 1

## Example Finding Surface Areas of Rectangular Prisms

Which rectangular prisms have a surface area of 54 ft²?

**a.**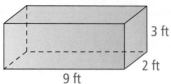
3 ft
2 ft
9 ft

**b.**
3 ft
3 ft
3 ft

**c.**
$4\frac{1}{5}$ ft
2 ft
3 ft

**d.**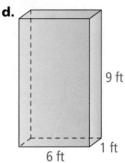
9 ft
1 ft
6 ft

## Solution

To find the surface areas of the prisms, you can use the formula S.A = L.A. + 2B. Use L.A. = $ph$ to find the lateral area, where $p$ represents the perimeter of the base, and $h$ represents the height of the prism. Use $B = bh$ to find the area of the base. You can also use the formula S.A. = $6s^2$ to find the surface area of the cube.

**a.**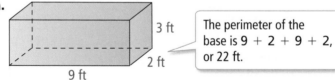
3 ft
2 ft
9 ft

The perimeter of the base is 9 + 2 + 9 + 2, or 22 ft.

L.A. = Lateral Area
  = $ph$
  = (9 + 2 + 9 + 2)(3)
  = (22)(3)
  = 66

B = Area of base
  = $bh$
  = (9)(2)
  = 18

S.A. = L.A. + 2B
  = 66 + 2(18)
  = 66 + 36
  = 102

Surface Area ≠ 54 ft²

**b.**
3 ft
3 ft
3 ft

S.A. = $6s^2$
  = $6(3)^2$
  = 6(9)
  = 54
Surface Area = 54 ft²

continued on next page >

# Part 1

**Solution** continued

**c.**

L.A. = Lateral Area
 = $ph$
 = $(3 + 2 + 3 + 2)\left(4\frac{1}{5}\right)$
 = $(10)\left(4\frac{1}{5}\right)$
 = $(10)\left(\frac{21}{5}\right)$
 = $\left(\frac{210}{5}\right)$
 = 42

$B$ = Area of base
 = $bh$
 = $(3)(2)$
 = 6

S.A. = L.A. + 2$B$
 = 42 + 2(6)
 = 42 + 12
 = 54

Surface Area = 54 ft$^2$

**d.**

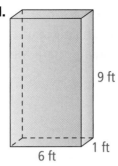

L.A. = Lateral Area
 = $ph$
 = $(6 + 1 + 6 + 1)(9)$
 = $(14)(9)$
 = 126

$B$ = Area of base
 = $bh$
 = $(6)(1)$
 = 6

S.A. = L.A. + 2$B$
 = 126 + 2(6)
 = 126 + 12
 = 138

Surface Area = 54 ft$^2$

# Part 2

## Example Finding Surface Areas of Triangular Prisms

Ms. Adventure went on a trip around the world. In the Netherlands, she tasted Dutch cheese. The piece of cheese has the shape of a triangular prism. How much surface area is there for mold to grown on?

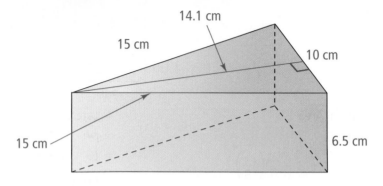

**Solution**

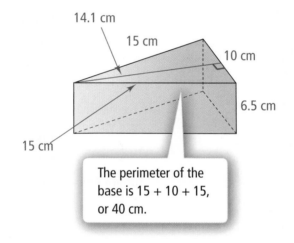

The perimeter of the base is 15 + 10 + 15, or 40 cm.

**Step 1** Find the lateral area.

| | |
|---|---|
| Use the formula for the lateral area of a prism. | L.A. = $ph$ |
| Substitute 40 for the perimeter of the base $p$ and 6.5 for the height of the prism $h$. | = (40)(6.5) |
| Multiply. | = 260 |

continued on next page >

## Part 2

**Solution** continued

Step 2 Find the area of the base.

> **Use the formula for the area of a triangle.** $\qquad B = \dfrac{1}{2}\,bh$

> **Substitute 10 for the base of a triangle _b_ and 14.1 for the height of triangle _h_.** $\qquad = \dfrac{1}{2}(10)(14.1)$

> **Multiply.** $\qquad = 70.5$

Step 3 Find the surface area of the prism.

> **Use the formula for the surface area of a prism.** $\qquad \text{S.A.} = \text{L.A.} + 2B$

> **Substitute 260 for the lateral area and 70.5 for the area of the base.** $\qquad = 260 + 2(70.5)$

> **Simplify.** $\qquad = 401$

There is a surface area of 401 cm² for mold to grow on.

## Part 3

### Intro

When a base of a prism is a regular polygon, you can decompose the polygon to finds its area.

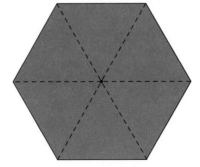

# Part 3

## Example  Finding Surface Areas of Hexagonal Prisms

Ms. Adventure wants to make a box like one she saw in Japan. She plans to cover the box with paper. The box has the shape of a regular hexagonal prism. To the nearest square inch, how much paper does Ms. Adventure need to cover the box?

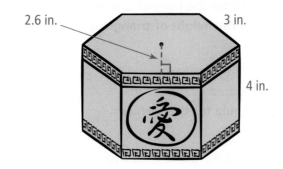

2.6 in.    3 in.

4 in.

### Solution

The box has the shape of a regular hexagonal prism. To find the amount of paper needed to cover the box, find its surface area. Use S.A. = L.A. + 2*B*.

**Step 1** Find the lateral area of the prism.

| | |
|---|---|
| **Use the formula for the lateral area of a prism.** | L.A. = $ph$ |
| **Substitute for the perimeter of the base *p* and the height of the prism *h*.** | = $(6 \cdot 3)(4)$ |
| **Simplify to find the perimeter.** | = $(18)(4)$ |
| **Multiply.** | = 72 in.$^2$ |

continued on next page >

**Solution** continued

**Step 2** Find the area of the hexagonal base.

$B = 6 \cdot$ area of one triangle

$\quad = 6 \cdot \frac{1}{2}bh$

$\quad = 6 \cdot \frac{1}{2}(3)(2.6)$

$\quad = 23.4$ in.$^2$

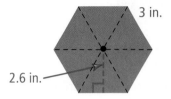

3 in.

2.6 in.

**Step 3** Find the surface area of the prism.

**Use the formula for the surface area of a prism.**   $\text{S.A.} = \text{L.A.} + 2B$

**Substitute 72 for L.A. and 23.4 for B.**   $= 72 + 2(23.4)$

**Simplify.**   $= 118.8$ in.$^2$

Ms. Adventure needs about 119 in.$^2$ of paper to cover the box.

**1.** Find the surface area of the cube. Simplify your answer.

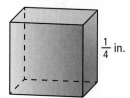

$\frac{1}{4}$ in.

**2.** Find the surface area of the triangular prism. The base of the prism is an isosceles triangle.

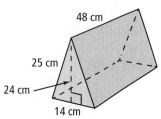

48 cm
25 cm
24 cm
14 cm

**3.** Find the surface area of the right triangular prism.

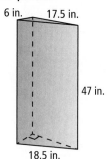

6 in.  17.5 in.
47 in.
18.5 in.

**4.** Find the surface area of the regular hexagonal prism.

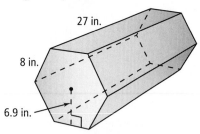

27 in.
8 in.
6.9 in.

**5. Gift Wrapping** A gift box has the shape of a rectangular prism. How much wrapping paper do you need to cover the box?

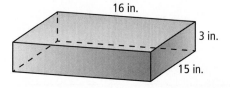

16 in.
3 in.
15 in.

**6. a. Multiple Representations** Find the surface area of the rectangular prism. The figure is not to scale.

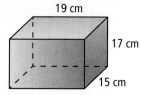

19 cm
17 cm
15 cm

**b.** Draw a net for the prism that is to scale.

**c.** Draw a more accurate sketch of the prism.

**7. a. Open-Ended** Design your own backyard shed in the shape of a cube. Choose exact dimensions for your shed.

**b.** Find the lateral area and surface area of the cube on which you based your design.

**c.** Find the ratio of its lateral area to its surface area.

**8. Think About the Process** A student wants to find the surface area of a triangular prism. Its bases are equilateral triangles with side lengths 9 cm and height 7.8 cm. The prism height is 15 cm. To find the surface area, the student first finds the lateral area of the triangular prism.

**a.** What should the student do first to find the lateral area?

**A.** The student should find the perimeter of a base, 27 cm.

**B.** The student should multiply the side length, 9 cm, by the triangle height, 7.8 cm.

**C.** The student should find the area of a base, 35.1 cm$^2$.

**D.** The student should find twice the area of a base, 70.2 cm$^2$.

**b.** What is the surface area?

**9. Error Analysis** The base of a prism is an equilateral triangle with area 84.9 cm². The area of each lateral face is 84 cm². Your friend incorrectly claims that the surface area is 253.8 cm².

**a.** What is the correct surface area?

**b.** What is your friend's error?

  **A.** Your friend added the areas of the bases and only one lateral face.

  **B.** Your friend added the areas of the bases and only two lateral faces.

  **C.** Your friend added the areas of only one base and one lateral face.

  **D.** Your friend added the areas of only one base and the three lateral faces.

**10. Reasoning** Two students find the surface area, S.A., of this regular hexagonal prism. One student multiplies the perimeter of the hexagon by the height of the prism to find the lateral area, L.A. The other student finds the area of each lateral face then multiplies by the number of faces.

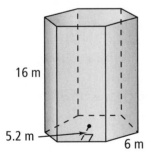

16 m

5.2 m

6 m

**a.** What is the L.A.?

**b.** What is the S.A.?

**c.** Explain why both approaches lead to the same S.A.

**11.** A box has the shape of a rectangular prism with height 29 cm. If the height is increased by 0.7 cm, by how much does the surface area of the box increase?

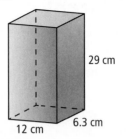

29 cm

12 cm   6.3 cm

**12. Think About the Process** A student correctly found the surface area of a regular hexagonal prism to be 550.2 yd². The teacher asked the student to explain how he found the surface area. The student said he first found the lateral area, 294 yd². Then he found the base area, 128.1 yd². What was the next step he likely described?

**a.** Double the lateral area to get ▇ yd².

**b.** Double the area of a base to get ▇ yd².

**c.** Divide the lateral area by 6 to get ▇ yd².

**d.** Multiply the perimeter of a base and the prism height to get ▇ yd².

**13.** One cube has edge length 2 cm. A larger cube has edge length 3 cm. What is the ratio of the surface area of the smaller cube to the surface area of the larger cube in simplest form?

**14. Challenge** A sculpture is to include 12 suspended identical tubes. The tubes are regular hexagonal prisms. The tubes have very thin walls and are open at each end. Each tube is 11 ft long with edges that are each 3 ft. The sculptor wants to paint the inside and outside of each tube. A can of paint covers 40 ft². How many cans of paint does the sculptor need? Round up to the nearest whole number.

**Vocabulary**
volume of a cube,
volume of a prism

CCSS: 7.G.B.6

## Key Concept

The **volume of a prism** is the number of unit cubes needed to fill the prism. The formula for the volume of a prism is the product of the base area and the height of the prism.

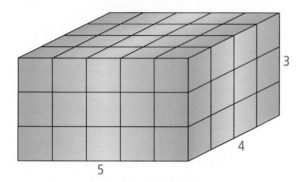

Each layer contains 5 · 4 cubes.
There are 3 layers of 20 cubes.
The volume of the prism is
3 · 20, or 60 cubic units.

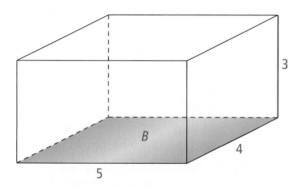

Volume = area of base · height
$$V = Bh$$

The volume of a cube is the number of unit cubes needed to fill the cube.
The formula for the volume of a cube is the edge length cubed.

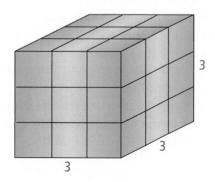

Each layer contains 3 · 3 cubes.
There are 3 layers.
The volume of the cube is
3 · 3 · 3, or 27 cubic units.
Volume = edge length cubed
$$V = s^3$$

### Example Finding Volumes of Prisms

Find the volume of each prism.

**a.**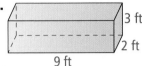
3 ft
2 ft
9 ft

**b.**
3 ft
3 ft
3 ft

**c.**
$4\frac{1}{5}$ ft
2 ft
3 ft

**d.**
9 ft
1 ft
6 ft

**Solution** · · · · · · · · · · · · · · · · · · · · · · · · · · · · · · · · · · · · · · · · · · · ·

To find the volumes of the prisms, you can use the formula $V = Bh$. Where $B$ is the area of the base and $h$ is the height of the prism. You can also use $V = s^3$ to find the volume of the cube.

**a.**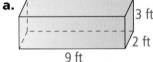
3 ft
2 ft
9 ft

$B =$ Area of the base

$= bh$ ⟵ *h* represents the height of the rectangular base.

$= (9)(2)$

$= 18$

$V = Bh$ ⟵ *h* represents the height of the prism.

$= (18)(3)$

$= 54$

Volume $= 54$ ft³

**b.** $V = s^3$

$= 3^3$

$= 27$

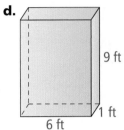
3 ft
3 ft
3 ft

Volume $= 27$ ft³

Volume $\neq 54$ ft³

continued on next page >

# Part 1

**Solution** continued

   **c.**    $B$ = Area of the base

           = $bh$

           = $(3)(2)$

           = $6$

    $V$ = $Bh$

           = $(6)\left(4\frac{1}{5}\right)$

           = $(6)\left(\frac{21}{5}\right)$

           = $\frac{126}{5}$

           = $25\frac{1}{5}$

   Volume = $25\frac{1}{5}$ ft$^3$

   Volume ≠ $54$ ft$^3$

   **d.**    $B$ = Area of the base

           = $bh$

           = $(6)(1)$

           = $6$

    $V$ = $Bh$

           = $(6)(9)$

           = $54$

   Volume = $54$ ft$^3$

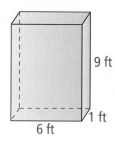

# Part 2

### Example Finding Volumes of Right Triangular Prisms

What is the volume of the right triangular prism?

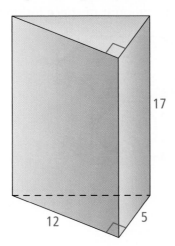

17

12    5

**Solution** · · · · · · · · · · · · · · · · · · · · · · · · · · · · · · · · · · · · · · · · · · · · · · · · · · · · · · · · · · · · · ·

Use $V = Bh$ to find the volume of the prism.

**Step 1** Find the area of the base.

| | |
|---|---|
| **Use the formula for the area of a triangle.** | $B = \frac{1}{2}bh$ |
| **Substitute 12 for the base of the triangle $b$, and 5 for the height of the triangle $h$.** | $= \frac{1}{2}(12)(5)$ |
| **Multiply.** | $= 30$ |

**Step 2** Find the volume of the prism.

| | |
|---|---|
| **Use the formula for the volume of a prism.** | $V = Bh$ |
| **Substitute 30 for the area of the base $B$, and 17 for the height of the prism $h$.** | $= (30)(17)$ |
| **Multiply.** | $= 510$ |

The volume of the right triangular prism is 510 cubic units.

# Part 3

### Example Finding Volumes of Hexagonal Prisms

Ms. Adventure's Japanese box has the shape of a regular hexagonal prism. To the nearest cubic inch what is the amount of space inside the box?

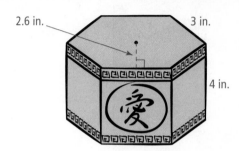

2.6 in.       3 in.

4 in.

### Solution · · · · · · · · · · · · · · · · · · · · · · · · · · · · · · · · · · · · · · · · · · · · ·

Use $V = Bh$ to find the volume of the prism.

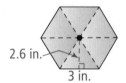

**Step 1** Find the area of the hexagonal base.

2.6 in.

3 in.

| | |
|---|---|
| **The area of the base is 6 times the area of one triangle.** | $B = 6 \cdot$ area of one triangle |
| **Use the formula for the area of a triangle.** | $= 6 \cdot \frac{1}{2}bh$ |
| **Substitute 3 for the base of the triangle $b$, and 2.6 for the height of the triangle $h$.** | $= 6 \cdot \frac{1}{2}(3)(2.6)$ |
| **Multiply to find the area of the triangle.** | $= 6 \cdot 3.9$ |
| **Simplify.** | $= 23.4$ |

**Step 2** Find the volume of the prism.

| | |
|---|---|
| **Use the formula for the volume of a prism.** | $V = Bh$ |
| **Substitute 23.4 for the area of the base $B$, and 4 for the height of the prism $h$.** | $= (23.4)(4)$ |
| **Multiply.** | $= 93.6$ |

The volume of the box is about 94 in.$^3$.

**1.** Find the volume of the rectangular prism.

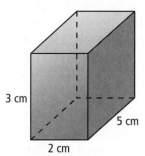

3 cm

5 cm

2 cm

**2.** Find the volume of the cube.

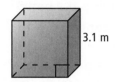

3.1 m

**3.** Find the volume of the triangular prism.

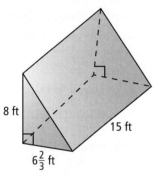

8 ft

15 ft

$6\frac{2}{3}$ ft

**4.** Find the volume of the triangular prism.

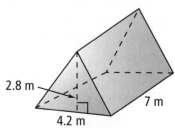

2.8 m

7 m

4.2 m

**5.** To the nearest cubic centimeter, what is the volume of the regular hexagonal prism? Do not round until the final answer. Then round to the nearest whole number as needed.

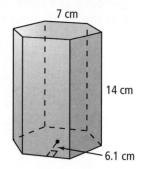

7 cm

14 cm

6.1 cm

**6.** An outdoor art display is a metal cube with edge length 57 feet. What is the volume of the cube in cubic feet? In cubic yards?

**7.** A tunnel for an amusement park ride has the shape of a regular hexagonal prism. To the nearest cubic meter, what is the volume of the regular hexagonal prism? Do not round until the final answer. Then round to the nearest whole number as needed.

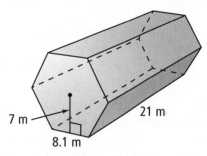

7 m

21 m

8.1 m

**8.** **Mental Math** Find the volume of a rectangular prism with length 5 ft, width 8 ft, and height 8 ft.

**9.** The walls of a farm silo form a regular hexagonal prism. To the nearest cubic foot, what is the volume of the silo?

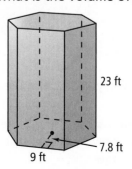

23 ft

7.8 ft

9 ft

**10. a. Writing** How does the volume of the larger cube compare to the volume of the smaller cube?

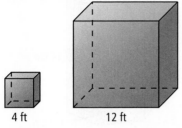

4 ft          12 ft

**A.** The volume of the larger cube is 27 times the volume of the smaller cube.

**B.** The volume of the larger cube is 9 times the volume of the smaller cube.

**C.** The volume of the larger cube is 3 times the volume of the smaller cube.

**D.** The volume of the larger cube is 12 times the volume of the smaller cube.

**b.** Use this and other examples to describe what happens to the volume of a cube if you triple the length of the edges.

**11. Think About the Process** The triangular prism has bases that are equilateral triangles. Each base has perimeter 63 cm. To find the volume of the prism, you need the area of a base.

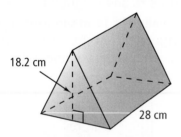

18.2 cm

28 cm

**a.** How can you find the area of a base?

**A.** Find half of the perimeter and multiply by the height of the triangle.

**B.** Multiply the perimeter of the base times the height of the triangle.

**C.** Divide the perimeter by 3 and multiply by the height of the triangle.

**D.** Divide the perimeter by 3 and multiply by one-half the height of the triangle.

**b.** What is the volume of the prism to the nearest cubic centimeter?

**12. Think About the Process** At a store, a 2.8 ft by 3 ft by 3.4 ft rectangular container costs $4.00. A 3 ft by 4 ft by 3.5 ft container costs $5.04.

**a.** How would you find which container is the better buy?

**A.** The container with the lower cost is always a better buy.

**B.** Divide the volume of each container by its cost to find the price per cubic foot.

**C.** The container with the greater volume is always a better buy.

**D.** Divide the cost of each container by its volume to find the price per cubic foot.

**b.** The ■ container is the better buy.

**13. Reasoning** Freezer A has interior dimensions 1 ft × 1 ft × 5 ft and sells for $499.99. Freezer B has interior dimensions of 1.5 ft × 1.5 ft × 4 ft and sells for $849.99. Which freezer is a better buy in terms of dollars per cubic foot? Show your work and explain your reasoning.

**14. a. Challenge** Find the volume of the figure shown.

**b.** Show three different ways to find the volume.

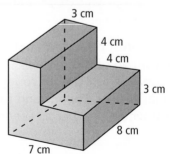

3 cm

4 cm

4 cm

3 cm

8 cm

7 cm

CCSS: 7.G.B.6

**Vocabulary**
lateral area of a pyramid, slant height of a pyramid, surface area of a pyramid

## Key Concept

The **slant height of a pyramid** is the height of a lateral face.

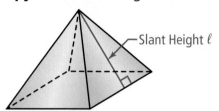

Slant Height $\ell$

The **lateral area of a pyramid** is the sum of the areas of the lateral faces.

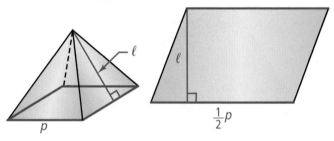

Lateral Area = $\frac{1}{2}$ perimeter of base · slant height

$$\text{L.A.} = \frac{1}{2} p\ell$$

The **surface area of a pyramid** is the sum of the lateral area and the area of the base.

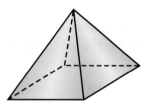

Surface Area = Lateral Area + area of base

$$\text{S.A.} = \text{L.A.} + B$$

### Example  Finding Surface Areas of Square Pyramids

What is the surface area of the square pyramid?

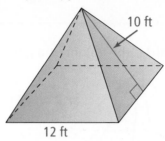

10 ft

12 ft

### Solution

Use S.A. = L.A. + $B$ to find the surface area.

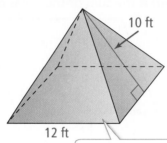

10 ft

12 ft

The perimeter of the base is 4 · 12, or 48 ft.

**Step 1** Find the lateral area.

| | |
|---|---|
| Use the formula for the lateral area of a pyramid. | L.A. $= \dfrac{1}{2}p\ell$ |
| Substitute 48 for the perimeter of the base $p$, and 10 for the slant height $\ell$. | $= \dfrac{1}{2}(48)(10)$ |
| Multiply. | $= 240$ |

**Step 2** Find the area of the base.

| | |
|---|---|
| Use the formula for the area of a square. | $= s^2$ |
| Substitute 12 for the side length $s$. | $= 12^2$ |
| Simplify. | $= 144$ |

continued on next page >

## Part 1

**Solution** continued

**Step 3** Find the surface area.

| | |
|---|---|
| **Use the formula for the surface area of a pyramid.** | S.A. = L.A. + B |
| **Substitute 240 for the lateral area L.A., and 144 for the area of the base B.** | = 240 + 144 |
| **Add.** | = 384 |

The surface area of the square pyramid is 384 in.².

## Part 2

### Example  Finding Surface Areas of Triangular Pyramids

Ms. Adventure brought home an assortment of tea from India. To the nearest square inch, how much cardboard was used to make the regular triangular pyramid package?

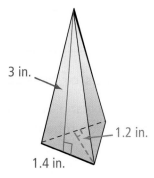

3 in.

1.2 in.

1.4 in.

**Solution** · · · · · · · · · · · · · · · · · · · · · · · · · · · · · · · · · · · · · · · · · · · · ·

Use S.A. = L.A. + B to find the surface area.

The perimeter of the base is 3 · 1.4, or 4.2 in.

**Step 1** Find the lateral area.

| | |
|---|---|
| **Use the formula for the lateral area of a pyramid.** | $\text{L.A.} = \frac{1}{2}p\ell$ |
| **Substitute 4.2 for the perimeter of the base p, and 3 for the slant height ℓ.** | $= \frac{1}{2}(4.2)(3)$ |
| **Multiply.** | = 6.3 |

continued on next page >

# Part 2

### Solution continued

**Step 2** Find the area of the base.

Use the formula for the area of a triangle. $\quad B = \frac{1}{2}bh$

Substitute 1.4 for the base of the $\quad\quad\quad = \frac{1}{2}(1.4)(1.2)$
triangle *b*, and 1.2 for the height of
the triangle *h*.

Multiply. $\quad\quad\quad\quad\quad\quad\quad\quad\quad\quad = 0.84$

**Step 3** Find the surface area.

Use the formula for the surface $\quad\quad$ S.A. = L.A. + B
area of a pyramid.

Substitute 6.3 for the lateral area L.A., $\quad = 6.3 + 0.84$
and 0.84 for the area of the base *B*.

Add. $\quad\quad\quad\quad\quad\quad\quad\quad\quad\quad = 7.14$

About 7 in.² of cardboard were used to make the tea package.

# Part 3

## Example  Finding Surface Areas of Hexagonal Pyramids

Ms. Adventure went camping in New Zealand. Her tent has the shape of a
regular hexagonal pyramid. To the nearest square foot, how much fabric was
used to make the tent?

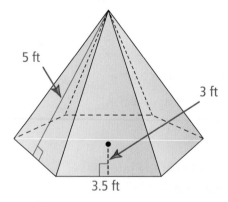

5 ft

3 ft

3.5 ft

continued on next page >

**Example** continued

**Solution** · · · · · · · · · · · · · · · · · · · · · · · · · · · · · · · · · · · · · · · · · · · · · · · · · ·

Use S.A. = L.A. + $B$ to find the surface area.

**Step 1** Find the lateral area.

| | |
|---|---|
| **Use the formula for lateral area.** | L.A. $= \frac{1}{2}p\ell$ |
| **Substitute 6 · 3.5, or 21, for the perimeter of the base $p$, and 5 for the slant height $\ell$.** | $= \frac{1}{2}(21)(5)$ |
| **Multiply.** | $= 52.5$ |

**Step 2** Find the area of the base.

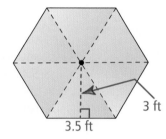

3 ft

3.5 ft

| | |
|---|---|
| **The area of the base is 6 times the area of one triangle.** | $B = 6 \cdot$ area of one rectangle |
| **Use the area formula for a triangle.** | $= 6 \cdot \frac{1}{2}bh$ |
| **Substitute 3.5 for the base of the triangle $b$, and 3 for the height of the triangle $h$.** | $= 6 \cdot \frac{1}{2}(3.5)(3)$ |
| **Simplify.** | $= 31.5$ |

**Step 3** Find the surface area.

| | |
|---|---|
| **Use the formula for the surface area of a pyramid.** | S.A. = L.A. + $B$ |
| **Substitute 52.5 for the lateral area L.A., and 31.5 for the area of the base $B$.** | $= 52.5 + 31.5$ |
| **Simplify.** | $= 84$ |

You need about 84 ft² of fabric to make the tent.

**1.** Find the surface area of the square pyramid.

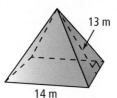

13 m

14 m

**2.** A piece of cheese has the shape of a regular triangular pyramid. Find the surface area of the cheese.

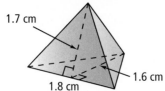

1.7 cm

1.6 cm

1.8 cm

**3.** Find the surface area of the regular hexagonal pyramid.

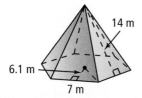

14 m

6.1 m

7 m

**4.** An iceberg has the shape of a regular hexagonal pyramid. Find the surface area of the iceberg to the nearest square foot.

20 ft

13 ft

11.3 ft

**5. Open-Ended** Think of an object that has the shape of a square pyramid. It could be pointed up, down, or to the left or right.

**a.** Sketch a square pyramid that has the shape of the object.

**b.** What information could you use to find the surface area of a square pyramid? Select all that apply.

**A.** the side length of the base

**B.** the lateral area

**C.** the slant height of the pyramid

**D.** the area of the base

**E.** the perimeter of the base

**F.** the height of the pyramid

**6. a. Writing** Explain how to find the surface area of the regular triangular pyramid.

**b.** Find the surface area of the regular triangular pyramid.

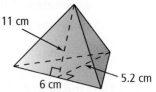

11 cm

6 cm

5.2 cm

(The figure is not to scale.)

**7. Think About the Process** You want to find the surface area of the square pyramid. You use the formula S.A. = L.A. + B, where L.A. represents the lateral area of the pyramid and B represents the area of the base.

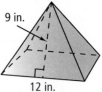

9 in.

12 in.

**a.** Which equations do you use for L.A. and B?

**A.** L.A. $= \frac{1}{2}(12^2)(9)$; $B = 9^2$

**B.** L.A. $= \frac{1}{2}(4 \cdot 9)(12)$; $B = 9^2$

**C.** L.A. $= (4 \cdot 12)(9)$; $B = 12^2$

**D.** L.A. $= \frac{1}{2}(4 \cdot 12)(9)$; $B = 12^2$

**b.** What is the surface area of the square pyramid?

**8. Reasoning** A building block has the shape of a regular triangular pyramid.

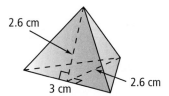

2.6 cm

3 cm    2.6 cm

**a.** What is true of the regular triangular pyramid if the slant height and the height of the triangular base are equal?

  **A.** The area of the base of the pyramid is larger than the area of the other three faces.

  **B.** The base of the pyramid is an equilateral triangle. The other three faces are isosceles triangles.

  **C.** The area of the base of the pyramid is smaller than the area of the other three faces.

  **D.** All four faces have the same area.

**b.** What is the surface area of the building block?

**9. a. Multiple Representations** Show two different ways to find the lateral area of the regular hexagonal pyramid.

  **b.** Find the surface area of the regular hexagonal pyramid.

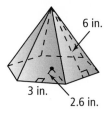

6 in.

3 in.    2.6 in.

**10. Think About the Process** To find the surface area of the regular triangular pyramid, find the lateral area and the area of the base. What is the next step?

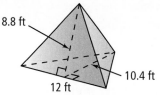

8.8 ft

10.4 ft

12 ft

(The figure is not to scale.)

  **A.** Subtract the area of the base from the lateral area.

  **B.** Subtract the lateral area from the area of the base.

  **C.** Add the lateral area and the area of the base.

  **D.** Multiply the lateral area by the area of the base.

**11. Crystals** A crystal has the shape of a regular hexagonal pyramid. You have a collection of 6 identical crystals. Find the total surface area of all the crystals.

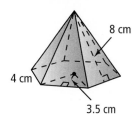

8 cm

4 cm

3.5 cm

**12.** Find the surface area of the regular triangular pyramid.

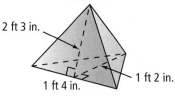

2 ft 3 in.

1 ft 2 in.

1 ft 4 in.

(The figure is not to scale.)

**13. Challenge** Steven buys material to make a tent. The tent will have the shape of a square pyramid with canvas material covering all five faces. The canvas material needed to make the tent costs $0.86 per square foot. How much does material for the tent cost?

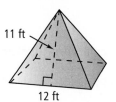

11 ft

12 ft

CCSS: 7.G.B.6

## Key Concept

The **volume of a pyramid** is the number of unit cubes needed to fill the pyramid.

The formula for the volume of a pyramid is $\frac{1}{3}$ the product of the base area and the height of the pyramid.

Suppose you have a pyramid and a prism with the same base and the same height. By turning these solid figures into containers, you can show a relationship between their volumes. Find out how many containers of the pyramid it takes to fill the prism.

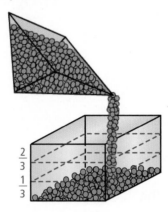

It takes three containers of the pyramid to fill the prism. So the volume of the prism is three times the volume of the pyramid. This means that the volume of the pyramid is $\frac{1}{3}$ the volume of the prism. The volume of a prism is the base times the height.

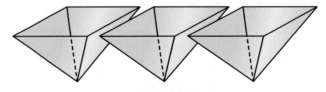

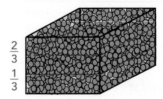

volume of pyramid $= \frac{1}{3}$(volume of prism)

volume of pyramid $= \frac{1}{3}$(area of base · height)

$$V = \frac{1}{3}Bh$$

# Part 1

## Example Finding Volumes of Square Pyramids

What is the volume of each square pyramid? Order them from least volume to greatest volume.

a.
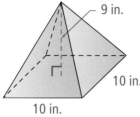

b.
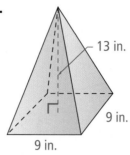

c.
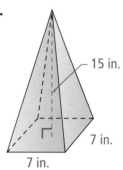

**Solution** · · · · · · · · · · · · · · · · · · · · · · · · · · · · · · · · · · · · · · · · · · · · · · · · · · · · · · · · ·

To find the volume of each pyramid, you can use the formula $V = \frac{1}{3}Bh$. Use $A = s^2$ to find the area of the square base of each pyramid.

a.
$$B = 10^2$$
$$= 100$$
$$V = \frac{1}{3}Bh$$
$$= \frac{1}{3}(100)(9)$$
$$= 300$$
Volume = 300 in.$^3$.

b.
$$B = 9^2$$
$$= 81$$
$$V = \frac{1}{3}Bh$$
$$= \frac{1}{3}(81)(13)$$
$$= 351$$
Volume = 351 in.$^3$.

c.
$$B = 7^2$$
$$= 49$$
$$V = \frac{1}{3}Bh$$
$$= \frac{1}{3}(49)(15)$$
$$= 245$$
Volume = 245 in.$^3$.

Shown in order from least to greatest volumes:

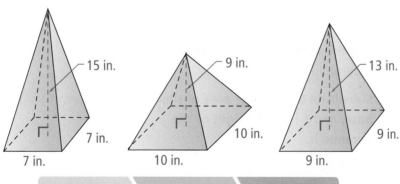

See your complete lesson at MyMathUniverse.com

# Part 2

### Example  Finding Volumes of Triangular Pyramids

Ms. Adventure's tea package has the shape of a regular triangular pyramid. To the nearest tenth of a cubic inch, how much tea can the package hold?

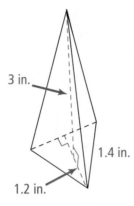

3 in.

1.4 in.

1.2 in.

**Solution** · · · · · · · · · · · · · · · · · · · · · · · · · · · · · · · · · · · · · · · · · · · · · · · · · · · · · · · · · ·

Use $V = \frac{1}{3}Bh$ to find the volume of the pyramid.

**Step 1** Find the area of the base.

| | |
|---|---|
| **Use the formula for the area of a triangle.** | $B = \frac{1}{2}bh$ |
| **Substitute 1.4 for the base of the triangle b, and 1.2 for the height of the triangle h.** | $= \frac{1}{2}(1.4)(1.2)$ |
| **Multiply.** | $= 0.84$ |

**Step 2** Find the volume of the pyramid.

| | |
|---|---|
| **Use the formula for the volume of a pyramid.** | $V = \frac{1}{3}Bh$ |
| **Substitute 0.84 for the area of the base, and 3 for the height of the pyramid h.** | $= \frac{1}{3}(0.84)(3)$ |
| **Multiply.** | $= 0.84$ |

The package can hold about 0.8 in.$^3$ of tea.

# Part 3

## Example  Finding Volumes of Hexagonal Pyramids

Ms. Adventure's tent has the shape of a regular hexagonal pyramid. To the nearest cubic foot, how much space is in the tent?

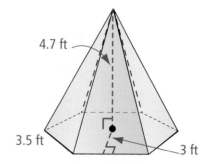

4.7 ft

3.5 ft

3 ft

**Solution**

Use $V = \frac{1}{3}Bh$ to find the volume of the pyramid.

**Step 1** Find the area of the base.

| | |
|---|---|
| The area of the base is 6 times the area of one triangle. | $B = 6 \cdot \text{area of one triangle}$ |
| Use the area formula for a triangle. | $= 6 \cdot \frac{1}{2}bh$ |
| Substitute 3.5 for the base of the triangle $b$, and 3 for the height of the triangle $h$. | $= 6 \cdot \frac{1}{2}(3.5)(3)$ |
| Multiply. | $= 31.5$ |

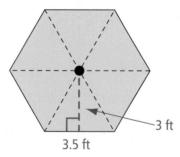

3 ft

3.5 ft

**Step 2** Find the volume of the pyramid.

| | |
|---|---|
| Use the formula for the volume of a pyramid. | $V = \frac{1}{3}Bh$ |
| Substitute 31.5 for the area of the base $B$, and 4.7 for the height of the pyramid $h$. | $= \frac{1}{3}(31.5)(4.7)$ |
| Multiply. | $= 49.35$ |

There is about 49 ft³ of space in Ms. Adventure's tent.

**1.** Find the volume of the square
pyramid.

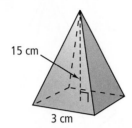

15 cm

3 cm

**2.** Find the volume of the regular
triangular pyramid. Do not round
until the final answer. Then round to
the nearest tenth as needed.

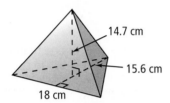

14.7 cm

15.6 cm

18 cm

**3.** Find the volume of the regular
triangular pyramid.

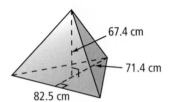

67.4 cm

71.4 cm

82.5 cm

**4.** A craftsperson uses the volume of a
gem to set the price. One gem is
shaped like a regular triangular
pyramid. Find the volume of the gem.
Do not round until the final answer.
Then round to the nearest tenth as
needed.

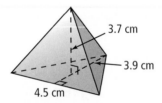

3.7 cm

3.9 cm

4.5 cm

**5.** Find the volume of the regular
hexagonal pyramid. Do not round
until the final answer. Then round to
the nearest tenth as needed.

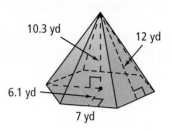

10.3 yd

12 yd

6.1 yd

7 yd

**6. Writing** A square-based pyramid and
a square-based rectangular prism have
the same base edge *b* and the same
height *h*.

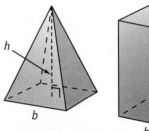 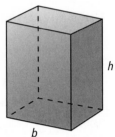

*h*

*b*

*h*

*b*

**a.** How does the volume of the prism
compare to the volume of the
pyramid?

   **A.** The volume of the prism is
   4 times the volume of the
   pyramid.

   **B.** The volume of the prism is
   2 times the volume of the
   pyramid.

   **C.** The volumes cannot be
   compared without the actual
   given measurements.

   **D.** The volume of the prism is 3
   times the volume of the pyramid.

**b.** Describe a situation that could use
this fact.

**7. Estimation** Estimate the volume of
the regular triangular pyramid. Round
each dimension to the nearest whole
number. Multiply the rounded
dimensions. Then, divide by 6.

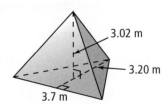

3.02 m

3.20 m

3.7 m

**8. Error Analysis** A student incorrectly gave the volume of this square pyramid as 3,675 mm³.

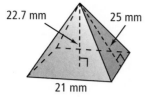

22.7 mm    25 mm

21 mm

a. What is the correct volume of the square pyramid? Do not round until the final answer. Then round to the nearest tenth as needed.

b. What error did the student most likely make?

  **A.** The student multiplied the three given measurements instead of using the formula.

  **B.** The student used the base edge length instead of the pyramid height in the formula.

  **C.** The student used the face height instead of the pyramid height in the formula.

  **D.** The student used the formula for the volume of a prism instead of a pyramid.

**9. Reasoning** The perimeter of a base of the regular triangular pyramid is 54 cm.

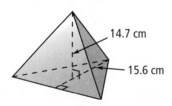

14.7 cm

15.6 cm

a. Find the volume of the pyramid.

b. Which expressions are equivalent to the volume of the pyramid? Select all that apply.

  **A.** $\left(\frac{1}{3}\right)\left(\frac{1}{2}\right)$(18)(15.6)(14.7)

  **B.** (18)(15.6)(14.7) ÷ 6

  **C.** $\left(\frac{1}{3}\right)$(54)(15.6)(14.7)

  **D.** (54)(15.6)(14.7) ÷ 18

**10. Concerts** A large tent for a summer concert series has the shape of a regular hexagonal pyramid. For ventilation, the contractor needs to know the amount of air inside the tent. What is the volume of the tent? Do not round until the final answer. Then round to the nearest tenth as needed.

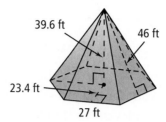

39.6 ft    46 ft

23.4 ft

27 ft

**11.** A pyramid-shaped building is 126 ft tall with a square base that is 99 ft on each side. What is the volume of the building in cubic feet? In cubic yards?

**12. Think About the Process**

  a. Will the volume of the square pyramid shown here be in a whole number of units?

9 ft

11 ft

  **A.** Yes, because the base edge is a multiple of 3.

  **B.** No, because the height and the base edge are not both multiples of 3.

  **C.** No, because neither the height nor the base edge is a multiple of 3.

  **D.** Yes, because the height is a multiple of 3.

  b. The volume is ■ ft³.

**13. Think About the Process**

  a. What is the volume of the regular hexagonal pyramid? Do not round until the final answer.

  b. Which measurement is NOT needed to find the volume of the hexagonal pyramid?

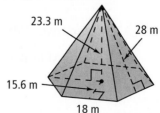

23.3 m    28 m

15.6 m

18 m

  **A.** 15.6 m      **B.** 28 m

  **C.** 23.3 m      **D.** 18 m

See your complete lesson at MyMathUniverse.com

CCSS: 7.G.B.6

## Part 1

### Example  Using Surface Areas in Real-World Problems

You plan to build a doghouse with the dimensions shown. You want to put shingles on the roof and paint the sides of the doghouse. Shingles cost $.99 per square foot. A 2-oz container of paint costs $2.99 and covers 3 square feet. How much will the whole project cost?

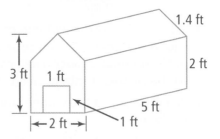

**Solution** · · · · · · · · · · · · · · · · · · · · · · · · · · · · · · · · · · · · · · · · ·

| **Know** | **Need** | **Plan** |
|---|---|---|
| • The dimensions of the doghouse<br><br>• The doghouse is made up of a rectangular prism and a triangular prism<br><br>• The costs of the shingles and the paint | The area to be covered by shingles and the area to be covered by paint | Find the area to be covered by shingles and multiply by the cost of the shingles. Find the area to be covered by paint and find how many containers of paint you need. Multiply the number of containers by the cost of the paint. Add the two costs together. |

cost of project = cost of shingles + cost of paint

**Step 1** Find the surface area of the roof.

$$\text{surface area of roof} = 2 \cdot \text{area of rectangle}$$
$$= 2 \cdot bh$$
$$= 2 \cdot (5)(1.4)$$
$$= 14$$

The surface area of the roof is 14 ft$^2$.

**Step 2** Find the cost of the shingles.

$$\text{cost of shingles} = \$.99 \cdot \text{surface area of roof}$$
$$= 0.99 \cdot 14$$
$$= 13.86$$

The cost of the shingles is $13.86.

continued on next page >

**Step 3** Find the area to be painted.

Notice that the height of the base of the triangular prism is the difference of the height of the doghouse and the height of the rectangular prism.

| area to be painted | = | lateral area of rectangular prism | − | area of doorway | + 2 · | area of base of triangular prism |
|---|---|---|---|---|---|---|
| | = | $ph$ | − | $s^2$ | + 2 · | $\frac{1}{2}bh$ |
| | = | $(2 + 5 + 2 + 5)(2)$ | − | $1^2$ | + 2 · | $\frac{1}{2}(2)(3 - 2)$ |
| | = | $(14)(2)$ | − | $1$ | + 2 · | $\frac{1}{2}(2)(1)$ |
| | = | $28$ | − | $1$ | + 2 · | $1$ |
| | = 29 | | | | | |

The area to be painted is 29 ft$^2$.

**Step 4** Find the number of containers of paint needed and the cost of the paint.

containers needed = area to be painted ÷ area each container covers

$$= 29 ÷ 3$$

$$= 9\frac{2}{3}$$

You will need 10 containers of paint.

The cost of paint is 10 · 2.99, or $29.90.

**Step 5** Find the cost of the project.

cost of project = cost of shingles + cost of paint

$$= 13.86 + 29.90$$

$$= 43.76$$

The cost of the project will be $43.76.

# Part 2

### Example Finding Surface Areas of Complex Figures

Ms. Adventure went to an Italian bakery in New York City. She bought a cake made of three layers of regular hexagonal prisms. Each layer is 3 inches high. Ms. Adventure plans to decorate the visible parts of the layers. To the nearest square inch, how much cake can she cover with decorations?

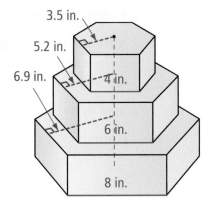

3.5 in.

5.2 in.

6.9 in.

4 in.

6 in.

8 in.

**Solution** · · · · · · · · · · · · · · · · · · · · · · · · · · · · · · · · · · · · · · · · · · · · · · · ·

To find the amount of cake Ms. Adventure can cover with decorations, find the surface area of the cake.

S.A. of cake = top area of top layer + L.A. of top layer
  + top area of middle layer + L.A. of middle layer
  + top area of bottom layer + L.A. of bottom layer

**Step 1** Find the area of the top base of the top layer.

$$\text{area of hexagon} = 6 \cdot \text{area of one triangle}$$

$$= 6 \cdot \tfrac{1}{2}bh$$

3.5 in.    4 in.

$$= 6 \cdot \tfrac{1}{2}(4)(3.5)$$

$$= 42$$

S.A. of cake = 42 + L.A. of top layer
  + top area of middle layer + L.A. of middle layer
  + top area of bottom layer + L.A. of bottom layer

**Step 2** Find the lateral area of the top layer.

$$\text{L.A.} = ph$$

$$= (6 \cdot 4)(3)$$

$$= (24)(3)$$

$$= 72$$

S.A. of cake = 42 + 72
  + top area of middle layer + L.A. of middle layer
  + top area of bottom layer + L.A. of bottom layer

continued on next page >

# Part 2

**Solution** continued

**Step 3** Find the area of the top of the middle layer.

top of middle layer = area of larger hexagon − area of smaller hexagon

$$= 6 \cdot \frac{1}{2}(6)(5.2) - 42$$

$$= 93.6 - 42$$

$$= 51.6$$

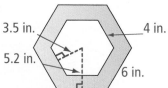

S.A. of cake = 42 + 72

    + 51.6 + L.A. of middle layer

    + top area of bottom layer + L.A. of bottom layer

**Step 4** Find the lateral area of the middle layer.

L.A. = *ph*

  = (6 · 6)(3)

  = (36)(3)

  = 108

S.A. of cake = 42 + 72

    + 51.6 + 108

    + top area of bottom layer + L.A. of bottom layer

**Step 5** Find the area of the top of the bottom layer.

top of bottom layer = area of larger hexagon − area of smaller hexagon

$$= 6 \cdot \frac{1}{2}(8)(6.9) - 93.6$$

$$= 165.6 - 93.6$$

$$= 72$$

S.A. of cake = 42 + 72

    + 51.6 + 108

    + 72 + L.A. of bottom layer

**Step 6** Find the lateral area of the bottom layer.

L.A. = *ph*

  = (6 · 8)(3)

  = (48)(3)

  = 144

S.A. of cake = 42 + 72 + 51.6 + 108 + 72 + 144

    = 489.6

Ms. Adventure can cover about 490 in.² of the cake with decorations.

See your complete lesson at MyMathUniverse.com

**1.** A glass bead has the shape of a rectangular prism with a smaller rectangular prism removed. What is the volume of the glass that forms the bead?

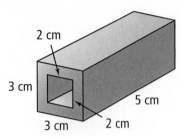

2 cm

3 cm

5 cm

3 cm  2 cm

(The figure is not to scale.)

**2.** The bottom part of this block is a rectangular prism. The top part is a square pyramid. You want to cover the block entirely with paper. How much paper do you need? Explain your reasoning.

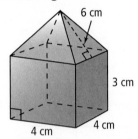

6 cm

3 cm

4 cm  4 cm

(The figure is not to scale.)

**3.** A landscaper uses tiles to make a walkway through a garden. Each tile is a regular hexagonal prism. The material used for the tiles weighs 2 g per cubic centimeter. How much does each tile weigh?

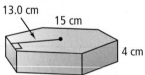

13.0 cm

15 cm

4 cm

(The figure is not to scale.)

**4.** Ben uses clay to make the rectangular prism. Naomi uses cardboard to make the triangular prism.

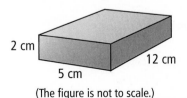

2 cm

12 cm

5 cm

(The figure is not to scale.)

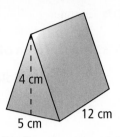

4 cm

12 cm

5 cm

(The figure is not to scale.)

**a.** Compare the volumes of the two prisms.

**b.** Describe two different methods by which you can compare the volumes.

**5.** A water tank has the shape of a regular hexagonal prism topped with a pyramid. Your friend incorrectly claims that the volume of the tank is 5,686.2 ft³.

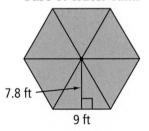

6 ft

27 ft

9 ft

(The figure is not to scale.)

**Base of Water Tank**

7.8 ft

9 ft

(The figure is not to scale.)

**a.** What is the correct volume?

**b.** What is your friend's error?

**A.** Your friend subtracted the volume of the pyramid from the volume of the prism.

**B.** Your friend only found the volume of the pyramid.

**C.** Your friend only found the volume of the prism.

**D.** Your friend subtracted the volume of the prism from the volume of the pyramid.

**6. Think About the Process** A baker just finished making a cake of two layers that are rectangular prisms. Each layer is 2 in. high.

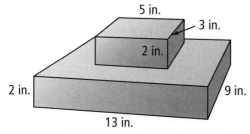

5 in.

3 in.

2 in.

2 in.

9 in.

13 in.

(The figure is not to scale.)

**a.** Which of these expressions represents the volume of the cake?

**A.** (2)(13)(9)(2)

**B.** (13)(9)(2)+(5)(3)(2)

**C.** (13)(9)(2)(5)(3)

**D.** (2)(5)(3)(2)

**E.** (13)(9)(2)−(5)(3)(2)

**b.** Find the volume of the cake.

**7. Think About the Process** A gift comes in a box that is a regular hexagonal prism. A sheet of wrapping paper covers 100 in.²

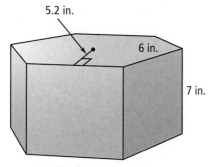

5.2 in.

6 in.

7 in.

(The figure is not to scale.)

**a.** How can you find the number of sheets you need to wrap the box?

**A.** Find the lateral area of the prism. Then divide it by 100 and round down to the nearest whole number.

**B.** Find the lateral area of the prism. Then divide it by 100 and round up to the nearest whole number.

**C.** Find the surface area of the prism. Then divide it by 100 and round up to the nearest whole number.

**D.** Find the surface area of the prism. Then divide it by 100 and round down to the nearest whole number.

**b.** If you have 4 sheets of wrapping paper, do you have enough to wrap the box? You may assume that no paper goes to waste.

**8. Challenge** You want to paint the outside walls and shingle the roof of this doghouse. It costs $0.98 to paint each square foot. Shingles cost $0.93 per square foot. How much will this project cost? You may assume that no paint or shingles go to waste.

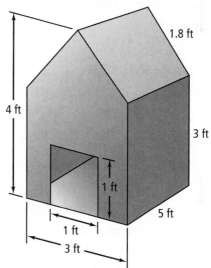

1.8 ft

4 ft

3 ft

1 ft

5 ft

1 ft

3 ft

(The figure is not to scale.)

# Populations and Samples

**Vocabulary**
bias, biased sample, inference, invalid inference, population, representative sample, sample of a population, subject, valid inference

CCSS: 7.SP.A.1

## Part 1

### Intro

A **population** is the complete set of items being studied.

A **sample of a population** is a part of the population. A sample is useful when you want to find out about a population, but you do not have the resources to study every member of the population.

Each member in the sample is called a **subject**.

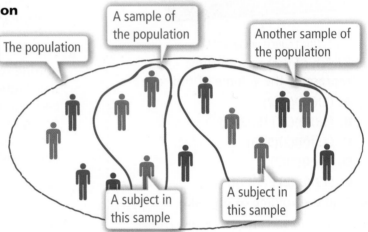

The population

A sample of the population

Another sample of the population

A subject in this sample

A subject in this sample

### Example  Understanding Populations and Samples

You are investigating the lengths of all of the words in a book. Determine whether each description is a *population* or a *sample*.

   **a.** All of the words on a page of the book
   **b.** Every other word in the book
   **c.** All of the words in the book
   **d.** One word in the book

continued on next page >

## Part 1

### Example continued

**Solution** · · · · · · · · · · · · · · · · · · · · · · · · · · · · · · · · · · · · · · · · · · · · · · · · · · · · · ·

    **a.** all of the words on a page of the book

        This is a part of all the words in the book, so this is a sample.

    **b.** every other word in the book

        This is a part of all the words in the book, so this is a sample.

    **c.** all of the words in the book

        This is the complete set of items you are investigating, so this is the population.

    **d.** one word in the book

        This is a part of all the words in the book, so this is a sample.

## Part 2

### Intro

A **bias** is a tendency toward a particular perspective that is different from the overall perspective of the population.

A sample has a bias toward "yes" if most of the subjects answer "yes" to a question.

A sample has a bias toward "no" if most of the subjects answer "no" to a question.

**Do you like sushi?**

Sample with a **bias** toward "no"

Sample with a **bias** toward "yes"

### Example  Analyzing Samples for Bias

You are studying the people in the United States. You want to know who spends at least two months every year within 200 miles of the ocean.

continued on next page >

# Part 2

**Example** continued

**a.** Which description is your population?

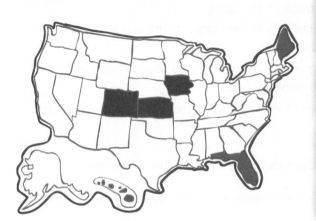

Everyone in Colorado, Iowa, and Kansas

Everyone in Florida, Hawaii, and Maine

100 people from each state

Everyone in the U.S.

**b.** Describe each sample as having bias or not having bias. Justify your reasoning.

## Solution

**a.** The population is "everyone in the United States." This includes all of the people who you are studying.

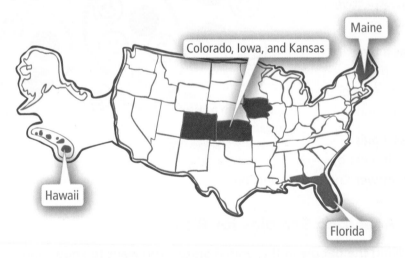

Maine

Colorado, Iowa, and Kansas

Hawaii

Florida

**b.** Colorado, Iowa, and Kansas are states that do not border the ocean, so the sample is not likely to include people who spend at least two months near the ocean. The sample has bias.

Florida, Hawaii, and Maine are states that border the ocean, so the sample is likely to include mostly people who spend at least two months near the ocean. The sample has bias.

"100 people from each state" includes people all across the United States, so the sample more accurately represents the population. The sample does not have bias.

# Key Concept

You are investigating the percentage of males in the population below. The population:

In a **representative sample**, the number of subjects in the sample with the trait being studied is proportional to the number of members in the population with that trait.

| 12 females | 4 males |
| 75% female | 25% male |

A representative sample:

| 6 females | 2 males |
| 75% female | 25% male |

> Accurately represents the population

In a **biased sample**, the number of subjects in the sample with the trait being studied is *not* proportional to the number of members in the population with that trait.

| 12 females | 4 males |
| 75% female | 25% male |

A biased sample:

| 4 females | 4 males |
| 50% female | 50% male |

> Does *not* accurately represent the population

# Part 3

## Intro

An **inference** is a judgment that is made by interpreting data.

A **valid inference** is true about the population. Valid inferences can be made when they are based on data from a representative sample.

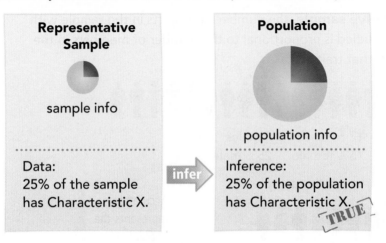

An **invalid inference** is false about the population, or does not follow from the data. A biased sample can lead to invalid inferences.

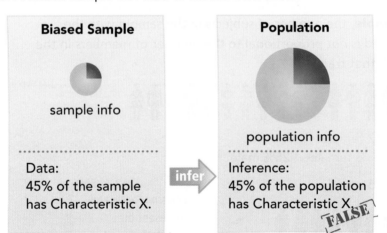

# Part 3

## Example Deciding If Inferences Are Valid Or Invalid

Suppose it is 200 years in the future. You collect a representative sample of humans and robots. Tell whether each inference is *valid* or *invalid*.

Representative Sample

- 20% of the population are robots.
- There are more humans than robots in the population.
- 25% of the population are robots.
- 2 out of every 8 members in the population are robots.

## Solution

There are 2 robots and 8 humans. The total number of subjects in the sample is $2 + 8 = 10$.

$\frac{2}{10}$, or 20%, of the sample are robots.

**Valid**

| 20% of the population are robots. |

| There are more humans than robots in the population. |

More humans than robots in the sample.

20%  **Invalid**

| 25% of the population are robots. |

| 2 out of every 8 members in the population are robots. |

There are 10 subjects not 8.

1. You are investigating the number of cats in each household in a state.

   a. Which description(s) are populations? Select all that apply.

      A. the number of cats in every other household on a street in the state

      B. the number of cats in all households of a city in the state

      C. the number of cats in all households in the state

      D. the number of cats in one household in the state

   b. Which description(s) are samples? Select all that apply.

      A. the number of cats in every other household on a street in the state

      B. the number of cats in all households of a city in the state

      C. the number of cats in all households in the state

      D. the number of cats in one household in the state

2. You are studying the quality of the yellow and blue sweaters being sold in a store. Determine whether the given set is a sample or a population.

   the quality of all the blue sweaters sold in the store

3. **Think About the Process** A survey asked people in France the following question, "How many children do you have?" Of the 887 people who responded, 5% reported having only 1 child.

   a. What is the difference between a sample and a population?

      A. A sample includes only the set of items with the trait being studied. The population includes every item being studied.

      B. A sample is a part of the population. A population includes the complete set of items being studied.

      C. A sample includes only the set of items with the trait being studied. The population includes all other items.

      D. A sample includes the complete set of items being studied. A population is a part of the sample.

   b. What is the sample for this survey?

      A. The sample is people in France who did not respond.

      B. The sample is the 887 people who responded.

      C. The sample is people who live in France.

      D. The sample is the 5% who reported having only one child.

4. A school district has all of the students in Grade 7 take a science test. Three samples are taken from the results. Which of these samples are likely to be unbiased? Select all that apply.

   A. 150 randomly selected students in Grade 7

   B. 100 students who do well in science class

   C. 25 Grade 7 students whose last name begins with a letter between B and T

5. At a concert, a representative sample is collected of men and women. The sample contains 6 men and 8 women. Which inference is valid for the population of people attending the concert?

   A. 43% of the population are men.

   B. There are more men than women in the population.

   C. 6 out of every 8 members in the population are men.

   D. 75% of the population are men.

See your complete lesson at MyMathUniverse.com

**6. Think About the Process** Your class would like to know what percentage of people in your town go water skiing every year.

> 150 people identified as outdoors enthusiasts
>
> 200 people randomly selected at local sporting goods stores
>
> 100 people randomly selected at the local grocery store

**a.** What factors might contribute to the bias of a sample? Select all that apply.

   **A.** The type of store the sample was taken in

   **B.** The time of day the sample was taken

   **C.** The interests of the people in the sample

   **D.** None of the above

**b.** Which of these samples are likely to contain bias? Select all that apply.

   **A.** 200 people randomly selected at local sporting goods stores

   **B.** 100 people identified as outdoors enthusiasts

   **C.** 150 people randomly selected at the local grocery store

   **D.** None of the above

**7. Writing** A movie company recently collected a representative sample of people who prefer dramas. The sample contains 29 men and 33 women.

**a.** Which inferences are valid for the population of people who prefer dramas? Select all that apply.

   **A.** There are more women than men in the population.

   **B.** 29 out of every 33 members in the population are men.

   **C.** 88% of the population are men.

   **D.** 47% of the population are men.

**b.** Write two other valid inferences.

**8. Survey** Out of a group of 20 volunteers, 15 people are chosen to participate in a survey about the number of miles they drive to work each week. What is the sample in this situation?

   **A.** the 5 people not selected to participate

   **B.** the 15 people selected to participate

   **C.** the people conducting the survey

   **D.** the 20 volunteers

**9. Open-Ended** A supermarket takes a survey of its customers and asks if they like apple juice.

**a.** Which of these samples is most likely to be unbiased?

   **A.** 357 people randomly selected from all the people in the store

   **B.** 353 people who purchase apple juice that day

   **C.** 449 people who purchased apple and grape juice that day

   **D.** 407 people who did not purchase apple juice that day

**b.** Describe two more possible sample sets, one biased and one unbiased.

**10.** A company takes a survey of people who subscribe to their website. The results indicate that 55% of their subscribers are over the age of 30. Which of the following is true of a representative sample of 700 subscribers?

   **I.** 45% of the subscribers are age 30 or younger.

   **II.** 385 of the subscribers are over 30.

   **III.** The number of subscribers 30 or younger is more than the number of subscribers over 30.

   **A.** I only      **B.** I and II only

   **C.** I and III only   **D.** I, II, and III

CCSS: 7.SP.A.2, Also 7.SP.A.1

## Key Concept

The number of orange golf balls in the population is proportional to the number of orange golf balls in the representative sample.

Population of 150 golf balls          Representative sample

Constant of proportionality of orange golf balls $= \dfrac{\text{Number of orange golf balls in sample}}{\text{Sample size}} = \dfrac{2}{6} = \dfrac{1}{3}$

> 1 orange golf ball for every 3 golf balls

There are about $\dfrac{1}{3} \cdot 150$, or 50, orange golf balls in the bucket.

The number of green golf balls in the population is proportional to the number of green golf balls in the representative sample.

Constant of proportionality of green golf balls $= \dfrac{\text{Number of green golf balls in sample}}{\text{Sample size}} = \dfrac{4}{6} = \dfrac{2}{3}$

> 2 green golf balls for every 3 golf balls

There are about $\dfrac{2}{3} \cdot 150$, or 100, green golf balls in the bucket.

# Part 1

## Example Estimating Populations from Samples

Suppose it is 200 years in the future. The population consists of humans and robots. You collect a representative sample.

If the population has 13,500 members, estimate the number of robots in the population.

### Solution

**Know**
- There are 2 robots in the sample of 10 subjects.
- The sample is a representative sample.
- There are 13,500 members in the population.

**Need**
- The number of robots in the population

**Plan**
- Find the constant of proportionality of robots.
- Write an equation:
  number of robots in population = constant of proportionality · population size

**Step 1** Find the constant of proportionality.

$$\text{constant of proportionality} = \frac{\text{number of robots in sample}}{\text{sample size}}$$

$$= \frac{2}{10}, \text{ or } \frac{1}{5}$$

> 1 robot for every 5 members of the population

**Step 2** Estimate the number in the population.

number of robots in population = constant of proportionality · population size

$$= \frac{1}{5} \cdot 13{,}500$$

$$= 2{,}700$$

> There are about 2,700 robots in the population.

# Part 2

## Example Identifying Representative Samples

A botanist wants to find the number of four-leaf clovers in a field. There are 700 clovers in the field. She has three samples of the population. If the actual number of four-leaf clovers in the field is 6, which sample best represents the population?

| Sample A | Sample B | Sample C | | | |
|---|---|---|---|---|---|
| 3 | 3 | 3 | 3 | 3 | 3 |
| 3 | 3 | 3 | 3 | 3 | 3 |
| 3 | 3 | 3 | 3 | 3 | 3 |
| 4 | 3 | 3 | 3 | 3 | 3 |
| 3 | 3 | 3 | 3 | 3 | 3 |
|   | 3 | 3 | 3 | 3 | 3 |
|   | 3 | 3 | 3 | 3 | 3 |
|   | 3 | 3 | 3 | 3 | 3 |
|   | 3 | 3 | 3 | 3 | 3 |
|   | 3 | 3 | 3 | 3 | 3 |
|   | 3 | 3 | 3 | 3 | 3 |
|   | 3 | 3 | 3 | 3 | 3 |
|   | 3 | 3 | 3 | 3 | 3 |
|   | 4 | 3 | 3 | 3 | 3 |
|   | 3 | 3 | 3 | 3 | 3 |
|   | 3 | 3 | 3 | 3 | 3 |
|   | 3 | 3 | 3 | 3 | 3 |
|   | 3 | 3 | 3 | 3 | 3 |
|   | 3 | 3 | 3 | 3 | 3 |
|   | 3 | 3 | 3 | 3 | 3 |
|   | 3 | 3 | 3 | 3 | 3 |
|   | 3 | 3 | 3 | 3 | 3 |
|   | 3 | 3 | 3 | 3 | 3 |
|   | 3 | 3 | 3 | 3 | 4 |

## Solution

**Step 1** Find the constant of proportionality.

$$\text{constant of proportionality} = \frac{\text{number of four-leaf clovers in sample}}{\text{sample size}}$$

| Sample | Sample A | Sample B | Sample C |
|---|---|---|---|
| Number of Four-leaf Clovers | 1 | 1 | 1 |
| Sample Size | 5 | 25 | 100 |
| Constant of Proportionality | $\frac{1}{5}$ | $\frac{1}{25}$ | $\frac{1}{100}$ |

continued on next page >

## Part 2

### Solution continued

**Step 2** Estimate the number in the population.

$$\begin{matrix} \text{number of four-leaf} \\ \text{clovers in population} \end{matrix} = \begin{matrix} \text{constant of} \\ \text{proportionality} \end{matrix} \cdot \begin{matrix} \text{population} \\ \text{size} \end{matrix}$$

| Sample | Sample A | Sample B | Sample C |
|---|---|---|---|
| Number of Four-leaf Clovers | $\frac{1}{5} \cdot 700 = 140$ | $\frac{1}{25} \cdot 700 = 28$ | $\frac{1}{100} \cdot 700 = 7$ |

The actual number of four-leaf clovers in the field is 6. Of Samples A, B, and C, Sample C is closest to the actual number. So Sample C best represents the population.

## Part 3

### Example Comparing Estimates of Populations

A computer factory has 670 computers in storage. Three inspectors each checked 50 of the computers in different areas of the storage room and noted the number of defective computers they found. Each inspector used his or her results to estimate the total number of defective computers in the factory.

> **Inspector A:** 4 defective computers
> **Inspector B:** 1 defective computer
> **Inspector C:** 2 defective computers

**a.** What was each inspector's estimate?

**b.** Suppose the actual number of defective computers in storage is 29. Which inspector's estimate is best? Explain.

### Solution

**a. Step 1** Find the constant of proportionality.

$$\text{constant of proportionality} = \frac{\text{number of defective computers in sample}}{\text{sample size}}$$

| Sample | Inspector A | Inspector B | Inspector C |
|---|---|---|---|
| Number of Sample Defective Computers | 4 | 1 | 2 |
| Sample Size | 50 | 50 | 50 |
| Constant of Proportionality | $\frac{4}{50}$, or $\frac{2}{25}$ | $\frac{1}{50}$ | $\frac{2}{50}$, or $\frac{1}{25}$ |

continued on next page >

# Part 3

## Solution continued

**Step 2** Estimate the number in the population.

$$\frac{\text{number of defective}}{\text{computers}} = \frac{\text{constant of}}{\text{proportionality}} \cdot \frac{\text{population}}{\text{size}}$$

| Sample | Inspector A | Inspector B | Inspector C |
|---|---|---|---|
| Number of Defective Computers | $\frac{2}{25} \cdot 670 = \frac{1{,}340}{25}$<br>$= 53.6$<br>$\approx 54$ | $\frac{1}{50} \cdot 670 = \frac{670}{50}$<br>$= 13.4$<br>$\approx 13$ | $\frac{1}{25} \cdot 670 = \frac{670}{25}$<br>$= 26.8$<br>$\approx 27$ |

**b.** Answers may vary. Sample: Inspector C's estimate is best. The estimate is 27, which is closest to the actual number of defective computers.

**1.** A bag contains red and blue marbles. In a representative sample of 30 marbles, there are 16 red marbles. If the bag has 180 marbles, estimate the number of red marbles and blue marbles in the bag.

**2.** A bucket of golf balls contains gray golf balls and white golf balls. You collect the representative sample shown. If the bucket contains 50 golf balls, about how many golf balls are white?

**3.** A farmer uses government reports to simulate three samples that note the number of acres ready for harvesting. Combine the samples to make one large sample. Use that sample to predict the number of acres ready for harvesting in a 700-acre corn field.

| | |
|---|---|
| **Sample X** | **34 out of 50 acres ready for harvesting** |
| **Sample Y** | **42 out of 50 acres ready for harvesting** |
| **Sample Z** | **39 out of 50 acres ready for harvesting** |

**4. Think About the Process** An Internet service provider (ISP) wants to know how many people in a region with population 11,000 use the Internet. The ISP obtains these three samples.

| | |
|---|---|
| **Sample 1** | **In a sample of 50 people, 33 said they use the Internet.** |
| **Sample 2** | **In a sample of 100 people, 66 said they use the Internet.** |
| **Sample 3** | **In a sample of 250 people, 165 said they use the Internet.** |

**a.** How can the ISP use the samples to make an estimate? Select all that apply.

**A.** Divide the population size by the size of the combined samples.

**B.** Divide the population size by the size of the largest sample.

**C.** Multiply the constant of proportionality for the combined samples by the population size.

**D.** Multiply the constant of proportionality for a sample by the population size.

**b.** The best estimate is that about ■ people in the region use the Internet.

**c.** Should the ISP be confident about this estimate?

**5. Reasoning** You want to find the number of students with October birthdays. In a school with 1,000 students, the actual number of students with October birthdays is 120. You do not know this, so you collect three samples. One sample finds 16 October birthdays in 25 students. Another sample finds 17 October birthdays in 50 students. The third sample finds 12 October birthdays in 100 students.

**a.** Which sample best represents the population?

**A.** 16 students with October birthdays in a sample of 25 students

**B.** 17 students with October birthdays in a sample of 50 students

**C.** 12 students with October birthdays in a sample of 100 students

**D.** All three samples are representative.

**b.** Use the sample to predict the number of students with October birthdays in a group of 1,500 students.

**c.** Explain how you know a sample is representative of a population.

See your complete lesson at MyMathUniverse.com

**6. Think About the Process** A water park has 1,000 guests. Three employees each asked 100 people if they went on the park's new water slide. Suppose the actual number of people that went on the new water slide is 610.

**Employee X** 65 out of 100 people went on the new water slide.

**Employee Y** 62 out of 100 people went on the new water slide.

**Employee Z** 57 out of 100 people went on the new water slide.

**a.** How can you use the information in the samples to find the best estimate of the total number of people who went on the new water slide?

**A.** Compare the actual number of people who went on the new water slide to the total population to find the best estimate.

**B.** Compare the constant of proportionality for each sample. The best estimate comes from the constant of proportionality closest to the total population.

**C.** Use each sample to estimate the number of people who went on the new water slide. The best estimate is the estimate closest to the total population.

**D.** Combine the samples to make one large sample. Use the large sample to estimate the total number of people who went on the new water slide.

**b.** The best estimate is that about ■ people went on the park's new water slide.

**7. Error Analysis** In a box of 60 pens there are black pens and blue pens. Jenna was asked to estimate the number of black pens in the box. She incorrectly said there are about 40 black pens in the box. Use the representative sample shown.

black pens    blue pens

**a.** Estimate the number of black pens in the box.

**b.** What mistake might Jenna have made?

**A.** She used 10 as the population size instead of 60.

**B.** She used $\frac{2}{3}$ as the constant of proportionality instead of $\frac{2}{5}$.

**C.** She used $\frac{2}{5}$ as the constant of proportionality instead of $\frac{2}{3}$.

**D.** She used 60 as the population size instead of 10.

**8. Multiple Representations** In a bowl of fruit salad there are strawberries, blueberries, grapes, and raspberries. In a representative sample of 30 pieces of fruit, there are 14 strawberries.

**a.** If the fruit salad has 270 pieces of fruit, estimate the number of strawberries in the fruit salad.

**b.** Draw a picture to represent the proportional relationship.

**9. Challenge** A bag contains 200 red and blue marbles. Three people each took samples of 25 marbles and noted the number of red marbles.

**Person A** 17 red marbles out of 25 marbles

**Person B** 12 red marbles out of 25 marbles

**Person C** 20 red marbles out of 25 marbles

**a.** Combine the samples to make one large sample. Use that sample to predict the number of red marbles in a similar bag that contains 300 marbles.

**b.** Explain how having a fourth sample would make the estimate better.

See your complete lesson at MyMathUniverse.com

# Convenience Sampling

CCSS: 7.SP.A.1

## Key Concept

A good statistical study should consider whether there is a sampling method that produces a representative sample of the population.

**Convenience sampling** is a sampling method in which you choose members of the population that are convenient and available.

When a researcher surveys members of a population that are convenient, the sample is called a convenience sample. A convenience sample is not necessarily a representative sample.

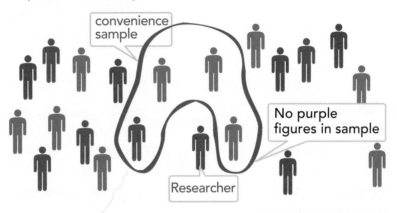

## Part 1

### Example  Identifying Convenience Sampling

Suppose you are doing research on the students at your school. Is each an instance of convenience sampling? Explain.

    **a.** You put an ad in the school newspaper for your research project. You accept the first 10 students who volunteer.

    **b.** You put the names of all of the students in a hat and put out 10 names at random.

    **c.** You choose the first 10 students you see.

### Solution

    **a.** Yes; your sample is based on the first 10 students who volunteered, so this is an instance of convenience sampling.

    **b.** No; you are choosing among the entire population at random, so this is not an instance of convenience sampling.

    **c.** Yes; since you are choosing the students who happen to be close to you and not sorting through the population in any way, this is an instance of convenience sampling.

# Part 2

## Example  Choosing Convenience Samples

Suppose you are a news reporter, investigating the town's opinion of the new shopping center. What are three ways to choose a convenience sample of town residents to interview? Are the samples that you choose representative samples? Explain.

### Solution

Convenience Sample #1: Ask people in the neighborhood near the new shopping center; yes, the sample is probably a representative sample because the people in this neighborhood may be mixed enough to represent the population.

Convenience Sample #2: Ask shoppers in the new shopping center; no, the sample is not a representative sample because the people shopping in the new shopping center probably like the new mall, so they do not represent the entire population.

Convenience Sample #3: Ask people commuting to work on the street; yes, the sample is probably a representative sample because the people on the street are likely to be a good mix of the population.

# Part 3

## Example Estimating Populations Using Convenience Samples

There are about 300 million Web sites in the world. Use the convenience sample to estimate the total number of Web sites that get more than a million hits per day. Is your estimate accurate? Explain.

http://www.digitsmath.com    Favorites

Convenience sample: 20 of my favorite Web sites
11 of them get more than a million hits per day

How many of the 300 million Web sites in the world get more than a million hits per day?

## Solution

**Step 1** Find the constant of proportionality of Web sites that get more than a million hits per day for the convenience sample.

$$\text{constant of proportionality} = \frac{\text{number of Web sites that get more than a million hits in sample}}{\text{sample size}}$$

$$= \frac{11}{20}$$

**Step 2** Estimate the number of Web sites with more than a million hits in the population.

$$\frac{\text{number of}}{\text{Web sites}} = \frac{\text{constant of}}{\text{proportionality}} \cdot \text{population size}$$

$$= \frac{11}{20} \cdot 300{,}000{,}000$$

$$= \frac{3{,}300{,}000{,}000}{20}$$

$$= 165{,}000{,}000$$

You can estimate that there are about 165 million Web sites out of the 300 million Web sites that get more than a million hits per day.

The convenience sample is based on a list of your favorite Web sites and may be biased toward popular Web sites with higher numbers of hits per day. So 165 million Web sites may not be an accurate estimate of the actual number.

1. Which of the following descriptions would be an example of a convenience sample? Select all that apply.

   **A.** A person accepts the first 27 people who respond to an email.

   **B.** A person chooses 27 names out of a hat at random.

   **C.** A person accepts the first 27 people who volunteer.

   **D.** None of the descriptions is an example of a convenience sample.

2. Victor is doing a study to see what the town thinks of the new grocery store. He chooses a convenience sample. He asks 13 people from the town who know people who work in the new grocery store. What bias is there in this convenience sample, if any?

   **A.** The bias is that Victor has 13 people in the sample.

   **B.** The bias is that Victor asks people in the town.

   **C.** The bias is that Victor asks people who know people who work in the new grocery store.

   **D.** There is not bias in this convenience sample.

3. Samuel is doing a report for his math class. He is doing a survey of what music people listen to. He asks 14 people at the beach. Is the convenience sample a representative sample of the entire population? Why?

   **A.** No, it is not representative because the ages of the people are probably mixed.

   **B.** Yes, it is representative because the ages of the people are probably mixed.

   **C.** Yes, it is representative because the ages of the people are in a specific age range.

4. Angela is doing a study to find what is the most popular fruit in her town. There are 9,000 people living in the town. She uses a convenience sample and finds that 3 people out of the 20 people asked say that the pineapple is the best fruit. Estimate the total number of people in the town who consider the pineapple to be the best fruit.

5. Tereza wants to know what movies people like in her town. She surveys high school students. Tereza estimates from the convenience sample that 16,000 people in the town like action movies. How accurate is the given estimate?

   **A.** The estimate is accurate because the group surveyed is random.

   **B.** The estimate is not accurate because the group surveyed is random.

   **C.** The estimate is not accurate because the group surveyed is a certain age group and must be biased.

   **D.** The estimate is accurate because the group surveyed is a certain age group and may be biased.

6. Petra is doing a survey.

   **a.** Which of the following descriptions is an example of convenience sampling?

   **A.** Petra surveys 4 students in every class in the school.

   **B.** Petra surveys every house in her town.

   **C.** Petra surveys the 15 players on her hockey team.

   **b.** How could you change the other descriptions to be examples of convenience sampling?

**7.** A class wants to know what sport people in the town enjoy. The class asks people at the mall. From the convenience sample the class estimates that 14,000 people enjoy basketball.

**a.** Which of the following is the best description of the estimate?

**A.** The estimate is not accurate because the group surveyed is random.

**B.** The estimate is not accurate because the group surveyed is a specific group and may be biased.

**C.** The estimate is accurate because the group surveyed is a specific group and may be biased.

**D.** The estimate is accurate because the group surveyed is random.

**b.** If an estimate is considered to be not accurate, how could it be made into an accurate estimate?

**8.** A city library is doing a survey to see what types of books people like to read. There are 160,000 people who live in the city. The library does a convenience sample. Out of the 250 people surveyed, 101 consider science fiction the best type of book. Estimate the total number of people in the city who consider science fiction the best type of book.

**9. Think About the Process** A contractor wants to know what the town thinks of his business. The contractor asks 11 people at a mall, "What is your opinion of the business?"

**a.** What should be the first step to see if the convenience sample is representative of the population?

**A.** The first step should be estimate part of the population.

**B.** The first step should be to make a generalization about the population using the convenience sample.

**C.** The first step should be to see if there is a bias within the sample.

**D.** The first step should be to do another sample.

**b.** Which of the following is the best description of the convenience sample?

**A.** The sample is not representative because people at the mall are probably not biased about the business.

**B.** The sample is representative because people at the mall are probably biased about the business.

**C.** The sample is representative because people at the mall are probably not biased about the business.

**D.** The sample is not representative because people at the mall are probably biased about the business.

**10. Think About the Process** Olivia works as a sports reporter for one of the small sports shows. There are 12,000 people who watch the show. Olivia wants to know what the most popular sport is, so she asks a convenience sample of people, "What is your favorite sport to watch?" She finds that of the 20 people sampled, 11 like watching soccer.

**a.** Which of the following is the constant of proportionality needed to estimate the total number of people who watch the show who like to watch soccer?

**A.** $\dfrac{20}{12,000}$      **B.** $\dfrac{12,000}{132,000}$

**C.** $\dfrac{11}{12,000}$      **D.** $\dfrac{11}{20}$

**b.** Estimate the total number of people who watch the show and like to watch soccer.

CCSS: 7.SP.A.1

## Key Concept

The population:

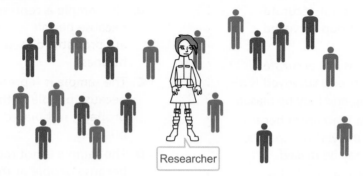

**Systematic sampling** is a sampling method in which you choose every *n*th member of the population, where *n* is a predetermined number.

A systematic sample is useful when the researcher is able to approach the population in a systematic, or methodical, way.

The population, arranged in a line:

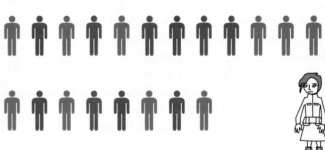

**Step 1** Assign numbers to the population. Assign each member of the population a unique number.

The population, with assigned numbers:

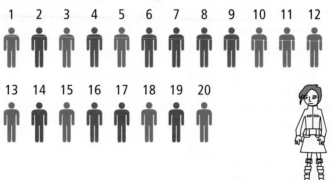

continued on next page >

# Key Concept

continued

**Step 2** Find the interval *n*. To find the interval *n*, you need to know the population size and the desired sample size.

There are 20 members in the population. Suppose you want a sample of 5 subjects.

$$\text{interval } n = \frac{\text{population size}}{\text{sample size}} = \frac{20}{5} = 4$$

The population, divided into groups of 4:

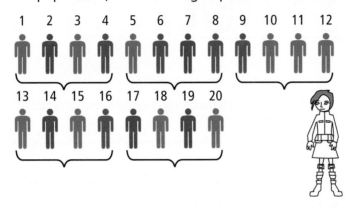

**Step 3** Find the starting number. To find the starting number, pick a number from 1 to *n* at random.

$$\text{Starting number} = 3$$

**Step 4** Collect a systematic sample. Collect a **systematic sample** by choosing the member with the starting number and then every 4th member until you reach the end of the population.

A systematic sample takes preparation to collect, but it usually produces a representative sample. Someone could introduce bias into the sample by arranging the population to make sure certain members are chosen.

$$\text{interval } n = 4$$
$$\text{Starting number} = 3$$

continued on next page >

# Key Concept

continued

The population, with a systematic sample represented:

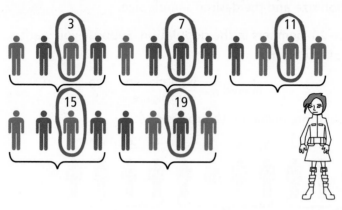

Numbers 3, 7, 11, 15, and 19 make up a systematic sample.

# Part 1

## Example  Identifying Systematic Sampling

Suppose you are doing research on the students at your school. Is each an instance of systematic sampling? Explain.

**a.** You make a list of students in your class and choose every seventh name, starting from the first name.

**b.** You have the students in your class count off by 4's. You choose the students who counted "3."

**c.** You make a list of the students and choose the first ten names on your list.

## Solution · · · · · · · · · · · · · · · · · · · · · · · · · · · · · · · · · · · · · · · · · · · · · · ·

**a.** Yes; you chose your sample using a starting point, the first person, and an interval, 7, so this is an instance of systematic sampling.

**b.** Yes; you choose your sample using a starting point, 3, and an interval, 4, so this is an instance of systematic sampling.

**c.** No; you chose the first 10 names, not by jumping intervals, so this is not an instance of systematic sampling.

# Part 2

### Example Choosing Systematic Samples

You want to estimate how often books in the science section of the library are checked out. There are 72 books in the section. You decide to sample 9 books in the section. Choose a systematic sample. Is your sample a representative sample? Explain.

**Solution** · · · · · · · · · · · · · · · · · · · · · · · · · · · · · · · · · · · · · · · · · ·

| Desired sample size |

| Population size |

You are sampling 9 books in the science section of 72 books.

First, find the interval $n$.

$$\text{interval } n = \frac{\text{population size}}{\text{sample size}}$$

$$= \frac{72}{9}$$

$$= 8$$

Choose the starting book by picking a number from 1 to 8 at random. The starting number is 4.

$$\text{interval } n = 8$$
Starting number: 4

Collect your systematic sample, starting at the 4th book and every 8th book from there.

The sample is most likely a representative sample because there does not seem to be a relevant pattern to the books that would introduce bias.

# Part 3

## Example  Estimating Populations Using Systematic Samples

Suppose you want to estimate the number of purple lights in a light display. You decide to take a systematic sample using an interval of 5 lights, starting from the second light.

Suppose there are a total of 300 light bulbs in the display. Using your systematic sample, how many purple bulbs do you estimate are in the display? How accurate is your estimate? Explain.

## Solution  · · · · · · · · · · · · · · · · · · · · · · · · · · · · · · · · · · · · · · · · · · · · · · · · · · · ·

The light display repeats colors in the same order every 5 bulbs. Since the interval of the systematic sample is also 5, the sample consists of only yellow light bulbs.

Start counting from the second light, which is yellow.

Count five lights. The next light is also yellow.

Using the systematic sample, there are only yellow lights (and therefore no purple lights) in the display.

This estimate is not accurate because the systematic sample is not a representative sample.

1. Caroline is doing research on the heights of players on her soccer team. Select each description that is an example of systematic sampling.

   A. Caroline chooses every seventh person on the team roster, starting with the second.

   B. Caroline randomly chooses one of her teammates.

   C. Caroline chooses the first 5 names on the team roster.

   D. Caroline chooses everyone on her team.

   E. Caroline has her teammates count off by 6 and chooses the ones who counted "3."

2. You are doing research on the students in your class. Which of the following descriptions is an example of systematic sampling?

   A. You make a list of the students and choose the first 5 names on your list.

   B. You choose every student whose birthday is in July.

   C. You choose every student in your class.

   D. You have the students count off by 5 and choose the students who counted "4."

3. **Think About the Process** The houses on a certain street are numbered in order with no gaps, starting at 1. The odd-numbered houses are always more expensive than the even-numbered houses. To research the average cost of the houses on this street, you decide take a systematic sample. You choose every eleventh house, starting at house number five.

   a. What factor should you consider when deciding if your sample is representative of the population?

      A. Any bias that may be present in the sample

   B. The names of the people that live in the houses

   C. The total number of houses on the street

   D. The time it took to get the sample

   b. Using your answer from the previous step, would the results from your systematic sample be representative of the population?

      A. Yes, because the pattern in the houses and the interval used introduce a bias in the systematic sample.

      B. No, because the pattern in the houses and the interval used introduce a bias in the systematic sample.

      C. No, because the pattern in the houses and the interval used do not introduce any bias in the systematic sample.

      D. Yes, because the pattern in the houses and the interval used do not introduce any bias in the systematic sample.

4. You are researching the average height of students in your class. You have the students line up in reverse alphabetical order. You take a systematic sample by measuring the height of every ninth student, starting with the fourth. Would the results from your systematic sample be representative of the class?

   A. No, because there seems to be a relevant pattern in the students that would introduce bias.

   B. No, because there does not seem to be a relevant pattern in the students that would introduce bias.

   C. Yes, because there seems to be a relevant pattern in the students that would introduce bias.

   D. Yes, because there does not seem to be a relevant pattern in the students that would introduce bias.

5. The trees in a city park form a line through the center of the park. The types of trees repeat in the order of elm, spruce, willow, pine, and birch throughout the line. You decide to take a systematic sample using an interval of 6 trees, starting from the first tree. In all, there are 150 trees in the park. Using your systematic sample, how many pine trees do you estimate are in the park?

6. **Writing** You are researching the average size of the apartments in a certain apartment building. The building has apartments numbered 1 to 96.

   a. Which of the following could represent the first three apartments you choose in a systematic sample of 16 apartments?

   **A.** 2, 9, 16      **B.** 1, 9, 18

   **C.** 3, 9, 15      **D.** 9, 15, 21

   b. Compare the advantages and disadvantages of systematic sampling with those of convenience sampling. Which method do you prefer? Explain.

7. The plants in your neighbor's garden are in the repeated order of sunflowers, lilacs, roses, and tulips. You decide to take a systematic sample using an interval of 7 plants, starting from the third plant. Using your systematic sample, you estimate that of the 56 plants in her garden, 14 are sunflowers. How accurate is your estimate? Explain.

   **A.** The estimate is not accurate. The pattern in the plants does not introduce any bias in the sample, so it is not representative of the population.

   **B.** The estimate is not accurate. The pattern in the plants introduces a bias in the sample, so it is not representative of the population.

   **C.** The estimate should be fairly accurate. The pattern in the plants does not introduce any bias in the sample, so it should be representative of the population.

   **D.** The estimate should be fairly accurate. The pattern in the plants does not introduce any bias in the sample, so it is not representative of the population.

8. a. **Reasoning** You are studying the colors of houses on a highly populated street. Decide whether or not each of the following descriptions is an example of systematic sampling. Select all that apply.

   **A.** You choose every eighth house on the street, starting with the second.

   **B.** You choose every house on the street.

   **C.** You choose the first and last 8 houses on the street.

   **D.** You list the houses alphabetically by owner's last name, and choose every fifth house on the list, starting at the fourth.

   b. Explain your reasoning for each decision.

9. **Think About the Process** In a pet store, birds are displayed in the repeated order of finch, canary, macaw, and parakeet. You take a systematic sample using an interval of 5 birds, starting from the third bird. In all, there are 80 birds in the store.

   a. Which of the following is the constant of proportionality needed to estimate the total number of finches in the store?

   **A.** $\frac{1}{20}$      **B.** 4

   **C.** 16      **D.** $\frac{1}{4}$

   b. You estimate there are ■ finches in the store.

| **Simple Random Sampling**

**Vocabulary**
simple random sampling

CCSS: 7.SP.A.1, 7.SP.A.2

## Key Concept

**Simple random sampling** is a sampling method in which every member of the population has an equal chance of being chosen for the sample.

**Step 1** Assign Numbers to Members

Like systematic sampling, you need a list of all of the members in a population. Assign a unique number to each member.

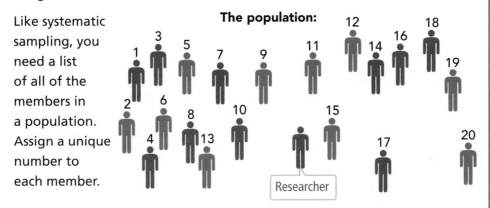

**Step 2** Generate Numbers at Random

Choose at random as many numbers as you need subjects in your sample.

9          12          3          1          19

**Step 3** Choose a Simple Random Sample

The members assigned to the chosen numbers are the subjects in the **simple random sample**.

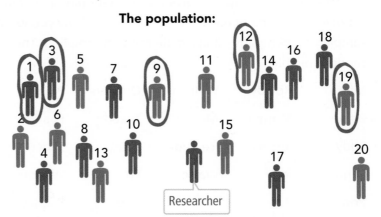

In this way, each member of the population has an equal chance of being chosen for the sample. A simple random sample takes some preparation to collect, but it usually produces a representative sample.

# Part 1

### Example Identifying Examples of Simple Random Sampling

Suppose you are doing research on the students in your class. Is each an instance of simple random sampling? Explain.

   **a.** You make an alphabetical list of the students in your class and select the first ten names on the list.

   **b.** You mix all of the students' names in a hat and select ten names, blindfolded.

   **c.** You assign a number starting from 1 to each student in your class. Then you pick ten of these numbers at random.

### Solution ·································································

   **a.** No; although you have a list of the members of the population, you did not randomly choose your subjects from that list. This is not an instance of simple random sampling.

   **b.** Yes; you have a list of the members of the population, and you selected the subjects at random. This is an instance of simple random sampling.

   **c.** Yes; you have a list of the members of the population, and you selected the subjects at random. This is an instance of simple random sampling.

# Part 2

### Example Choosing Simple Random Samples

Suppose you are studying a group of 35 penguins in an aquarium. The list gives the name of each penguin. Describe how you would collect a sample of 7 penguins using simple random sampling. Then choose a simple random sample.

| | | | | | | |
|---|---|---|---|---|---|---|
| Milo | Rowdy | William | Quakers | Pingo | Flapper | Big Ma |
| Baby | Stormie | Marcher | Tuxedo | Pearl | Meiko | Spencer |
| Eddy | Snowy | Ice Cube | Rainy | Slider | Blizzard | Flipper |
| Penny | Iggy | Watson | PK | Waddles | Oscar | Crystal |
| Princess | BJ | Honey | Bob | Stanley | Jackson | Bruce |

continued on next page >

# Part 2

**Example** continued

**Solution** · · · · · · · · · · · · · · · · · · · · · · · · · · · · · · · · · · · · · · · · · · · · · · · · · · · · · · · · · · ·

**Step 1** Assign a number to each penguin listed.

| Penguin Name | Number | Penguin Name | Number | Penguin Name | Number |
|---|---|---|---|---|---|
| Milo | 1 | Meiko | 13 | PK | 25 |
| Rowdy | 2 | Spencer | 14 | Waddles | 26 |
| William | 3 | Eddy | 15 | Oscar | 27 |
| Quackers | 4 | Snowy | 16 | Crystal | 28 |
| Pingo | 5 | Ice Cube | 17 | Princess | 29 |
| Flapper | 6 | Rainy | 18 | BJ | 30 |
| Big Ma | 7 | Slider | 19 | Honey | 31 |
| Baby | 8 | Blizzard | 20 | Bob | 32 |
| Stormie | 9 | Flipper | 21 | Stanley | 33 |
| Marcher | 10 | Penny | 22 | Jackson | 34 |
| Tuxedo | 11 | Iggy | 23 | Bruce | 35 |
| Pearl | 12 | Watson | 24 | | |

**Step 2** Generate seven random integers from 1 to 35:
20, 2, 16, 31, 8, 13, 27

continued on next page >

## Part 2

### Solution continued

**Step 3** Highlight the penguins that correspond to the seven random integers.

| Penguin Name | Number |
|---|---|
| Milo | 1 |
| Rowdy | 2 |
| | 3 |
| | 4 |
| | 5 |
| Flapper | 6 |
| Big Ma | 7 |
| Baby | 8 |
| Stormie | 9 |
| Marcher | 10 |
| Tuxedo | 11 |
| Pearl | 12 |

2 is an example of a penguin in the simple random sample.

| Penguin Name | Number |
|---|---|
| Meiko | 13 |
| Spencer | 14 |
| Eddy | 15 |
| Snowy | 16 |
| Ice Cube | 17 |
| Rainy | 18 |
| Slider | 19 |
| Blizzard | 20 |
| Flipper | 21 |
| Penny | 22 |
| Iggy | 23 |
| Watson | 24 |

| Penguin Name | Number |
|---|---|
| PK | 25 |
| Waddles | 26 |
| Oscar | 27 |
| Crystal | 28 |
| Princess | 29 |
| BJ | 30 |
| Honey | 31 |
| Bob | 32 |
| Stanley | 33 |
| Jackson | 34 |
| Bruce | 35 |

## Part 3

### Example  Using Simple Random Samples to Make Inferences

You are studying a population of 35 penguins. The table shows the seven penguins in your simple random sample. Based on this sample, how many penguins in the population weigh between 30 and 40 pounds? Explain.

| Number | Penguin | Weight (lb) |
|---|---|---|
| 2 | Rowdy | 28 |
| 8 | Ice Baby | 35 |
| 13 | Meiko | 42 |
| 16 | Snowflake | 24 |
| 20 | Blizzard | 31 |
| 27 | Oscar | 39 |
| 31 | Honey | 34 |

continued on next page >

# Part 3

**Example** continued

**Solution** · · · · · · · · · · · · · · · · · · · · · · · · · · · · · · · · · · · · · · · · · · · ·

There are 4 penguins out of 7 that are between 30 and 40 pounds.

| Number | Penguin | Weight (lb) |
|--------|---------|-------------|
| 2 | Rowdy | 28 |
| 8 | Ice Baby | 35 |
| 13 | Meiko | 42 |
| 16 | Snowflake | 24 |
| 20 | Blizzard | 31 |
| 27 | Oscar | 39 |
| 31 | Honey | 34 |

**Step 1** Find the constant of proportionality of penguins that are between 30 and 40 pounds.

$$\text{constant of proportionality} = \frac{\text{number of penguins between 30 and 40 lbs in sample}}{\text{size of sample}}$$

$$= \frac{4}{7}$$

**Step 2** Estimate the number of penguins between 30 and 40 pounds in the population.

$$\begin{matrix}\text{penguins between} \\ \text{30 and 40 lbs}\end{matrix} = \begin{matrix}\text{constant of} \\ \text{proportionality}\end{matrix} \cdot \text{population size}$$

$$= \frac{4}{7} \cdot 35$$ ← There are 35 penguins in the population.

$$= 4 \cdot \frac{35}{7}$$

$$= 4 \cdot 5$$

$$= 20$$

There are about 20 penguins in the population that weigh between 30 and 40 pounds.

1. Your science class is studying the temperature on the first day of each month for one year. Which sample is a simple random sample?

   **A.** the temperature on the first day of six months, selected randomly

   **B.** the temperature on the first day of this month

   **C.** the temperature on the first day of June, July, and August

   **D.** none of the above

2. A seventh grade teacher asks 30 students in her class if they like apple juice.

   **a.** Select each process the teacher could use to create a random sample of 12 students.

   **A.** Select the 12 students whose desks are closest to the window.

   **B.** Assign each student a number, then select 12 random numbers.

   **C.** Select the last 12 students who enter the classroom after lunch.

   **D.** Choose 12 student names out of a hat.

   **b.** Do you think the teacher would use the same process to create a random sample if the population were all of the students in seventh grade? In the school? Explain.

3. You are studying the weather during the month of January. The table shows the weather in your simple random sample of seven days. Use the simple random sample to estimate the number of foggy days in January.

   **Daily Weather**

   | Day | Weather |
   | --- | --- |
   | 1 | Foggy |
   | 2 | Humid |
   | 3 | Sunny |
   | 4 | Foggy |
   | 5 | Humid |
   | 6 | Rainy |
   | 7 | Foggy |

4. Your class is competing in a state-wide reading competition. A simple random sample of your class indicates that 4 students read a total of 15 books last month. About how many books do you expect your class of 29 students to have read after one month? After five months?

5. **Reasoning** For a project, you are studying what types of music people like to listen to. You ask 100 people to complete your survey, then randomly select 32 people to create a sample. Is this sample representative of the population?

   **A.** Yes, because it contains more than half of the subjects.

   **B.** No, because it is a simple random sample.

   **C.** Yes, because it is a simple random sample.

   **D.** No, because it contains less than half of the subjects.

6. **Error Analysis** A researcher is studying a population of 39 toads. She believes that if she chooses the 13 oldest toads collected, she can create a random sample of 13 toads.

   **a.** What type of sample did the researcher take?

   **A.** She took a systematic sample.

   **B.** She took a convenience sample.

   **C.** It is impossible to determine what type of sample it is.

   **b.** How could the researcher create a simple random sample of 13 toads? Select all that apply.

   **A.** She could organize the toads in order by age and chose every third toad.

   **B.** She could assign a letter to each toad and choose 13 letters from a hat.

   **C.** She could assign a number to each toad and choose 13 numbers at random.

   **D.** None of the above.

See your complete lesson at MyMathUniverse.com

**7. Think About the Process** You are given the following population.

28 students in your class

**a.** What is a good first step when creating a simple random sample of a population?

**A.** Subtract the number of subjects you want in the sample from the number of subjects in the population.

**B.** Ask for volunteers from the population.

**C.** Divide the number of subjects in the population by the number of subjects you want in the sample.

**D.** Assign a number or letter to each subject in the population.

**b.** Describe a process you could use to create a simple random sample of 9 subjects from the given population.

**A.** Assign each student a number and randomly select 9 even numbers.

**B.** Assign each student a number and randomly select 9 numbers less than 14.

**C.** Assign each student a number and randomly select 9 numbers.

**D.** Assign each student a number and randomly select 9 odd numbers.

**8. Mental Math** To study the height of 300 seventh graders, a teacher takes a simple random sample of 30 students. In the sample, the teacher finds that 13 of the students are between 5′5″ and 5′7″ tall. About how many of the students in the total population are between 5′5″ and 5′7″ tall?

**9. Think About the Process** A survey is given to 1,000 people. You take a simple random sample of 400 people and find that 152 of the people go to the movies at least once a month.

**a.** How do you find the constant of proportionality for a certain trait in a simple random sample?

**A.** Subtract the number of subjects with that trait from the number of subjects in the sample.

**B.** Divide the number of subjects in the sample by the number of subjects with that trait.

**C.** Divide the number of subjects with that trait by the number of subjects in the sample.

**D.** Multiply the number of subjects with that trait and the number of subjects in the sample.

**b.** Of the people who took the survey, ■ go to the movies less than once a month.

**10. Challenge** To predict the performance of his fourth period class on their next quiz, a teacher randomly selects 10 students from the class and takes the mean of their scores on the last quiz.

**a.** Is this sample representative of the class's performance on the quiz?

**A.** No, because it is a simple random sample.

**B.** Yes, because it is a simple random sample.

**C.** Yes, because the students were chosen based on their class average.

**D.** No, because the students were chosen from the best students in the class.

**b.** Could the teacher use this sample to predict the performance of other classes? Explain.

# Key Concept

**Convenience Sampling is best when...**

- you do not have access to all of the members of the population

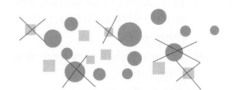

- you do not have time or resources to use a more accurate sampling method

- the members available are representative of the population, or it is not important that the sample be representative

**Systematic Sampling is best when...**

- the whole population is available, or a stream of representative members are available

- there is no pattern to the arrangement of the population or the stream of members

**Simple Random Sampling is best when...**

- the whole population is available

- the characteristics of the population are unknown

# Part 1

## Example Identifying Sampling Methods

Suppose the new music teacher wants to find out how many students in the school can play a musical instrument. Identify the sampling method in each description. Does each description produce a representative sample? Explain.

Simple Random                    Systematic                    Convenience

**a.** Survey every 5th student who enters the music room.
**b.** Survey the students in the school whose names are picked out of a hat.
**c.** Survey the students in the homeroom closest to the music room.
**d.** Survey all of the students in the next band practice.
**e.** Survey every 10th student who enters the school cafeteria.

## Solution

**a.** Systematic sampling

No; students who enter the music room probably play some sort of instrument and are more likely to play a musical instrument than students who do not go in the music room. So the sample has bias toward playing a musical instrument.

**b.** Simple random sampling

Yes; the random aspect of this method most likely produces a representative sample.

**c.** Convenience sampling

Yes; students in each homeroom are probably a good representation of the population because students were most likely assigned to a homeroom at random. So the sample is representative.

**d.** Convenience sampling

No; students in the band play an instrument, so the sample has bias toward playing a musical instrument.

**e.** Systematic sampling

Yes; the order in which students enter the cafeteria is random, in general, so the sample is representative.

# Part 2

## Example Comparing Systematic and Simple Random Sampling

Suppose you are a city developer. You want to determine how many of each model home there are in a neighborhood of 200 houses. Describe how you would choose a sample of 20 houses using either systematic sampling or simple random sampling. Justify your choice of sampling method.

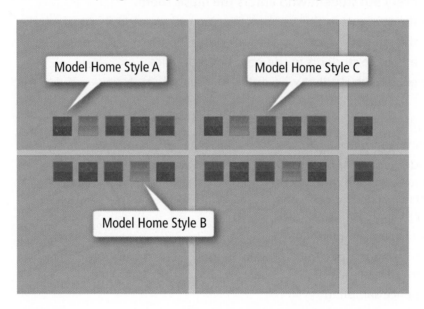

Model Home Style A

Model Home Style C

Model Home Style B

## Solution

Systematic Sampling

Find the interval:

total houses ÷ desired sample size = interval

$$200 \div 20 = 10$$

Sample every 10th house.

If there is a pattern to the line of houses that repeats every 10 houses, your sample may only include one type of model, regardless of which house you start at.

Might *not* produce a representative sample.

Simple Random Sampling

Assign a unique number from 1 to 200 to each house. Generate 20 numbers between 1 and 200 at random, and sample those houses.

Produces a representative sample.

Simple random sampling is the best choice because each type of house is equally likely to be chosen.

# Part 3

> **Example** **Comparing Convenience and Systematic Sampling**

Suppose you are an inspector at a toy factory that makes 600 toys per day. Six machines each make toys and place them on the conveyor belt. Describe how you would choose a sample of at least 75 toys from one day's production using either convenience or systematic sampling. Justify your choice of sampling method.

**Solution** ·····················································

> **Know**
> • Population: 600 toys
> • Six machines make the toys
> • You collect a sample from the conveyor belt

⬇

> **Need**
> The better method of choosing a sample of at least 75 toys

⬇

> **Plan**
> Make a table to consider the pros and cons of each sampling methods.

| Sampling Method | Pros | Cons |
|---|---|---|
| Convenience | • It is easy to take a sample of the next 75 toys on the conveyor belt. | • The sample represents only a fraction of the time that the toys are being produced, so it does not give a representative sample of toys from the whole day. <br> • It is difficult to catch toys that are defective if a machine malfunctions at a time other than when the sample is taken. |
| Systematic | • It generates a sample of toys produced throughout the day. | • You need to spend the entire day to collect the sample. <br> • The machines place the penguins on the conveyor belt in the same order each time. So, if you choose an interval that is a multiple of 2, 3, or 4 your sample would not include toys from all of the machines. |

Use systematic sampling with an interval of 5. This will give a representative sample of $\frac{600}{5}$ or 125 toys produced by all six machines throughout the day.

1. Employees at a water park want to find out how many customers like to ride their newest water slide.

   a. The employees surveyed every eighth customer waiting in line for the new water slide. Identify the sampling method they used.

   b. Does the description produce a representative sample?

2. Company X wants to determine how many cyclists at a certain bike path ride a Company X bike. About 210 cyclists ride on the bike path each day. The company wants a sample of 23 cyclists. You come up with two different sampling methods. One is a systematic sampling where you record the type of bike for every 9th cyclist that enters the trail. The other is a simple random sampling where 210 cyclists are given individual numbers and 23 of those numbers are chosen at random. Which method should you use and why?

   A. Simple random sampling, because systematic sampling will produce a biased sample.

   B. Systematic sampling, because simple random sampling will produce a biased sample.

   C. Systematic sampling, because it is easier to ask every 9th cyclist as they enter the path than to do the simple random sampling.

   D. Simple random sampling, because you cannot evenly divide 210 by 23, and it is easier to do than systematic sampling.

3. You want to know how many students in your school are left-handed. There are 160 students in your school and you want to choose a sample of 29 students. Should you use convenience sampling or systematic sampling? Explain you answer.

4. To estimate the percentage of defects in a recent manufacturing batch, a quality control manager at Company Y selects every 13th car that comes off the assembly line. She starts the count with the ninth car and continues until she obtains a sample of 140 cars.

   a. Identify the sampling method that is being used.

   b. Explain your reasoning.

5. The school's recycling club is thinking about using its funding to purchase reusable water bottles for every student in the school. The club came up with the ideas below to find out if students would use the water bottles.

   Survey students at the basketball courts.

   Survey students at the gym.

   Survey every fifth student that enters the school.

   Survey every fourth student that leaves the cafeteria.

   a. Which of the following descriptions are convenience sampling methods? Select all that apply.

   A. Survey students at the basketball courts.

   B. Survey students at the gym.

   C. Survey every fifth student that enters the school.

   D. Survey every fourth student that leaves the cafeteria.

   b. Which of the following descriptions are systematic sampling methods? Select all that apply.

   A. Survey every fourth student that leaves the cafeteria.

   B. Survey every fifth student that enters the school.

   C. Survey students at the gym.

   D. Survey students at the basketball courts.

   c. Find another description that uses the convenience sampling method and another that uses the systematic sampling method.

See your complete lesson at MyMathUniverse.com

6. **Think About the Process** Your school needs to get new lab coats for the science room as soon as possible and wants to know what color the students would prefer. There are 700 students in your school and the staff wants to choose a sample of 50 students.

a. How can you decide if they should use convenience sampling or systematic sampling?

b. Should they use convenience sampling or systematic sampling? Justify your choice of sampling method.

A. They should use systematic sampling, because convenience sampling will produce a biased sample.

B. They should use convenience sampling, because the decision is not that important and should be made fast.

C. They should use systematic sampling, because convenience sampling will not produce a representative sample.

D. They should use convenience sampling, because systematic sampling will produce a biased sample.

7. **Think About the Process** A deli wants to find out if their customers are satisfied. The deli managers came up with the methods below.

Survey 15 customers whose names were chosen out of a hat.

Send a survey to 70 customers chosen at random.

Survey every third customer that enters the deli.

Survey every fourth customer that orders a turkey sandwich.

a. How can you determine which descriptions are simple random sampling?

A. Find the descriptions where the whole population is available and the characteristics of the population are known.

B. Find the descriptions where the whole population is available and the characteristics of the population are unknown.

C. Find the descriptions where the whole population is not available and the characteristics of the population are unknown.

b. Which of the following descriptions are simple random sampling methods? Select all that apply.

A. Survey every fourth customer that orders a turkey sandwich.

B. Survey 15 customers whose names were chosen out of a hat.

C. Send a survey to 70 customers chosen at random.

D. Survey every third customer that enters the deli.

c. How can you determine which descriptions are systematic sampling?

d. Which of the following descriptions are systematic sampling methods? Select all that apply.

A. Survey 15 customers whose names were chosen out of a hat.

B. Send a survey to 70 customers chosen at random.

C. Survey every fourth customer that orders a turkey sandwich.

D. Survey every third customer that enters the deli.

CCSS: 7.SP.A.1, 7.SP.A.2

## Part 1

### Example  Determining If Inferences Are Valid

During the final episode of a national TV singing competition, the announcer congratulates the winner as "the singer who the country has declared number one!" Is this a valid inference? Explain.

#### Solution

The statement is not a valid inference. The sample has bias because the callers are only a section of the population that watches the TV show, including the singers' families and friends calling multiple times, rather than a random sample of each citizen of the country.

## Part 2

### Example  Using Samples to Estimate Populations

Suppose you are a wildlife researcher. You want to know the total number of fish in a lake. You catch and tag 50 fish from the lake. Then you release them. A week later, you catch another 50 fish from the lake. 15 of them are tagged. How many fish are in the lake?

#### Solution

**Step 1** Find the constant of proportionality.

$$\text{constant of proportionality} = \frac{\text{number of tagged fish in sample}}{\text{sample size}}$$

$$= \frac{15}{50}$$

$$= \frac{3}{10}$$

continued on next page >

# Part 2

**Solution** continued

**Step 2** Estimate the total number of fish in the lake.

$$\frac{\text{number of tagged}}{\text{fish in lake}} = \frac{\text{constant of}}{\text{proportionality}} \cdot \text{population size}$$

$$50 = \frac{3}{10} \cdot \text{population size}$$

$$50(10) = \frac{3}{10}(10) \cdot \text{population size} \quad \text{[Multiply each side by 10.]}$$

$$\frac{500}{3} = \frac{3}{3} \cdot \text{population size} \quad \text{[Divide each side by 3.]}$$

$$166.7 \approx \text{population size}$$

There are about 167 fish in the lake.

# Part 3

## Example  Comparing Samples to Make Conclusions

The manager of a grocery store wants to know how many bananas to buy for next week. Both of the assistant managers on duty collect sample data from the customers in the store. Compare the assistant managers' conclusions. Do you agree with *either*, *neither*, or *both*? Explain.

"Are you planning to buy bananas next week?"

**Assistant Manager 1:**
A convenience sample of 23 out of 25 people said yes, so buy enough bananas for everyone.

**Assistant Manager 2:**
A systematic sample of 15 out of 30 people in the entire store said yes, so buy enough bananas for half the customers.

**Solution** · · · · · · · · · · · · · · · · · · · · · · · · · · · · · · · · · · · · · · · · · · · · · · · · · · · · · · · · · · · ·

Answers may vary. Sample: The second assistant manager's conclusion is more reliable. The convenience sample seems biased because the first assistant manager could have been collecting data only from customers in the fruit department. It seems likely that these customers might purchase bananas every week. The systematic sample collected data from customers all over the store, not just from the customers in the fruit department.

1. A newspaper conducted a telephone survey to find the percent of houses in a certain city with at least one cat. An article printed that one half of homes in the city have at least one cat. Is this a valid inference?

   **A.** Yes, because the sample has no bias since every home would respond to a telephone survey.

   **B.** No, because not everyone reads the newspaper.

   **C.** Yes, because one half of homes in the state have at least one cat.

   **D.** No, because the sample has bias since not every home would respond to a telephone survey.

2. A bag is filled with marbles. You take out and mark 60 marbles. Then you put the marbles back in the bag and mix the marbles. In a sample of 10 marbles, 2 of the marbles are marked. About how many marbles are in the bag?

3. For a project, Neil asked people at a mall, "Do you prefer exercising or playing computer games?" Out of 100 people asked, 54 answered "exercising" and 46 answered "playing computer games." Neil concludes that the most popular activity is exercising. Is this a valid inference? Explain.

   **A.** Yes, because the people asked are a representative sample of the population.

   **B.** No, because 54 people said exercising out of the 154 who were asked.

   **C.** No, because there is bias in the question since it asks for only two activities.

   **D.** Yes, because 54 people said exercising out of the 100 who were asked.

4. A scientist asked five of his doctor friends if they thought the new Brand X medicine that he developed was effective. Three responded "yes." The scientist used the results to write a TV advertisement claiming that "3 out of 5 doctors prefer Brand X medicine." Is the inference valid?

   **A.** Yes, because the doctors asked are a representative sample of the population of doctors.

   **B.** No, because the doctors asked are not a representative sample of the population of doctors.

   **C.** Yes, because 3 doctors said yes out of 5 who were asked.

   **D.** No, because 3 doctors said yes out of 8 who were asked.

5. **Think About the Process** To determine the number of perch in a lake, a conservationist catches 342 perch, tags them, and releases them. Later 99 perch are caught, and it is found that 60 of them are tagged.

   **a.** What is the first step in estimating how many perch there are in the lake?

   **A.** Multiply the number of tagged perch in the sample by the population size.

   **B.** Divide the number of tagged perch in the sample by the number in the sample.

   **C.** Multiply the number of tagged perch in the sample by the number in the sample.

   **D.** Divide the number of tagged perch in the sample by the number of tagged perch.

   **b.** There are about ■ perch in the lake.

6. Shantel and Syrus are researching what types of novels people prefer. They decide to survey people at the mall. Shantel uses systematic sampling and asks every ninth person at the entrance. She finds that 26% prefer fantasy novels. Syrus uses convenience sampling and asks every person in only one store. He finds that 47% prefer fantasy novels.

   a. Whose inference do you agree with? Explain.

   b. What mistake might the incorrect friend have made?

7. To determine the number of squirrels in a conservation area, a researcher catches and marks 114 squirrels. Then the researcher releases them. Later 97 squirrels are caught and it is found that 33 of them are tagged. About how many squirrels are in the conservation area? Round to the nearest whole number as needed.

8. **Think About the Process** A factory tests samples of its parts to look for defects. Worker X uses a convenience sample of all the parts made from one machine and finds 5 parts with defects out of 20. Worker X concludes that 25% of all parts in the factory contain a defect. Worker Y uses a simple random sample of various machines and finds 8 parts with defects out of 40. Worker Y concludes that 20% of all parts in the factory contain a defect.

   a. What factors can you use to compare the workers' conclusions? Select all that apply.

   A. The sample size

   B. Any bias in the sampling method

   C. If the sample represents the actual number of parts with defects

   D. The percent of parts that have defects

   b. Whose inference do you agree with? Explain.

   A. Worker Y because the convenience sample seems biased.

   B. Worker X because the simple random sample seems biased.

   C. Both Worker X and Worker Y because both represent the number of parts with defects without bias.

   D. Neither Worker X nor Worker Y because both samples seem biased.

9. In a random sample of 10% of the daily production, a manufacturing company finds 80 defective parts. In another random sample, 2 out of 10 parts are defective. Find the approximate number of parts the company makes each day.

10. **Challenge** A business is asking customers if they are satisfied with the service. The business uses three different sampling methods and the conclusions are shown.

   **Method 1:** Simple random sample; $\frac{408}{1,000}$ said they are satisfied with the service, so about 40% are satisfied.

   **Method 2:** Convenience sample; $\frac{302}{500}$ said they are not satisfied with the service, so about 60% are not satisfied.

   **Method 3:** Systematic sample; $\frac{98}{200}$ said they are satisfied with the service, so about 50% are satisfied.

   a. Which method do you agree with?

   A. **Method 2** since it is the best representation of the population and has the least bias.

   B. **Method 1** since it is the best representation of the population and has the largest sample size.

   C. **Method 3** since it is the best representation of the population and has the highest percent of satisfaction.

   D. All methods are a good representation of the population.

   b. If the business makes a conclusion about its customers, how accurate is the judgment?

CCSS: 7.SP.A.1, 7.SP.B.4

## Part 1

### Intro

A measure of center is a single, central value that summarizes a set of data.

The **mean** of a set of data values is the sum of the data divided by the number of data values.

data set: $-5, -1, 3, 6, 8, 8, 9$

$$\text{mean} = \frac{\text{sum of the data values}}{\text{the number of data values}}$$

$$= \frac{-5 + -1 + 3 + 6 + 8 + 8 + 9}{7}$$

$$= \frac{28}{7}$$

$$= 4$$

The mean is a measure of center.

For an odd number of data values, the **median** is the middle value when the data values are arranged in numerical order.

data set: $-5, -1, 3, 6, 8, 8, 9$

median

The median is a measure of center.

For an even number of data values, the **median** is the average of the two middle items when the data values are arranged in numerical order.

data set: $-5, -1, 3, 6, 7, 8, 8, 9$

median

$$\text{median} = \frac{6 + 7}{2}$$

$$= \frac{13}{2}$$

$$= 6.5$$

The median is a measure of center.

# Part 1

### Example  Finding Mean and Median Intervals

At Yellowstone National Park, Data Girl and Ms. Adventure watch Jewel Geyser erupt. Data Girl records the time intervals between eruptions.

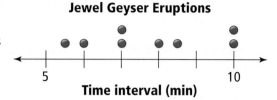

**Jewel Geyser Eruptions**

Time interval (min)

**a.** Find the mean and median intervals between eruptions.

**b.** Using the measure of center, what inference can you make about how often Jewel Geyser erupts?

### Solution · · · · · · · · · · · · · · · · · · · · · · · · · · · · · · · · · · · · · ·

**a.** Find the mean interval.

There are eight values in the data set. Use the formula for the mean.

$$\text{mean} = \frac{\text{sum of the data values}}{\text{the number of data values}}$$

$$= \frac{5\frac{1}{2} + 6 + 7 + 7 + 8 + 8\frac{1}{2} + 10 + 10}{8}$$

$$= \frac{62}{8}$$

$$= 7.75$$

> $0.75 = \frac{3}{4}$, and $\frac{3}{4}$ of a minute is 45 seconds.

The mean interval between eruptions is 7 minutes 45 seconds.

Find the median interval.

Make sure the time intervals are listed in order.

$$5\frac{1}{2}, 6, 7, 7, 8, 8\frac{1}{2}, 10, 10$$

> There is an even number of data values. Take the average of the middle two values to find the median.

$$\text{median} = \frac{7 + 8}{2}$$

$$= 7.5$$

The median interval between eruptions is 7 minutes 30 seconds.

**b.** Sample: The mean and median are close together. The dot plot shows that the two values at 10 minutes are higher than the rest of the data, so the median may describe the more typical central value. You can make the inference that Jewel Geyser erupts about every 7 minutes and 30 seconds.

## Part 2

**Intro**

A measure of variability is a single value that describes the spread of values in a data set.

The **range** of a data set is the difference between the greatest and the least values.

data set: −5, −1, 4, 7, 8, 8, 11

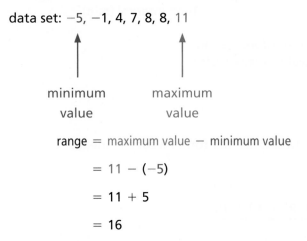

$$\text{range} = \text{maximum value} - \text{minimum value}$$

$$= 11 - (-5)$$

$$= 11 + 5$$

$$= 16$$

The **quartiles** of a data set divide the data set into four parts with the same number of data values in each part.

data set: −5,    −1,    4,    7,    8,    8,    11

| first quartile | second quartile (median) | third quartile |

The **interquartile range** (**IQR**) is the difference between the first and third quartiles of the data set. It represents the spread of the middle 50% of the data values.

data set: −5, −1, 4, 7, 8, 8, 11

| first quartile | third quartile |

$$\text{interquartile range} = \text{third quartile} - \text{first quartile}$$

$$= 8 - (-1)$$

$$= 8 + 1$$

$$= 9$$

# Part 2

## Example  Finding Ranges and Interquartile Ranges

Ms. Adventure and Data Girl are visiting different hot springs in Yellowstone. Data Girl makes a box plot of the temperatures she records.

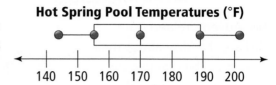

**Hot Spring Pool Temperatures (°F)**

140  150  160  170  180  190  200

a. Find the range and interquartile range of the temperatures.

b. Describe the variability of temperatures in the hot spring pools at Yellowstone.

## Solution

a.

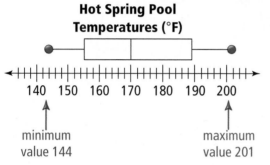

**Hot Spring Pool Temperatures (°F)**

140  150  160  170  180  190  200

minimum value 144          maximum value 201

range = maximum value − minimum value

= 201 − 144

= 57

b.

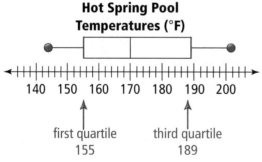

**Hot Spring Pool Temperatures (°F)**

140  150  160  170  180  190  200

first quartile 155          third quartile 189

interquartile range = third quartile − first quartile

= 189 − 155

= 34

c. Sample: The range is 57°F and the interquartile range is 34°F. This means that the temperatures of the hot springs are spread out evenly throughout the data set.

# Part 3

## Example Using Median and Range to Make Inferences

Ms. Adventure and Data Girl are thinking about their next trip. They sample the flight prices of two airlines at random.

Find the median and the range for each airline. Based on the two values, make an interference about which airline they will most likely choose. Justify your reasoning.

| Beta Air | Park Air |
|----------|----------|
| $400 | $398 |
| $402 | $447 |
| $413 | $428 |
| $399 | $465 |
| $722 | $409 |

## Solution

**Step 1** Find the median and range.

median
↓

**Beta Air**  $399, $400, $402, $413, $722
**Park Air**  $398, $409, $428, $447, S465

↑
median

The median flight price on Beta Air is $402. The median flight price on Park Air is $428.

Range = maximum value − minimum value

**Beta Air**    722 − 399 = 323
**Park Air**    465 − 398 = 67

The range of flight prices on Beta Air is $323. The range of flight on Park Air is $67.

**Step 2** Make an inference.

The median is not affected by stray data values, while the range is. Since there is an unusually high price in one of the samples, use the median to make your inference.

Sample inference: The median price of Beta Air flights is lower than the median price of Park Air flights. Ms. Adventure and Data Girl will most likely choose Beta Air.

1. Compute the mean and median of the following data set.

150  122  168  196  104  189  118

2. What is the interquartile range of this box plot?

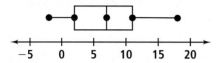

3. The data set 55, 65, 40, 40, 30, 50, 64, 45, 40, and 41 shows the admission price (in dollars) for one-day tickets to 10 theme parks in the United States. What is the interquartile range of the data values?

4. A random sample is taken from two different groups of people. The age of each subject in the sample is recorded.

**Ages of People**

| Sample from Group A | Sample from Group B |
|---|---|
| 18 | 41 |
| 19 | 24 |
| 38 | 37 |
| 31 | 42 |
| 38 | 41 |

a. Find the mean age for the sample from each group.

b. If a person is chosen at random from each group, which group's person is likely to be younger?

5. a. **Writing** Find the mean and median of the data set 1,199, 958, 1,240, 1,094, 1,153, and 957.

b. Describe a situation you could model using this data set. Interpret the mean and median in the context of your situation.

6. **Estimation** Simple random samples are taken from two groups of mice in a laboratory to study their weights. See **Figure 1**.

a. Compare the ranges of Data Set $X$ and Data Set $Y$. Fill in the answer line to complete your choice.

A. The range of Data Set $X$ is about ■ times greater than the range of Data Set $Y$.

B. The range of Data Set $Y$ is about ■ times greater than the range of Data Set $X$.

C. The ranges of Data Set $X$ and Data Set $Y$ are equal.

D. It is impossible to compare the ranges of the data sets.

b. What can you conclude about Data Set $Y$?

A. The weights of the mice in Data Set $Y$ have less variability than the mice in Data Set $X$.

B. Data Set $Y$ contains more mice than Data Set $X$.

C. The weights of the mice in Data Set $Y$ have greater variability than the mice in Data Set $X$.

D. Data Set $Y$ contains fewer mice than Data Set $X$.

7. **Estimation** Two machines in a factory work at different speeds. On five random days, the number of items built by each machine is recorded in the table. About how many times faster is Machine $Y$ compared to Machine $X$?

| Number of Items Built | | | | | |
|---|---|---|---|---|---|
| **Machine X** | 14 | 13 | 18 | 19 | 21 |
| **Machine Y** | 89 | 83 | 91 | 92 | 104 |

**(Figure 1)**

| Weight of Mice in Laboratory (grams) | | | | | | |
|---|---|---|---|---|---|---|
| **Data Set X** | 104 | 147 | 127 | 117 | 157 | 174 |
| **Data Set Y** | 176 | 74 | 143 | 242 | 205 | 158 |

**8. a.** Reasoning  Use the range and interquartile range to describe the variability of the data set 8, −4, −8, −2, −3, 7, 9, 16, and −9.

**b.** For this data set, is the range or the interquartile range a better measure of the variability?

    **A.** The interquartile range, because the range is too large.

    **B.** The range, because the value 16 is a stray data value.

    **C.** The interquartile range, because the value 16 is a stray data value.

    **D.** The range, because the interquartile range is too small.

**9. Think About the Process**  The annual salaries of the employees of a local cable network office are shown below.

$26,800   $12,200   $34,500   $22,900
$28,800   $19,700

**a.** What is the first step when finding the mean of a data set?

    **A.** Find the sum of the data values.

    **B.** Write the data values in order from least to greatest.

    **C.** Subtract the least data value from the greatest data value.

    **D.** Choose the middle value of the data set.

**b.** The mean annual salary is $ ■.

**c.** The median annual salary is $ ■.

**10. Hotel Rooms**  Before going on vacation, Leo randomly samples the cost of hotel rooms at two different hotels. Which hotel is Leo likely to choose?

**Cost per Night ($)**

| Hotel S | Hotel T |
|---------|---------|
| 108 | 107 |
| 137 | 129 |
| 178 | 182 |
| 238 | 213 |
| 407 | 241 |

**A.** Leo is likely to choose Hotel S.

**B.** Leo is likely to choose Hotel T.

**C.** It is impossible to compare the two hotels.

**11. Mental Math**  Find the interquartile range of the data set 32.6, 98.5, 16.6, 22.4, 99.8, 72.6, 68.2, 51.8, and 49.3.

**12.** Find the range and the interquartile range of the data set 35.6, 7.4, 6.2, 27.7, −28.4, −32.2, −27.9, 17.1, and −35.2.

**13. Think About the Process**

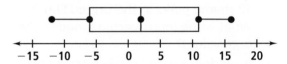

**a.** What is always true about the interquartile range of a data set? Select all that apply.

    **A.** The interquartile range is less than the range.

    **B.** The interquartile range contains about 50% of the data set.

    **C.** The interquartile range contains the median of the data set.

    **D.** The interquartile range is greater than the range.

**b.** The interquartile range is ■.

**14. a. Challenge**  Find the mean and median of the data set 781, 866, 358, 514, 162, 313, 670, 715, and 247.

**b.** Add four more numbers to the data set to create a new data set with the same mean and median.

# Multiple Populations and Inferences

**Vocabulary**
comparative
inference

CCSS: 7.SP.A.1, 7.SP.B.4, Also 7.SP.B.3

## Part 1

### Intro

When you analyze a group, you usually have a question that you want answered about that group.

Use one population when you have a question about a trait of the whole group.

*"How many students in my school play a sport?"*

We are all the students in the school.

Use two populations when you want to compare two groups or two parts of a group.

*"Are students who play a sport generally taller than students who don't play a sport?"*

We play sports.　　We don't play sports.

Use the number of populations needed to answer the question you have.

*"How many students play a sport in each grade?"*

Grade 6　　　Grade 7　　　Grade 8

## Part 1

### Example  Determining the Number of Populations

A teacher gave a test to each of her three math classes. To answer each question, should the teacher consider the classes as *three* populations or as one population?

- What was the highest score overall?
- Which is the top-scoring class?
- What is the mean score in each class?
- Who is the top-scoring student in each class?
- What is the mean score of all the students?
- How does the range of scores compare among classes?

**Solution** · · · · · · · · · · · · · · · · · · · · · · · · · · · · · · · · · · · · · · · · · · · ·

One Population

These questions ask about a trait among all of the students, so the classes should be considered one combined population.

- What was the highest score overall?
- What is the mean score of all the students?

Three Populations

These questions ask about how the classes compare to each other, so the classes should be considered three separate populations.

- Which is the top-scoring class?
- Who is the top-scoring student in each class?
- What is the mean score in each class?
- How does the range of scores compare between classes?

## Part 2

### Example  Describing Multiple Populations

A researcher is analyzing United States census data. For each question, how many population(s) should the researcher use? Describe the population(s).

**a.** Do more people live in Maine or in Hawaii?

**b.** Is the median number of people per residence greater in Chicago, Los Angeles, or Philadelphia?

**c.** What is the age of the oldest U.S. citizen?

**d.** What percent of each state's population is male?

continued on next page >

# Part 2

**Example** continued

**Solution** · · · · · · · · · · · · · · · · · · · · · · · · · · · · · · · · · · · · · · · · · · · · ·

**a.** The researcher should use 2 populations. Description:
- population of Hawaii
- population of Maine

**b.** The researcher should use 3 populations. Description:
- population of Chicago
- population of Los Angeles
- population of Philadelphia

**c.** The researcher should use 1 population. Description:
- the population of the entire United States

**d.** The researcher should use 50 populations. Description:
- the population of each of the 50 states

# Key Concept

You can make inferences about populations using random samples from each population.

When you make a judgment by interpreting a set of data, you are making an inference.

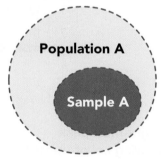

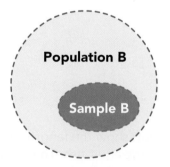

**Inference:**
Based on **Sample A**, 65% of **Population A** loves to sing.

**Inference:**
Based on **Sample B**, 30% of **Population B** loves to sing.

An inference that compares two things is called a **comparative inference**.

**Comparative Inference:**
Based on Sample A and Sample B, a greater percent of Population A loves to sing than Population B.

# Part 3

## Example Making Comparative Inferences

The table shows the lengths of a random sample of koi fish from two koi ponds.

a. Make a conjecture about why there are two peaks in the dot plots of both samples.

b. Based on your conjecture, make a comparative inference about the fish in the two ponds.

| Pond A | | Pond B | |
|---|---|---|---|
| 2 | 8 | 5 | 10 |
| 4 | 9 | 6 | 10 |
| 5 | 10 | 6 | 10 |
| 5 | 10 | 7 | 10 |
| 5 | 10 | 7 | 10 |
| 5 | 10 | 7 | 10 |
| 6 | 11 | 7 | 11 |
| 6 | 11 | 7 | 11 |
| 6 | 11 | 8 | 11 |
| 6 | 11 | 8 | 11 |
| 6 | 11 | 8 | 11 |
| 6 | 11 | 8 | 11 |
| 6 | 11 | 8 | 11 |
| 6 | 11 | 8 | 12 |
| 7 | 11 | 8 | 12 |
| 7 | 11 | 8 | 12 |
| 7 | 12 | 9 | 12 |
| 7 | 12 | 9 | 12 |
| 7 | 12 | 9 | 13 |
| 7 | 14 | 9 | 13 |

## Solution

Sample:

a. The dot plots show the lengths of koi fish. The right-most peak represents the adult fish. The left-most peak, showing koi of shorter length, represents the baby fish.

b. In the dot plot for Pond B the two peaks are closer together than they are in the dot pot for Pond A. So, there is less difference in length between the baby fish and the adult fish in Pond B than between the baby fish and the adult fish in Pond A.

1. You are researching the different cell phones offered by 5 major companies. For which question should you consider the cell phones as multiple populations to find the answer?

   **A.** Which is the largest cell phone overall?

   **B.** What is the total number of different cell phones the 5 companies offer?

   **C.** How many of the cell phones can connect to a computer?

   **D.** Which company offers the greatest number of different cell phones?

2. **Think About the Process** David is studying the mountains on each of the seven continents in the world. He asks the following question.

   How many mountains are there in the world?

   **a.** Select each factor he should consider when deciding which population(s) to use.

      **A.** Use only one population.

      **B.** Use all populations that are required to answer the question.

      **C.** Do not use any populations that are not required to answer the question.

      **D.** Use as many populations as you can think of.

   **b.** List or describe the population(s) he should use.

      **A.** The populations of mountain ranges on each of the seven continents

      **B.** The populations of mountain ranges in North America and in Asia

      **C.** The populations of mountain ranges in each of North America, Asia, and Europe

      **D.** The population of all mountain ranges in the world

3. Ivan is researching the television viewing habits of the people at his school. Which population(s) should he use to find out if a higher percentage of students or teachers watch television every night?

   **A.** the population of Ivan's grade

   **B.** the population of teachers, the population of boys, and the population of girls

   **C.** the population of teachers and the population of students

   **D.** the population of all people at the school

4. Anita is choosing universities to apply to. Some are private schools and some are state schools. She writes a list of questions.

   **a.** For which question should she consider the universities as one population to find the answer?

      **A.** Do the private or state schools have a lesser mean tuition?

      **B.** Which universities have the least amount of tuition for each type?

      **C.** Which university offers the most scholarships?

      **D.** Which type offers more scholarships?

   **b.** Explain why she might want to ask each of these questions.

**5. Think About the Process** The bar graphs show samples of the distances players on two soccer teams had to travel to get to the soccer field for their game.

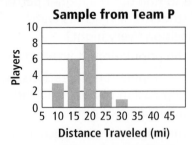

**Sample from Team P**

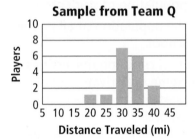

**Sample from Team Q**

**a.** What is the first step in finding the median of each sample?

  **A.** Find the sum of the values in the sample.

  **B.** Arrange the values in the sample in order from least to greatest.

  **C.** Find the number of values in the sample.

  **D.** Divide the number of values in the sample by 2.

**b.** The median of the sample from Team P is ▩ mi.

**c.** The median of the sample from Team Q is ▩ mi.

**d.** Make a comparative inference about the distance traveled by the players on the two teams.

  **A.** Most of the players on Team Q live closer to the field than the players on Team P.

  **B.** There are more players on Team P than on Team Q.

  **C.** There are more players on Team Q than on Team P.

  **D.** Most of the players on Team P live closer to the field than the players on Team Q.

**6. Houses** The dot plots show samples of the number of rooms in homes on two adjacent streets.

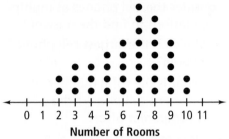

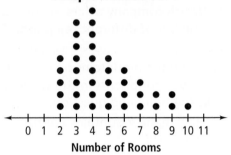

**a.** Find the median of each sample.

**b.** Make a comparative inference about the homes on the two streets.

**7.** A local movie store sells 8 different categories of movies.

  **a.** How many populations should you use to answer the following question?

  Which is the least expensive movie in the store?

  **b.** Give two more questions you could ask about the movies in the store. Explain how many populations you should use to answer each.

CCSS: 7.SP.B.4

## Key Concept

You can compare two data sets by comparing their individual data values. A quicker way to make a general comparison of two data sets is to compare their measures of center.

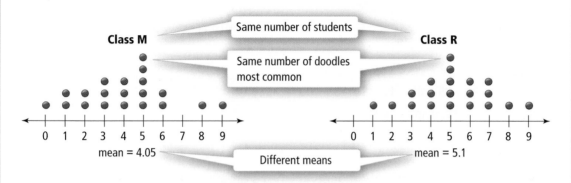

## Part 1

### Example  Making Comparative Inferences Based on Medians

A biology student is studying two species of endangered parrots. What is the median wingspan of each sample? Make a comparative inference based on the median values.

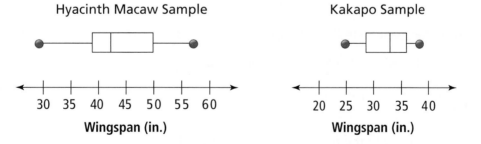

continued on next page >

## Part 1

**Example** continued

**Solution** · · · · · · · · · · · · · · · · · · · · · · · · · · · · · · · · · · · · · · · · · · · · · ·

Results of a Study of Endangered Parrots

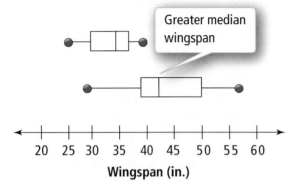

Greater median wingspan

Kakapo Sample

Hyacinth Macaw Sample

Wingspan (in.)

Comparative Inference

The Hyacinth Macaw population generally has a greater wingspan than the Kakapo population.

## Part 2

**Example  Making Comparative Inferences Based on Means**

A biology student is studying two species of endangered parrots. What is the mean weight of each sample? Make a comparative inference based on the mean values.

Hyacinth Macaw Sample (lb): 2.8, 3.7, 3.9, 3.0, 3.1, 3.4, 2.9, 3.2

Kakapo Sample (lb): 3.9, 4.5, 5.3, 6.7, 7.4, 8.1, 6.4, 8.1

**Solution** · · · · · · · · · · · · · · · · · · · · · · · · · · · · · · · · · · · · · · · · · · · · · · · ·

**Step 1** Calculate the mean value of each sample.

There are 8 subjects in each sample.

$$\text{mean} = \frac{\text{sum of data values}}{\text{number of data values}}$$

continued on next page >

## Part 2

**Solution** continued

Hyacinth Macaw Sample:

$$\text{mean} = \frac{2.8 + 3.7 + 3.9 + 3.0 + 3.1 + 3.4 + 2.9 + 3.2}{8}$$

$$= \frac{26}{8}$$

$$= 3.25$$

Kakapo Sample:

$$\text{mean} = \frac{3.9 + 4.5 + 5.3 + 6.7 + 7.4 + 8.1 + 6.4 + 8.1}{8}$$

$$= \frac{50.4}{8}$$

$$= 6.3$$

The mean weight of the Hyacinth Macaw is 3.25 lb and the mean weight of the Kakapo is 6.3 lb.

**Step 2** Make a comparative inference based on the mean values.

Sample: From the mean values, you can infer that the Hyacinth Macaws in this population are generally lighter than the Kakapos in this population.

## Part 3

**Intro**

If you have different comparative inferences based on each measure of center, you can draw a conclusion about the situation by looking more closely at the data sets.

No stray data values.
Use the mean.

Stray data value.
Use the median.

# Part 3

## Example  Making Conclusions from Data

A biology student is studying two species of endangered parrots. One species can fly and the other cannot. Using the data, which species would the student conclude can fly? Explain.

| HMws | Kws | HMwt | Kwt |
|------|------|------|-----|
| 30 | 25 | 2.8 | 3.9 |
| 37 | 26 | 3.7 | 4.5 |
| 39 | 30 | 3.9 | 5.3 |
| 41 | 33 | 3.0 | 6.7 |
| 45 | 34 | 3.1 | 7.4 |
| 48 | 35 | 3.4 | 8.1 |
| 52 | 36 | 2.9 | 6.4 |
| 57 | 37.5 | 3.2 | 8.1 |

**Solution** · · · · · · · · · · · · · · · · · · · · · · · · · · · · · · · · · · · · · · · · · · · · ·

Sample:

The Hyacinth Macaw population generally has a larger wingspan and is lighter than the Kakapo population,

Using the data, the biology student might conclude that the Hyacinth Macaw is able to fly and the Kakapo is not.

**1.** The box plots show the number of people that went to two restaurants for lunch over a few days.

### Restaurant 1

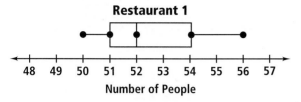

Number of People

### Restaurant 2

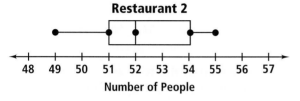

Number of People

**a.** Which of the following is the best description of the medians?

  **A.** The median for Restaurant 1 is greater.

  **B.** The median for Restaurant 2 is greater.

  **C.** The medians are the same.

**b.** Which of the following is the best inference based on the median values?

  **A.** More people generally eat at Restaurant 1 for lunch.

  **B.** The same amount of people generally eat at each restaurant for lunch.

  **C.** More people generally eat at Restaurant 2 for lunch.

**c.** When making an inference, does the inference always apply to the entire population of the two samples being compared? Explain.

**2. Think About the Process** The following dot plots show the ages of two groups of tourists.

### Group 1

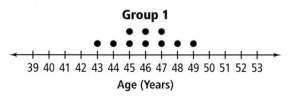

Age (Years)

### Group 2

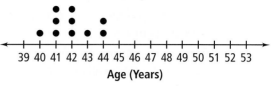

Age (Years)

**a.** What is the first step to finding the mean age for each group?

  **A.** The first step should be to average the minimum and maximum values that have dots.

  **B.** The first step should be to count the ages that have dots and just average those numbers.

  **C.** The first step should be to count the number of dots for each age.

  **D.** The first step should be to find the middle number of all the dots.

**b.** The mean age for Group 1 is ▧ years.

**c.** The mean age for Group 2 is ▧ years.

**d.** Which is a correct inference based on the mean values?

  **A.** Group 1 is generally older than Group 2.

  **B.** Group 2 is generally older than Group 1.

  **C.** The groups are generally the same age.

**3.** The box plots show the number of people that go to town meetings in two towns. The data is over the period of one year.

### Town 1

Number of People

### Town 2

Number of People

**a.** Which of the following is the best inference based on the median values?

  **A.** More people generally go to the meetings in Town 1.

  **B.** The same amount of people in each town generally go to the meetings.

  **C.** More people generally go to the meetings in Town 2.

**b.** Which of the following is another conclusion that a person might make from the median values?

  **A.** The meetings in Town 2 are more important.

  **B.** The meetings in both towns are equally important.

  **C.** The meetings in Town 1 are more important.

**4. Mental Math** A student is studying two different breeds of dogs. The following are the weights of 6 of each breed of dog.

| Dog Breed 1 Weight (lb) | | |
|---|---|---|
| 61 | 59 | 48 |
| 54 | 50 | 46 |

| Dog Breed 2 Weight (lb) | | |
|---|---|---|
| 44 | 38 | 43 |
| 46 | 45 | 36 |

**a.** Find the mean weight of each population.

**b.** Which of the following is a correct inference based on the mean values?

  **A.** Dog Breed 2 generally weighs more than Dog Breed 1.

  **B.** Dog Breed 1 generally weighs more than Dog Breed 2.

  **C.** Dog Breed 1 and Dog Breed 2 generally weigh about the same.

**c.** Explain how you could use mental math to compare the means of the two types of dogs.

**5.** The box plots show different heights of two trees.

**Tree 1**

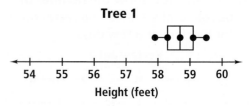

Height (feet)

**Tree 2**

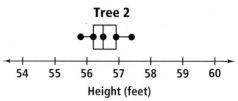

Height (feet)

**a.** Which of the following is the best description of the medians?

  **A.** The median for Tree 2 is greater.

  **B.** The medians are about the same.

  **C.** The median for Tree 1 is greater.

**b.** Are you always able to make a clear inference from the data you are given? Explain.

**6. Think About the Process** A family is comparing natural stones used for kitchen countertops. They go to various stores to compare the price of two types of stones. The mean price per square foot of Stone 1 is $78 and the mean price per square foot for Stone 2 is $118.

**a.** Which is a correct inference based on the mean values?

  **A.** Stone 2 is generally more expensive than Stone 1.

  **B.** Stone 1 is generally more expensive than Stone 2.

  **C.** Stone 1 and Stone 2 generally cost the same.

**b.** Use the mean price to draw a conclusion. Do you think the stone with the greater mean price is more or less rare than the other stone?

**c.** Which is a reasonable conclusion?

  **A.** Stone 2 is a rarer stone.

  **B.** Stone 1 is a rarer stone.

  **C.** The rareness of each stone is the same.

# Using Measures of Variability

CCSS: 7.SP.B.4

## Key Concept

You can compare two data sets by comparing their individual data values. A quicker way to make a general comparison of the spreads of two data sets is to compare their measures of variability.

**Number of Doodles on Last Night's Homework**

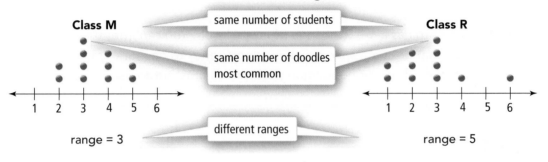

## Part 1

### Example  Making Comparative Inferences Based on Range

A psychologist is studying how spending time outdoors affects people's moods. He surveys two samples of people chosen at random. What is the range of mood levels for each sample? Make a comparative inference about the populations based on range.

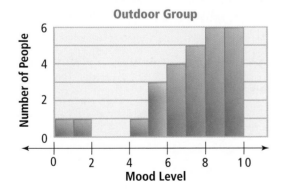

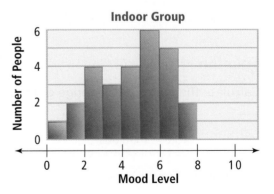

continued on next page >

## Part 1

> **Example** continued

### Solution

Calculate the range of mood levels for each sample.

> range = maximum − minimum

Outdoor Group range ≈ 10 − 0

= 10

Indoor Group range ≈ 8 − 0

= 8

The Outdoor Group has a greater range of mood levels. You can infer that the population that does not spend time outdoors tends to be more similar in their mood levels than the population that spends time outdoors.

## Part 2

> **Example** **Making Comparative Inferences Based on IQR**

A psychologist is studying how spending time outdoors affects people's moods. He surveys two samples of people chosen at random. What is the interquartile range of mood levels for each sample? Make a comparative inference about the populations based on IQR.

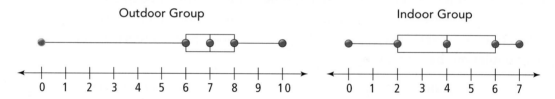

Outdoor Group

Indoor Group

### Solution

Calculate the interquartile range of mood levels for each group.

> IQR = third quartile − first quartile

Outdoor Group IQR = 8 − 6

= 2

Indoor Group IQR = 6 − 2

= 4

The Indoor Group has a greater interquartile range of mood levels. You can infer that the mood levels of the population that spends time outdoors are more consistent than those of the mood levels of the population that spends time indoors.

# Part 3

### Example Making Conclusions from the Variability of Data

A psychologist is studying how spending time outdoors affects people's moods by surveying two groups of people chosen at random. Using the data, what might the psychologist conclude about the populations? Explain.

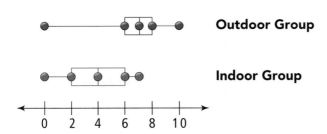

**Mood Level**

Outdoor Group

Indoor Group

## Solution

The interquartile range shows the middle 50% of the data, so it is not affected by stray data values. This means that the IQR gives a more accurate description of where the data in each group fall.

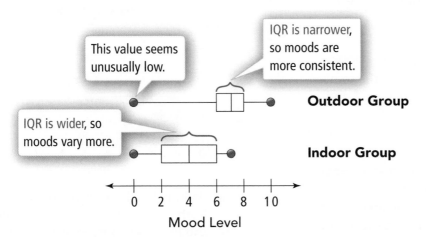

This value seems unusually low.

IQR is narrower, so moods are more consistent.

**Outdoor Group**

IQR is wider, so moods vary more.

**Indoor Group**

Mood Level

The psychologist might conclude that spending time outdoors generally helps to keep the population's mood levels more stable and consistent.

**1.** A group of 10 people were asked to rate books, shown in the histograms.

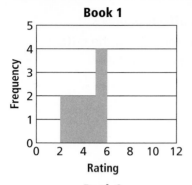

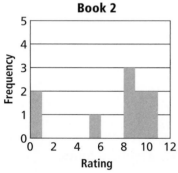

**a.** Find the range of the ratings for each sample.

**b.** Make a comparative inference about the ratings of the books.

   **A.** The ratings vary to the same degree for both Book 1 and Book 2.

   **B.** The ratings vary less for Book 1 than for Book 2.

   **C.** The ratings vary less for Book 2 than for Book 1.

**2.** The box plots show the amount of time two groups of students spend reading in one week.

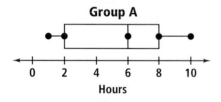

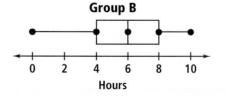

**a.** What is the interquartile range of hours spent reading for Group A?

**b.** What is the interquartile range of hours spent reading for Group B?

**c.** Is the interquartile range for Group A less than or greater than the interquartile range for Group B?

**3.** The following histograms represent the number of cars parked in two parking lots during the 9 hours the lots are open. What might you conclude about the populations based on the range?

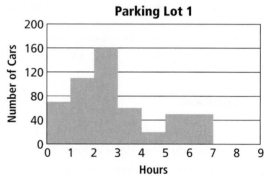

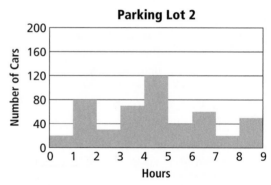

**A.** Parking Lot 1 and Parking Lot 2 both consistently have cars during the first few hours they are open.

**B.** Parking Lot 2 consistently has cars during its last few of hours while Parking Lot 1 has cars throughout the entire time it is open.

**C.** Parking Lot 1 consistently has cars during its first few of hours while Parking Lot 2 has cars throughout the entire time it is open.

**D.** Parking Lot 1 and Parking Lot 2 both have cars throughout the entire time they are open.

**4. Think About the Process** The histograms show the number of hours students watch television in one week.

**Group 1**

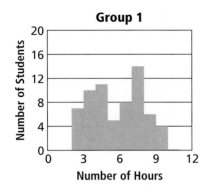

**Group 2**

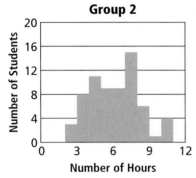

**a.** How can you make a comparative inference about the students in Group 1 and Group 2?

**A.** Find and compare the maximum hours for each group.

**B.** Find and compare the median hours for each group.

**C.** Find and compare the range of hours for each group.

**D.** Find and compare the mean hours for each group.

**b.** Make a comparative inference about the number of hours students watch television in each group.

**A.** The number of hours students watch TV varies less for the students in Group 2 than for those in Group 1.

**B.** The number of hours students watch TV varies less for the students in Group 1 than for those in Group 2.

**C.** The number of hours students watch TV varies to the same degree for both groups.

**5. Think About the Process** The box plots show the wait times for the most popular ride at an amusement park and at a water park.

**Amusement Park**

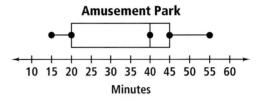

**Water Park**

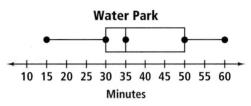

**a.** How can you make a comparative inference about the populations based on the interquartile range (IQR)?

**A.** Find and compare the maximum of the wait times for each park.

**B.** Find and compare the IQR of the wait times for each park.

**C.** Find and compare the median of the wait times for each park.

**D.** Find and compare the range of the wait times for each park.

**b.** Make a comparative inference about the populations based on the IQR.

**A.** The wait times at the amusement park and the water park are equally consistent.

**B.** The wait times at the amusement park are more consistent than those at the water park.

**C.** The wait times at the water park are more consistent than those at the amusement park.

# Exploring Overlap in Data Sets

CCSS: 7.SP.B.3, Also 7.SP.B.4

## Part 1

### Intro

The **mean absolute deviation (MAD)** is a measure of variability that describes how far the data values are spread out from the mean of a data set.

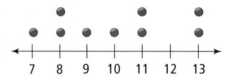

**Step 1** Find the mean of the data set.

$$\frac{7 + 8 + 8 + 9 + 10 + 11 + 11 + 13 + 13}{9} = 10$$

**Step 2** Find the deviation of each data value from the mean.

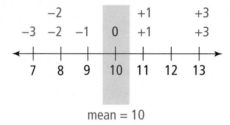

mean = 10

**Step 3** Find the absolute deviations, or the absolute value of the deviations.

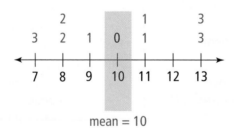

mean = 10

**Step 4** Find the mean absolute deviation. The mean absolute deviation of the data set is the mean of the absolute deviations.

$$MAD = \frac{\text{sum of absolute deviations}}{\text{number of data values}}$$

$$= \frac{(3 + 2 + 2 + 1 + 0 + 1 + 1 + 3 + 3)}{9}$$

$$= \frac{16}{9}$$

$$\approx 1.8$$

continued on next page >

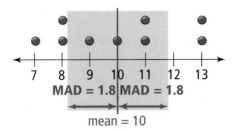

MAD = 1.8 | MAD = 1.8

mean = 10

## Example Calculating Mean Absolute Deviation

Calculate the mean absolute deviation for the heights of second graders. The mean is about 50 inches. Round to the nearest whole number.

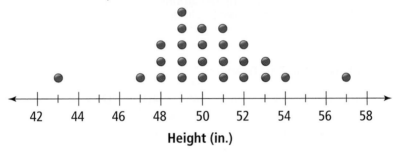

Sample of 2nd Grade Students

Height (in.)

**Solution** · · · · · · · · · · · · · · · · · · · · · · · · · · · · · · · · · · · · · · · · · · · · · · ·

Step 1 Find the deviations from the mean.

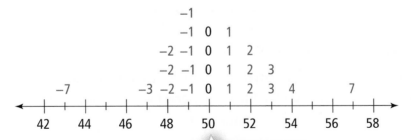

Deviations of 2nd Grade Students

The mean is about 50 inches.

continued on next page >

# Part 2

## Solution continued

Step 2 Find the absolute deviations from the mean.

### Absolute Deviations of 2nd Grade Students

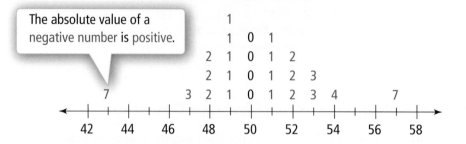

The absolute value of a negative number is positive.

Step 3 Find the mean absolute deviation.

$$\text{MAD} = \frac{\text{sum of absolute deviations}}{\text{number of data values}}$$

There are 25 subjects in the sample.

MAD of the 2nd Graders:

$$\frac{1(7) + 1(3) + 3(2) + 5(1) + 4(0) + 4(1) + 3(2) + 2(3) + 1(4) + 1(7)}{25}$$

$$= \frac{7 + 3 + 6 + 5 + 0 + 4 + 6 + 6 + 4 + 7}{25}$$

$$= \frac{48}{25}$$

$$\approx 2$$

The mean absolute deviation for the heights of second graders is about 2 inches.

## Key Concept

Suppose you have a data set A with mean $x$ and mean absolute deviation $m$.
Suppose you also have data set B with mean $y$ and mean absolute deviation $n$.

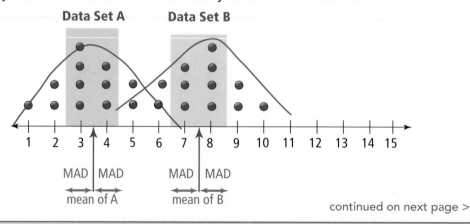

continued on next page >

When two data sets have approximately the same variability, you can use their mean absolute deviation to describe the distance between their means. You can express this distance as a multiple of the mean absolute deviation.

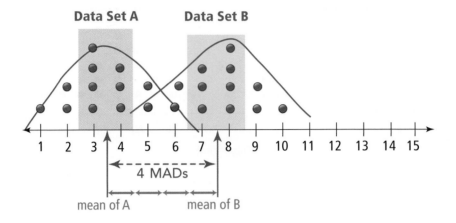

The centers of data set A and data set B are about 4 mean absolute deviations apart. The greater the distance between the means of the data sets, the more multiples of the mean absolute deviation you need to describe that distance.

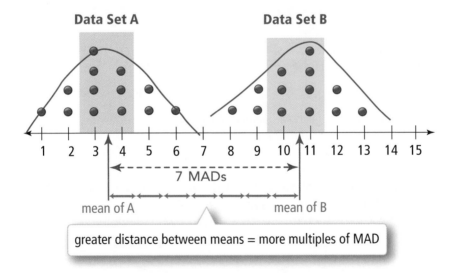

greater distance between means = more multiples of MAD

The less the distance between the means of the data sets, the fewer multiples of the mean absolute deviation you need to describe that distance.

# Part 2

## Example  Comparing Data Using Multiples of MAD

The mean of the 2nd grade heights is 50. The mean of the 7th grade heights is 61. The mean absolute deviation of each data set is 2. How do the means compare? Express the difference as a multiple of the MAD.

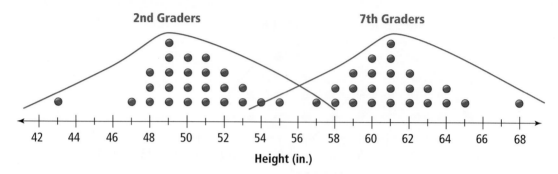

## Solution

**Step 1** Find the distance between the means.

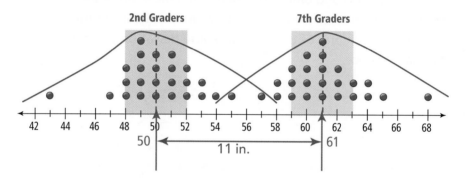

distance between means = mean of 7th graders − mean of 2nd graders
$$= 61 - 50$$
$$= 11$$

**Step 2** Find the number of multiples of the MAD needed to span the distance between the means.

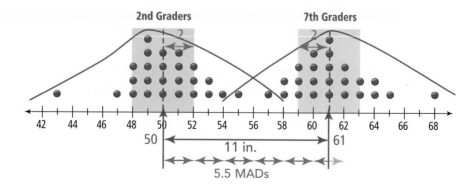

continued on next page >

Part 2

## Part 2

**Solution** continued

$$\text{number of multiples} = \frac{\text{distance between means}}{\text{MAD}}$$

$$= \frac{11}{2}$$

$$= 5.5$$

## Part 3

### Intro

If two data distributions have similar variability, you can describe the visual overlap between them by using a multiple of the mean absolute deviation.

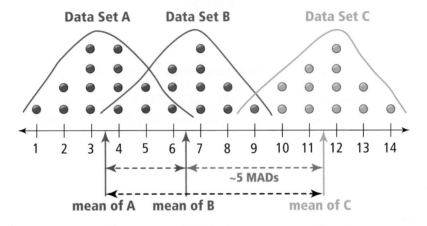

The lower the number of multiples, the more visual overlap there is between two data sets.

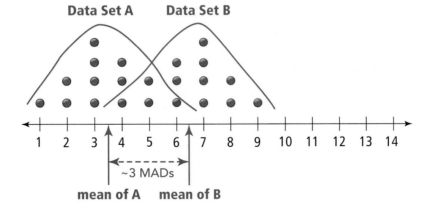

continued on next page >

# Part 3

**Intro** continued

The greater the number of multiples, the less visual overlap there is between two data sets.

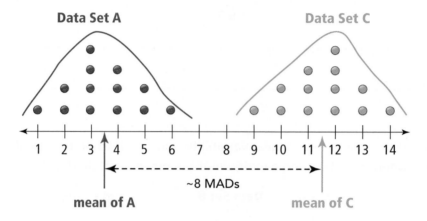

## Example  Sketching Data Distributions Using Multiples of MAD

The red curve has a mean of 300 and a MAD of 25. Sketch a second data distribution that is four mean absolute deviations away from the mean of the red curve.

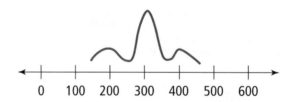

**Solution** · · · · · · · · · · · · · · · · · · · · · · · · · · · · · · · · · · · · · · · · · · · · · · · · · · · · · ·

**Step 1** Find the distance of 4 MADs.

$$4 \text{ MADs} = 4(25)$$

$$= 100$$

Four MADs is equivalent to 100 units.

continued on next page >

# Part 3

**Solution** continued

> **Step 2** Find the mean of the second distribution.
>
> The distance between the two means is 100 units.

mean of red curve + 100

      = 300 + 100

      = 400

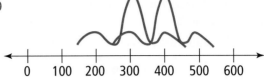

or

mean of red curve − 100

      = 300 − 100

      = 200

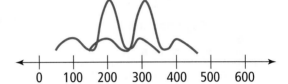

See your complete lesson at MyMathUniverse.com

1. You ask 8 classmates how many pens and pencils they have in their bags. The mean number of pens is 11. The mean number of pencils is 8. Calculate and compare the mean absolute deviations (MAD) for the number of pens and pencils.

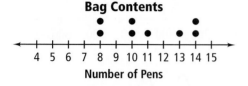

2. The mean height of Group A plants (gray dots) is 53 inches. The mean height of Group B plants (black dots) is 65 inches. Heights that are common are shown with a star. The mean absolute deviation of each data set is 2. The distance between the means is 6 times the mean absolute deviation of either group. What degree of visual overlap is there between the two distributions?

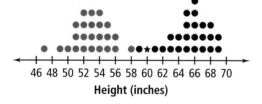

3. The curve has a mean of 800 and a mean absolute deviation (MAD) of 20. Which second data distribution is four mean absolute deviations greater than the mean of the initial curve?

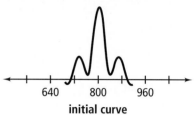

A.

B.

C.

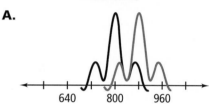

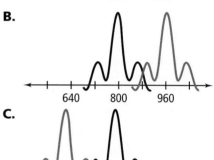

4. You think a coin is not fair. You have 10 friends each toss the coin 4 times and tell you the number of heads. The mean number of heads is 3.1.

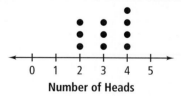

a. Find the mean absolute deviation of the data.

b. Explain how you can use the data to show that the coin is either fair or not fair.

**5.** The following shows the number of fish caught by the same 10 boaters on two different lakes. The mean number of fish caught in Lake A is 9. The mean number of fish caught in Lake B is 13. The mean absolute deviation (MAD) for both dot plots is 1.4. How much overlap is there in the distribution of fish caught in the lakes?

**Lake A**

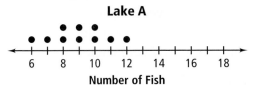

**Number of Fish**

**Lake B**

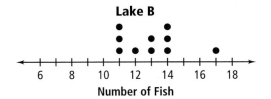

**Number of Fish**

**A.** There are 4 boaters that caught the same number of fish in the two lakes. There is a majority of overlap between the two distributions.

**B.** There are 2 boaters that caught the same number of fish in the two lakes. There is a little overlap between the two distributions.

**C.** There are no boaters that caught the same number of fish in the two lakes. There is no overlap between the two distributions.

**6. Think About the Process** The following dot plots show the ages of two groups of tourists. The mean age of Group 1 is 45.5 years. The mean age of Group 2 is 44.9 years.

**Group 1**

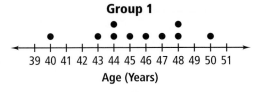

**Age (Years)**

**Group 2**

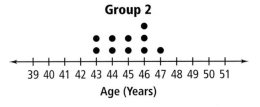

**Age (Years)**

**a.** What is the first step to finding the mean absolute deviation (MAD) for each group?

**b.** What is the Group 1 MAD?

**c.** What is the Group 2 MAD?

**d.** Which of the following is a correct inference from the MAD values?

**A.** The spread of ages is less for Group 1 than the spread of ages for Group 2.

**B.** The spread of ages is greater for Group 1 than the spread of ages for Group 2.

**C.** The spreads of ages are the same for Group 1 and Group 2.

**7. Think About the Process** The curve has a mean of 180 and a mean absolute deviation (MAD) of 20.

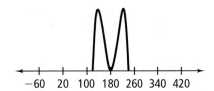

**a.** If a second data distribution is four mean absolute deviations less than the mean of the blue curve, what is its mean?

**b.** Choose the graph that shows the second data distribution.

**A.**

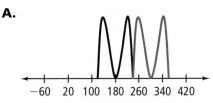

**B.**

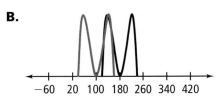

**C.**

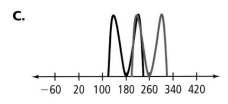

CCSS: 7.SP.B.4

## Part 1

### Example  Making Decisions Using Measures of Center and Variability

The table shows pizza delivery times to your house in the past year. You are hosting a party that starts in half an hour. From which pizza place should you order the pizza? Use measures of center and variability to justify your choice.

| Pizza Company A | Pizza Company B |
|---|---|
| 20 | 10 |
| 28 | 30 |
| 35 | 50 |
| 47 | 55 |
| 55 | 60 |

### Solution

**Know**

Delivery times of both pizza companies over the past year

**Need**

Decide which pizza company will most likely deliver in 30 minutes.

**Plan**

- Use the median, IQR, and range of both companies to make comparative inferences about the past delivery times.
- Make a list of pros for each company to help you make a decision.

continued on next page >

# Part 1

## Solution continued

**Measures of Center and Variability**

| | Pizza Company A | Pizza Company B |
|---|---|---|
| Median | 35 | 50 |
| Range | = 55 − 20<br>= 35 | = 60 − 10<br>= 50 |
| IQR | = 51 − 24<br>= 27 | = 57.5 − 20<br>= 37.5 |

> Pizza Company B has a larger maximum value and a smaller minimum value.

> Range and IQR are narrower for Pizza Company A.

Advantage of Pizza Company A:

Seems more consistent in their delivery times.
Median delivery time is a little over 30 minutes.
Pizza Company B has the longest delivery time of 60 minutes.

Advantages of Pizza Company B:

Has the fastest delivery time of 10 minutes.

Sample Answer 1: If you want to take a risk, choose Pizza Company B because they have delivered quickly at least once before.

Sample Answer 2: If you want to have a more accurate idea of when the pizza will arrive, go with Pizza Company A.

# Part 2

## Example Making Inferences Using Measures of Center and Variability

The education board is analyzing the weight (lb) of student backpacks in two schools. They take a random sample of 24 students from each school. Using the measures of center and variability of the two samples, what can the education board infer?

**Solution**

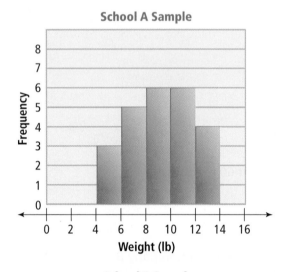

There is one weight in the School B sample that is much heavier than the rest of the sample weights. Use the median and the IQR to make an inference because this data value should not affect the overall analysis.

| School A | School B |
|----------|----------|
| 4 | 2 |
| 5 | 3 |
| 5 | 3 |
| 6 | 3 |
| 6 | 3 |
| 7 | 4 |
| 7 | 4 |
| 7 | 4 |
| 8 | 4 |
| 8 | 5 |
| 8 | 5 |
| 9 | 5 |
| 9 | 5 |
| 9 | 6 |
| 10 | 6 |
| 10 | 6 |
| 10 | 6 |
| 11 | 6 |
| 11 | 6 |
| 11 | 7 |
| 12 | 8 |
| 12 | 8 |
| 12 | 9 |
| 13 | 15 |

continued on next page >

# Part 2

**Solution** continued

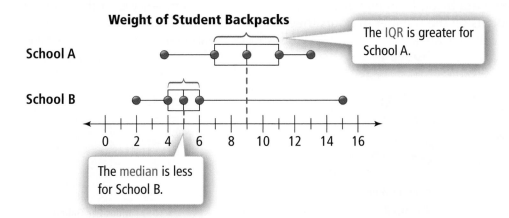

**Weight of Student Backpacks**

School A

The IQR is greater for School A.

School B

The median is less for School B.

The education board might infer from the medians that the backpacks at School B are generally lighter than at School A.

The board might infer from the interquartile ranges that the students at School B carry similar amounts in their backpacks.

**1. Think About the Process** The graphs show data taken from two groups of students on the number of hours they exercise in a week.

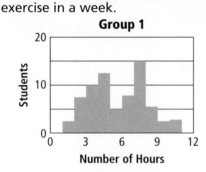

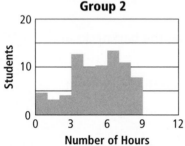

**a.** How can you decide which measure of center and variability to use to make a comparative inference about the number of hours the students exercise in each group? Select all that apply.

**A.** The median and interquartile range (IQR) are used when the sample size is small.

**B.** The mean and range are used when the sample size is small.

**C.** The mean and range are used when there are no unusual values in the data set.

**D.** The median and interquartile range (IQR) are used when dealing with a set of data that has an unusual value.

**b.** Make a comparative inference about the number of hours students exercise in each group.

**A.** The students in Group 2 exercise more than those in Group 1.

**B.** The students in Group 1 exercise as much as those in Group 2.

**C.** The students in Group 1 exercise more than those in Group 2.

**2.** A car manufacturer wants to know what fuel efficiency is for the models of Car X and Car Y. The histograms show a random sample of 31 cars of each model.

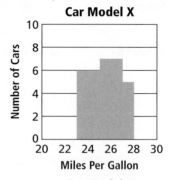

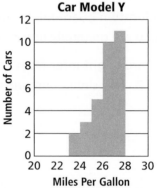

**a.** Select each measure of center or variability the car manufacturer should use.

**A.** Range

**B.** Interquartile range

**C.** Mean

**D.** Median

**b.** What can the researcher infer?

**A.** The car manufacturer might infer from the medians that Car Model X is more fuel efficient than Car Model Y.

**B.** The car manufacturer might infer from the medians that Car Model Y is more fuel efficient than Car Model X.

**C.** The car manufacturer might infer from the means that Car Model Y is more fuel efficient than Car Model X.

**D.** The car manufacturer might infer from the means that Car Model X is more fuel efficient than Car Model Y.

See your complete lesson at MyMathUniverse.com

**3.** Grade 6 and Grade 8 students were asked how long it takes them to get to school in the morning. The data shows the results of a survey taken by five Grade 6 and five Grade 8 students.

**Time Needed to Get to School (min)**

| Grade 6 | Grade 8 |
|---------|---------|
| 3 | 8 |
| 6 | 9 |
| 3 | 10 |
| 7 | 12 |
| 4 | 6 |

**a.** What are the measures of center and variability for Grade 6?

**b.** What are the measures of center and variability for Grade 8?

**c.** What can you infer about the relationship between grade level and the amount of time it takes to get to school?

**A.** More than half of the students in Grade 6 spend less time getting to school than half of the students in Grade 8.

**B.** More than half of the students in Grade 8 spend less time getting to school than half of the students in Grade 6.

**C.** More than half of the students in Grade 8 spend more time getting to school than half of the students in Grade 6.

**D.** More than half of the students in Grade 6 spend more time getting to school than half of the students in Grade 8.

**c.** Which measures work best for this situation? Why?

**4. Think About the Process** The dot plots show the race times of the students of Classroom X and Classroom Y.

**Class X**

**Class Y**

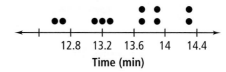

**a.** How do you decide which class has less variability in speed? Select all that apply.

**A.** Compare the median for each class.

**B.** Compare the range for each class.

**C.** Compare the interquartile range for each class.

**D.** Compare the mean for each class.

**b.** Which class has less variability in speed?

**c.** Explain what the variability of a sample represents.

CCSS: 7.SP.C.5, 7.SP.C.6

## Part 1

### Intro

You can use words to describe the likelihood that an event will occur.

| Still in a slump, playoff spot for Wolves impossible | Economy unlikely to recover this year | Scientists say another earthquake in this region is as likely as not | Showers likely in the afternoon | Congress certain to pass the new tax law |
|---|---|---|---|---|

**Impossible    Unlikely    As Likely as Not    Likely    Certain**

### Example  Describing the Likelihood of Events

Describe each event with one of the following words or phrases. Choose the one that best describes the likelihood that the event will occur.

Certain    Impossible    As Likely As    Likely    Unlikely

**a.** You will go swimming on a hot day this summer.
**b.** There will be children wearing costumes on Halloween.
**c.** Your hair will grow 5 inches in one day.
**d.** You flip a coin and it lands heads up.
**e.** A student in your class will become famous next year.

### Solution

**a.**

What a great idea! I'll probably go!

You will go swimming on a hot day this summer : Likely

**b.**

Somewhere there will definitely be kids wearing costumes on Halloween!

There will be children wearing costumes on Halloween: Certain

**c.**

That will never happen!

Your hair will grow 5 inches in one day: Impossible

**d.**

Half of the time, it's heads.

You flip a coin and it lands heads up: As Likely as Not

**e.**

That's improbable.

A student in your class will become famous next year: Unlikely

# Key Concept

The **probability of an event** is a number from 0 to 1 that measures the likelihood the event will occur. The closer the value is to 0, the less likely the event is. The closer the value is to 1, the more likely it is.

|  | Impossible | Unlikely | As Likely as Not | Likely | Certain |
|---|---|---|---|---|---|
| **Probability (fraction):** | 0 | $\frac{1}{4}$ | $\frac{1}{2}$ | $\frac{3}{4}$ | 1 |
| **Probability (decimal):** | 0 | 0.25 | 0.50 | 0.75 | 1 |
| **Probability (percent):** | 0% | 25% | 50% | 75% | 100% |

# Part 2

## Intro

If you choose a flag at random from this group of flags, each flag has the same chance of being selected. The probability that you choose the flag with stripes in its design is $\frac{1}{4}$.

Read *P* (stripes) as "The probability of stripes."

$$P(\text{stripes}) = \frac{1}{4} = 0.25 = 25\%$$

Probability written three ways

## Example  Describing Likelihood Based on Probabilities

Suppose you choose one flag at random. Use the probability in the table to classify choosing each design as *impossible, unlikely, as likely as not, likely,* or *certain*. Write each probability three ways.

| Type | Likelihood | Probability |
|---|---|---|
| a stripe | ▪ | $P(\text{stripe})$ = 0.65 = ▪ = ▪ |
| a triangle | ▪ | $P(\text{triangle})$ = 50% = ▪ = ▪ |
| a circle | ▪ | $P(\text{circle})$ = $\frac{1}{5}$ = ▪ = ▪ |

continued on next page >

## Part 2

**Example** continued

**Solution** · · · · · · · · · · · · · · · · · · · · · · · · · · · · · · · · · · · · · · · · · · · · · ·

*P*(stripes) is between 0.5 and 1, so you are *likely* to choose a flag with stripes in its design.

*P*(triangle) is 0.5, so you are as *likely as not* to choose a flag with a triangle in its design.

| Type | Likelihood | Probability |
|------|-----------|-------------|
| a stripe | likely | $P(\text{stripe}) = 0.65 = 65\% = \frac{13}{20}$ |
| a triangle | as likely as not | $P(\text{triangle}) = 50\% = 0.5 = \frac{1}{2}$ |
| a circle | unlikely | $P(\text{circle}) = \frac{1}{5} = 0.2 = 20\%$ |

*P*(circle) is between 0 and 0.5, so you are *unlikely* to choose a flag with a circle in its design.

## Part 3

### Intro

Airlines call a person who reserves a ticket for a flight and then does not board the flight a "no-show."

Because of no-shows, airlines often sell more tickets for a flight than there are seats on the airplane. This is called overbooking a flight.

### Example  Finding Expected Amounts Based on Probabilities

An airline believes that the probability of a passenger being a no-show on an afternoon flight is 10%.

$$p(\text{no–show}) = 0.1$$

The airline expects $\frac{1}{10}$ of the ticketed passengers not to show up.

The airline overbooked two afternoon flights.

210 tickets were sold for a flight with 200 seats.

330 tickets were sold for a flight with 300 seats.

On which flight should the airline expect to have more empty seats?

continued on next page >

# Part 3

**Example** continued

**Solution** ·······································································

| **Know** | **Need** | **Plan** |
|---|---|---|
| • $P$(no-show) = 0.1<br>• Number of tickets sold for a flight with 200 seats: 210<br>• Number of tickets sold for a flight with 300 seats: 330 | The flight that is expected to have more empty seats | • Use the probability statement to find the expected number of no-shows for each flight.<br>• To find the number of people expected to show up for each flight, subtract the number of no-shows from the number of tickets sold.<br>• To find the number of empty seats on each flight, subtract the number of people expected to show up from the number of seats on the flight. |

For the 200-seat airplane:

$$0.1(210) = 21$$  The airline expects 21 no-shows.

$$210 - 21 = 189$$  The airline expects 189 people to be on the flight.

$$200 - 189 = 11$$  The airline expects 11 empty seats on the flight.

For the 300-seat airplane:

$$0.1(330) = 33$$  The airline expects 33 no-shows.

$$330 - 33 = 297$$  The airline expects 297 people to be on the flight.

$$300 - 297 = 3$$  The airline expects 3 empty seats on the flight.

The airline expects 11 empty seats on the 200-seat plane and 3 empty seats on the 300-seat plane. So they should expect to have more empty seats on the 200-seat plane.

1. Which of these statements is best described as "unlikely"?

   **A.** The moon will rise in the west tomorrow.

   **B.** A meteorite lands next to you.

   **C.** A popular beach is crowded on a hot summer day.

   **D.** You flip a fair coin and get a tail.

2. Choose the word or phrase that best describes the likelihood of the statement below. Then explain your choice.

   All of the 21 students in a class have the same birthday.

   **A.** Unlikely     **B.** As likely as not

   **C.** Certain     **D.** Impossible

3. Suppose you have a bag of colored plastic disks and you choose one without looking. The probability the disk you choose is green is $P(\text{green}) = \frac{25}{50}$.

   **a.** Write this probability as a decimal.

   **b.** What best describes the probability?

       **A.** as likely as not

       **B.** likely

       **C.** unlikely

4. Suppose you have a bag of colored elastic bands and you choose one without looking. The probability the elastic band you choose is red is $P(\text{red}) = 0.35$.

   **a.** Write this probability as a percent and a fraction.

   **b.** What best describes the probability?

       **A.** as likely as not

       **B.** unlikely

       **C.** likely

5. Based on the records for the past several seasons, a sports fan believes the probability the red team wins is 0.55. The fan also believes the probability the blue team wins is 0.60. In a season with 180 games, how many fewer games should the fan expect the red team to win?

6. **Open-Ended** After many years of planting the same crop, a farmer knows that the probability of a certain type of seed sprouting is 86% when planted in his field.

   **a.** Of 1700 seeds planted, how many should the farmer expect to sprout?

   **b.** Describe how the farmer may have found this probability.

7. **Writing** A car comes to an intersection in a city and the light is red.

   **a.** Which word or phrase describes the likelihood of the statement?

       **A.** unlikely

       **B.** likely

       **C.** impossible

       **D.** as likely as not

   **b.** Write similar statements for the same situation that have different likelihoods. Explain why you believe the likelihoods are what you claim.

8. **a. Reasoning** Which of these statements has a likelihood best described as "certain"?

   **A.** A woman who has been in space comes to your birthday party.

   **B.** You flip a coin and get a head or a tail.

   **C.** You roll a standard six-sided number cube and get a value other than 3.

   **D.** A woman drives a car 2,607 miles in 1 hour.

   **b.** Explain what it is about the statement that makes you think it is certain.

**9. Think About the Process** Suppose you have a bag of 40 marbles and 20 of the marbles are white. If you choose one without looking, the probability you choose a white marble is $\frac{20}{40}$.

a. How do you change the fraction to a decimal?

   **A.** Divide the numerator by the denominator.

   **B.** Multiply the numerator and denominator by 3.

   **C.** Divide the denominator by the numerator.

   **D.** Multiply the numerator by the denominator.

b. The probability $\frac{20}{40}$ as a decimal is ■.

c. What best describes the probability?

   **A.** Likely      **B.** Unlikely

   **C.** As likely as not

**10. Error Analysis** Each player in a game has a 1 out of 50 chance of winning. The probability of winning is $\frac{1}{50}$. One player incorrectly thinks this means the probability of winning is 0.5.

a. What is the correct probability as a decimal?

b. How do you think the player found the incorrect decimal?

   **A.** The player divided 50 by 100.

   **B.** The player divided 100 by 50.

   **C.** The player divided 50 by 1.

   **D.** The player divided 1 by 50.

c. What best describes the probability?

   **A.** as likely as not

   **B.** likely

   **C.** unlikely

**11. Genetics** The probability of parents passing on a particular trait to their child is 0.28.

a. Write this probability as a percent and a fraction.

b. What best describes the probability?

   **A.** as likely as not   **B.** likely

   **C.** unlikely

**12. Mental Math** After many studies, a researcher finds that the probability of a word recognition program correctly interpreting a hand-written word is $\frac{9}{10}$. How many words would the researcher expect the program to interpret correctly out of 40 words?

**13. Think About the Process** Suppose you have a bag of 25 marbles and 3 of the marbles are white. If you choose one without looking, the probability you choose a white marble is P(white) = 0.12.

a. How do you change the decimal to a percent? Select all that apply.

   **A.** Divide the decimal by 100 and add a percent symbol.

   **B.** Multiply the decimal by 100 and add a percent symbol.

   **C.** Write the decimal as a fraction with denominator 100. The numerator is the percent.

   **D.** Write a percent symbol after the decimal.

b. Write P(white) as a percent.

c. Write P(white) as a fraction.

d. What best describes the probability?

   **A.** Likely      **B.** Unlikely

   **C.** As likely as not

**14.** To play a certain board game, the players roll 3 six-sided number cubes. The probability that the sum of the 3 numbers is 13 is $\frac{7}{72}$. If the players roll the number cubes 648 times during a game, how many times should the players expect the sum 13 to occur?

**15. Challenge** Suppose you have a bag with 20 letter tiles in it and 3 of the tiles are the letter Y. If you pick a letter tile at random from the bag, the probability that it is the letter Y is $\frac{3}{20}$. Suppose another bag has 500 letter tiles in it and 170 of the tiles are the letter Y.

a. Write the probability of picking a tile that is the letter Y as a fraction and as a percent.

b. From which bag are you more likely to pick a tile that is the letter Y?

**Vocabulary**
action, event, outcome, sample space

CCSS: 7.SP.C.7

## Part 1

### Intro

In probability situations, an **action** is a process with an uncertain result.

Rolling a number cube is an action with an uncertain result.

An **outcome** is a possible result of an action.

One possible result of rolling a standard number cube is rolling a 3.

The set of all possible outcomes is the **sample space** for the action.

The sample space for rolling a standard number cube is 1, 2, 3, 4, 5, 6.

### Example  Listing Outcomes in a Sample Space

The band director chooses one trumpet player at random to lead the band in the holiday parade. List all of the outcomes in the sample space for this action. How many outcomes are in the sample space?

Action: Choose one trumpet player to lead the band.

James   Jenny   Raul   Seth   Sara   Maria   Jenny   Julie

### Solution · · · · · · · · · · · · · · · · · · · · · · · ·

Action: Choose one trumpet player to lead the band.

Sample Space: James, Jenny, Raul, Sara, Seth, Maria, Jenny, Julie

Number of outcomes in the sample space: 8

Each trumpet player is one possible outcome.

# Part 2

## Intro

An **event** is a single outcome or group of outcomes from a sample space.

Sample Space for Rolling a Number Cube

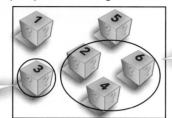

*Rolling a 3* is an event with one outcome.

*Rolling an even number* is an event with three outcomes.

## Example  Listing Outcomes of an Event

The band director will choose one trumpet player at random to lead the band in the holiday parade. Which trumpet players are in each event? Find the sample space for each event.

Jenny   Jenny   Maria   Sara   James   Raul   Seth   Julie

Event: Choose a boy.        Event: Choose a person wearing a striped shirt.

## Solution

Event: Choose a boy.

James, Raul, Seth

There are three boys in the sample space.

Event: Choose a person wearing a striped shirt.

Raul, Sara

There are two people in the sample space who are wearing striped shirts.

# Part 3

## Example Identifying Actions, Samples Spaces, and Events

Use the information below to complete the table.

Roll a number cube

Spin the spinner.

1, 2, 3, 4, 5, 6

Red, blue, green

Roll a number less than 3

The spinner stops on *blue*.

| | | |
|---|---|---|
| Action | | |
| Sample space | | |
| Event | | |

### Solution

| | | |
|---|---|---|
| Action | Roll a number cube. | Spin the spinner. |
| Sample space | 1, 2, 3, 4, 5, 6 | Blue, red, green |
| Event | Roll a number less than 3. | The spinner stops on blue. |

These are actions with uncertain results.

The sample space lists all possible results of the action.

An event consists of one or more of the possible outcomes.

## Key Concept

Probability allows you to analyze actions or situations for which the result is uncertain.

Action: Choose one button.

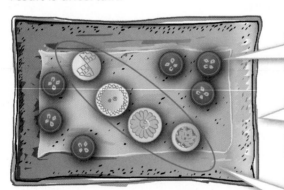

Outcome Each possible result – each button – is an outcome of the action

Sample Space The set of all possible outcomes – all the buttons – is the sample space for the action.

Event An event is a group of one or more possible outcomes. The four buttons in this group satisfy the event "choose a white button."

1. To meet a deadline, a manager chooses some workers to come in on a Saturday. The table shows the shirts five employees are wearing that day. Identify the outcomes for the following event. Event: The worker is wearing a solid shirt.

**Design of Shirts**

| Worker | Shirt |
|--------|-------|
| 1 | striped |
| 2 | purple |
| 3 | white |
| 4 | striped |
| 5 | white |

2. Use the given information to identify the action, the sample space, and the event.

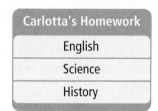

   **Roll a 6.**

   **1, 2, 3, 4, 5, 6**

   **Roll the number cube.**

3. Is the following an action, a sample space, or an event?

   **English, science, and history**

   | Carlotta's Homework |
   |---------------------|
   | English |
   | Science |
   | History |

4. Cara is picking out a snack. She has an orange, a banana, a pear, and an apple to choose from. Cara is going to pick one at random and wants to know what the chance is she will pick a banana. Identify the action, the sample space, and the event.

5. Classify the following as an action, sample space, or event.

   **a.** Tossing a fair coin

   **b.** Rolling an even number with a fair number cube

6. **Error Analysis** A teacher writes the four numbers shown. She asks the students to list the outcomes if two different numbers from the table are chosen at random. A student claims the outcomes for the action are 2, 3, 4, and 8.

   **a.** Which of the following are the correct outcomes for the action?

   **A.** 2 and 3, 2 and 8, 3 and 4, 3 and 8

   **B.** 2 and 2, 3 and 3, 4 and 4, 8 and 8

   **C.** 2 and 3, 2 and 4, 2 and 8, 3 and 4, 3 and 8, 4 and 8

   **D.** 2 and 3, 4 and 8

   **b.** What error did the student likely make?

7. **Number Cubes** When one number cube is rolled, the following six outcomes are possible. Identify the outcomes for each event. Event A: The number cube comes up odd. Event B: The number cube comes up 3 or more.

   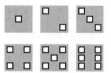

8. Use the given information to identify the action, the sample space, and the event.

   **The number chosen is a multiple of 5.**

   **choosing an odd number at random between 20 and 30**

   **21, 23, 25, 27, 29**

**9. Multiple Representations** Suppose you have 12 flashcards. The flashcards are yellow, green, blue, and red. The numbers on the flashcards are shown. You pick a flashcard at random. Identify the outcome for the event. Event: A flashcard that is green and odd.

**Flashcards**

| Color | Numbers |
|-------|---------|
| Yellow | 1, 2, 3 |
| Green | 4, 5, 6 |
| Blue | 7, 8, 9 |
| Red | 10, 11, 12 |

**a.** What is the outcome for the given event?

**b.** Draw pictures of the flashcards and the one you pick.

**10. Think About the Process** You have one spin of the spinner.

**a.** What part of the spinner represents a possible outcome?

   **A.** Each letter represents a possible outcome.

   **B.** Each number represents a possible outcome.

   **C.** Each color represents a possible outcome.

   **D.** Each sector of the spinner represents a possible outcome.

**b.** What is the sample space for this action? How many outcomes are in the sample space?

   **A.** The sample space is 1, 2, 3, 4, 5, 6, 7, 8. There are 8 outcomes.

   **B.** The sample space is 1, 1, 5, 5, *B*, *B*. There are 6 outcomes.

   **C.** The sample space is 1 light gray, 1 dark gray, 5 dark gray, 5 light gray, *B* dark gray, *B* white, *Z* light gray, *Z* dark gray. There are 8 outcomes.

   **D.** The sample space is 1, 5, *B*, *Z*. There are 4 outcomes.

**11. a. Challenge** List the outcomes in the sample space for the action. Action: Choose at random a multiple of three which lies between 2 and 20, inclusive.

**b.** Use the shapes given and identify the outcomes for the event. Event: Choose the multiples of three that are within the triangle-shaped figures in the diagram.

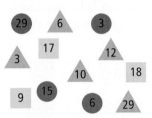

**12. Think About the Process** You have to list the outcomes in the sample space for the action shown below.

Choosing an odd number at random between 20 and 30

**a.** Which of these would be the best first step?

   **A.** Find the outcomes for other sample spaces.

   **B.** Find the total number of possible outcomes in the sample space.

   **C.** Find the lowest possible outcome in the sample space.

**b.** List all the outcomes in the sample space for this action.

**Vocabulary**
experimental probability, relative frequency, trial

CCSS: 7.SP.C.6

## Part 1

### Intro

In a probability experiment, you carry out or observe an action repeatedly. Each observation of the action is a **trial**. Keep track of the total number of trials and the frequency of each possible outcome.

You can use a ratio to find the **relative frequency** of a given event in the sample space of the experiment.

$$\text{relative frequency of an event} = \frac{\text{number of times event occurs}}{\text{total number of trials}}$$

You can conduct many probability experiments using numbers cubes, spinners, coins, and cards.

### Example  Finding Relative Frequencies

A spinner spins 40 times. The data found is shown in the table.

Find the relative frequency of each event as a fraction and as a decimal.

Event 1: Spin a 2.

Event 2: Spin an odd number.

| Experiment Table | | | | |
|---|---|---|---|---|
| Outcome | 1 | 2 | 3 | 4 |
| Frequency | 10 | 12 | 4 | 14 |
| Number of Trials: 40 | | | | |

### Solution

Event 1

$$\text{relative frequency of "spin of 2"} = \frac{\text{number of times 2 occurs}}{\text{total number of trials}}$$

$$= \frac{12}{40}$$

$$= \frac{3}{10}, \text{ or } 0.3$$

Event 2

$$\text{relative frequency of "spin an odd number"} = \frac{\text{number of times 1 or 3 occurs}}{\text{total number of trials}}$$

$$= \frac{14}{40}$$

$$= \frac{7}{20}, \text{ or } 0.35$$

# Key Concept

You can use relative frequencies to estimate the probability of an event. A probability found this way is an **experimental probability**.

The greater the number of trials, the closer the experimental probability will be to the actual probability of the event.

$$P(\text{event}) = \frac{\text{number of times event occurs}}{\text{total number of trials}}$$

# Part 2

## Example Finding Experimental Probabilities

A cashier in a grocery store asks each customer what type of bag to use. The table shows how many customers requested each type of bag during the cashier's three-hour shift. Find the experimental probability that a customer asks for plastic bags. Write the probability as a fraction and as a percent. Round to the nearest percent.

**Answers to "What type of bag would you like?"**

| Type of Bag | Number of Customer Requests |
|---|---|
| Plastic | 18 |
| Paper | 6 |
| Customer's own reusable bag | 8 |

**Solution** · · · · · · · · · · · · · · · · · · · · · · · · · · · · · · · · · · · · · · · · · · · · · · · · · · · · · ·

**Step 1** Identify the event.

The event is "A customer asks for plastic bags."

**Step 2** Find the probability.

$$P(\text{event}) = \frac{\text{number of times event occurs}}{\text{total number of trials}}$$

The total number of customers who asked for plastic bags is 18.

$$= \frac{18}{32}$$

The total number of customers is 18 + 6 + 8, or 32.

$$= \frac{9}{16}$$

The experimental probability that a customer asks for plastic bags is $\frac{9}{16}$.

$$\frac{9}{16} = 0.5625$$

The experimental probability that a customer asks for plastic bags is about 56%.

1. The heights of the students in a class are (in inches) 76, 75, 56, 62, 69, 65, 74, 69, 66, 58, 72, 60, 70, 71, 65, 67, 63, 59, 56, and 57. What is the experimental probability that a student chosen at random is 5 feet 6 inches tall?

2. A survey asked 125 people to choose a number from 1 to 5. The results are shown in the table.

**Experiment Table**

| Number | 1 | 2 | 3 | 4 | 5 | Number of Trials |
|---|---|---|---|---|---|---|
| Frequency | 15 | 30 | 35 | 20 | 25 | 125 |

   **a.** What is the relative frequency for each number?

   The relative frequency for 1 is ■.
   The relative frequency for 2 is ■.
   The relative frequency for 3 is ■.
   The relative frequency for 4 is ■.
   The relative frequency for 5 is ■.

   **b.** Predict the relative frequency for each number if 250 people were surveyed.

3. **Think About the Process** The heights of the students in a class are (in inches) 63, 61, 56, 72, 74, 72, 60, 74, 67, 69, 70, 67, 65, 69, 73, 72, 69, 65, 68, and 75.

   **a.** What steps do you need to take before finding the experimental probability that a randomly chosen student is less than 5 feet tall? Select all that apply.

   **A.** Find the number of students that are less than 5 feet tall.

   **B.** Convert feet to inches.

   **C.** Find the total number of students.

   **D.** Find the number of students that are greater than 5 feet tall.

   **E.** Divide the total number of students by 100.

   **F.** Divide the number of students that are less than 5 feet tall by 100.

   **b.** What is the experimental probability that a randomly chosen student is less than 5 feet tall?

4. **Think About the Process** A city council wants to know if the residents of the city would like a dog park. They sent out a survey to every household in the city. The results of the households that responded are shown in the table.

**Dog Owners**

| Number of Dogs in Household | Number of Households |
|---|---|
| 0 | 513 |
| 1 | 209 |
| 2 or more | 134 |

   **a.** What is an appropriate first step in finding the experimental probability that a household has more than one dog?

   **A.** Find the product of the number of households with one dog and the number with two or more dogs.

   **B.** Find the difference of the number of households with two or more dogs and the number with no dogs.

   **C.** Find the sum of the number of households for each category.

   **D.** Find the difference of the number of households with no dogs and the number with one dog.

   **b.** What is the experimental probability that a household has more than one dog?

   **c.** Do you think the city council should approve a dog park? Explain.

**5.** Your friend is playing a game where he rolls a number cube labeled 1 through 6 and spins the spinner. He records the sum of the numbers on the cube and spinner. The results are shown in the table in **Figure 1**.

**a.** Find the relative frequency of "a sum greater than 4 and less than 9."

**b.** Suppose your friend wins if the sum is greater than 4 and less than 9. Otherwise, you win. Is this a game you would want to play? Explain.

**6. Challenge** A store is giving out cards labeled 1 through 10 when customers enter the store. If the card is an even number, you get a 15% discount on your purchase that day. If the card is an odd number greater than 6, you get a 30% discount. Otherwise, you get a 20% discount. The table in **Figure 2** shows the results of 500 customers.

**a.** What is the relative frequency for each discount?

**b.** If the manager of the store wants approximately half of the customers to receive the 20% discount, does this seem like an appropriate method? Explain.

**(Figure 1)**

| Game Results | | | | | | | | | |
| --- | --- | --- | --- | --- | --- | --- | --- | --- | --- |
| Sum | 2 | 3 | 4 | 5 | 6 | 7 | 8 | 9 | 10 | Number of Trials |
| Frequency | 3 | 6 | 8 | 9 | 10 | 11 | 8 | 5 | 3 | 63 |

**(Figure 2)**

| Discounts | | | | | | | | | |
| --- | --- | --- | --- | --- | --- | --- | --- | --- | --- |
| Card Number | 1 | 2 | 3 | 4 | 5 | 6 | 7 | 8 | 9 | 10 |
| Frequency | 63 | 43 | 42 | 60 | 66 | 51 | 55 | 60 | 55 | 5 |

See your complete lesson at MyMathUniverse.com

**Theoretical Probability**

CCSS: 7.SP.C.7, 7.SP.C.7a

## Key Concept

Sometimes you can find the probability of an event through reasoning about the outcomes in the sample space. A probability found this way is a **theoretical probability**.

When all outcomes of an action are equally likely, you can use the theoretical probability formula.

$$P(\text{event}) = \frac{\text{number of favorable outcomes}}{\text{number of possible outcomes}}$$

*Favorable* outcomes are the outcomes in the sample space that satisfy the event.

## Part 1

### Intro

The theoretical probability of an event depends on the number of favorable outcomes and the number of possible outcomes.

Here are two views of the same number cube, showing its six faces. Find the theoretical probability of rolling a zero.

**Step 1** Check that all outcomes are equally likely.

Each side is equally likely to land facing up.

**Step 2** Find the number of outcomes in the sample space.

Step 2: The sample space has six possible outcomes.

| 0 | 1 | 2 | 3 | 4 | 0 |

Step 3: Two outcomes are zero.

**Step 3** Count the number of favorable outcomes.

continued on next page >

See your complete lesson at MyMathUniverse.com

# Part 1

**Intro** continued

**Step 4** Use the theoretical probability formula.

$$P(\text{event}) = \frac{\text{number of favorable outcomes}}{\text{number of possible outcomes}}$$

**Step 5** Find the probability.

$$P(0) = \frac{\text{number of zeros}}{\text{number of possible outcomes}} = \frac{2}{6}, \text{ or } \frac{1}{3}$$

## Example  Finding Theoretical Probabilities

Action: One spin of the spinner.

Find the probability that the spinner stops on each type of sector.

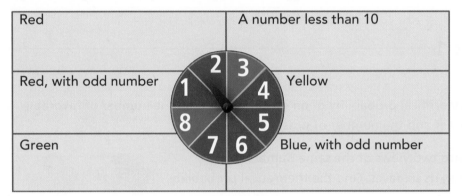

| Red | A number less than 10 |
|---|---|
| Red, with odd number | Yellow |
| Green | Blue, with odd number |

## Solution · · · · · · · · · · · · · · · · · · · · · · · · · · · · · · · · · · · · · · · · · · · · · · · · · · · · · · · · · · · · · · · ·

Each sector is one outcome in the sample space, so the sample space contains 8 outcomes.

The spinner has eight equal sectors, so all of the outcomes are equally likely. You can use the theoretical probability formula.

$$P(\text{event}) = \frac{\text{number of favorable outcomes}}{\text{number of outcomes in sample space}}$$

$$P(\text{red}) = \frac{3}{8}$$

The probability that the spinner stops on a red sector number is $\frac{3}{8}$.

$$P(\text{red, with an odd number}) = \frac{1}{8}$$

The probability that the spinner stops on a red sector with an odd number is $\frac{1}{8}$.

$$P(\text{number less than 10}) = \frac{8}{8} = 1$$

continued on next page >

## Part 1

### Solution continued

The probability that the spinner stops on a number less than 10 is 1.

Every sector is numbered less than 10.

$$P(\text{green}) = \frac{2}{8}$$
$$= \frac{1}{4}$$

The probability that the spinner stops on a green sector is $\frac{1}{4}$.

$$P(\text{event}) = \frac{\text{number of favorable outcomes}}{\text{number of outcomes in sample space}}$$
$$P(\text{yellow}) = \frac{0}{8}$$
$$= 0$$

The probability that the spinner stops on a yellow sector is 0. None of the sectors is yellow.

$$P(\text{blue, with odd number}) = \frac{2}{8} = \frac{1}{4}$$

The probability that the spinner stops on a blue sector with an odd number is $\frac{1}{4}$.

## Part 2

### Intro

Will a baby be a boy or a girl?

**Theoretical Probability**

- Based on reasoning about equally likely outcomes in a sample space
- Compares the number of favorable outcomes to the number of possible outcomes

If the outcomes *boy* and *girl* are equally likely, then

$$P(\text{boy}) = \frac{\text{number of boys in sample space}}{\text{number of possible outcomes}}$$

$$= \frac{1}{2}, \text{ or } 50\%$$

**Experimental Probability**

- Based on observing outcomes of repeated trials of an action
- Compares the number of times the event occurs to the total number of trials

continued on next page >

# Part 2

**Intro** continued

**Births in One Year (U.S.)**

| Boys | Girls | Total |
|------|-------|-------|
| 2,110,558 | 2,027,791 | 4,138,349 |

$$P(\text{boy}) = \frac{\text{number of boys}}{\text{total number of births}}$$
$$= \frac{2,110,558}{4,138,349}$$
$$= 0.51\% \text{ or } 51\%$$

## Example  Classifying Probabilities as Experimental or Theoretical

Classify each probability as *experimental* or *theoretical*.

**a.** A soccer player took 12 shots on goal and scored once.

$P(\text{soccer players scores on a shot}) = \frac{1}{2}$

**b.** You roll a standard number cube 50 times and get eight 3s.

$P(3) = \frac{8}{50}$

**c.** You choose one tulip at random from the vase.

$P(\text{red}) = \frac{5}{12}$

## Solution

**a.** A soccer player took 12 shots on goal and scored once.

$P(\text{soccer player scores on a shot}) = \frac{1}{12}$

This is an example of *experimental* probability.

> This situation involves the outcomes of 12 repeated trials.

**b.** You roll a standard number cube 50 times and get eight 3s.

$P(3) = \frac{8}{50}$

This is an example of *experimental* probability.

> This situation involves the outcomes of 50 repeated trials.

**c.** You choose one tulip at random from the vase.

$P(\text{red}) = \frac{5}{12}$

This is an example of *theoretical* probability.

> This situation involves choosing 1 of 12 equally likely outcomes.

# Part 3

## Intro

A **simulation** of a real-world situation is a model used to find probabilities.

You can use objects such as coins, number cubes, and spinners to simulate probability situations. You assign each outcome in the sample space to one outcome of the coin, number cube, or spinner.

| For a situation with: | 2 equally likely outcomes | 6 equally likely outcomes | 8 equally likely outcomes |
|---|---|---|---|
| You could | toss a coin. | roll a number cube. | use a spinner. |

## Example Comparing Predictions and Simulations

A class has the same number of boys as girls. Each day the teacher chooses one student at random to take attendance. The school year has 180 days.

**a.** How many days would you expect the teacher to choose a boy to take attendance?

**b.** Use the Probability Tool to simulate this situation with a coin toss. How do the results compare to your answer to part (a)?

The teacher chooses a girl.          The teacher chooses a boy.

## Solution

**a.** The class has the same number of boys as girls, so the outcomes are equally likely. The probability of choosing a boy is $\frac{1}{2}$. In 180 days, you would expect the teacher to choose $\frac{1}{2}$ (180) or 90 boys.

**b.** Sample simulation data:

**Coin Toss Results**

| Girls (Heads) | Boys (Tails) | Total |
|---|---|---|
| 81 | 99 | 180 |

In the simulation, the teacher chooses a boy 99 times, which is more than the number of times predicted using theoretical probability.

**1.** Find the theoretical probability of the event P(12) when rolling a 12-sided die.

**2.** Find the theoretical probability of the event P(less than 8) when rolling a 12-sided die.

**3.** The spinner at the right is divided into eight equal parts. Find the theoretical probability of landing on the given section(s) of the spinner.

P(odd) = ■

**4.** The probability of selecting a consonant at random from the alphabet is $\frac{21}{26}$.

   **a.** Decide whether the situation is an example of experimental probability or theoretical probability.

   **b.** Describe another example that is the other type of probability.

**5.** **Think About the Process** A student has a one-dollar bill, a five-dollar bill, and a ten-dollar bill in a box. The student selects a bill from the box 47 times and selects the one-dollar bill 15 times.

   **a.** Which of the following formulas should be used to calculate the experimental probability?

   **A.** P(event)
   $= \frac{\text{number of favorable outcomes}}{\text{number of possible outcomes}}$

   **B.** P(event) = total number of trials − number of times event occurs

   **C.** P(event)
   $= \frac{\text{number of times event occurs}}{\text{total number of trials}}$

   **D.** P(event) = total number of trials + number of times event occurs

   **b.** What is the experimental probability of selecting the one-dollar bill?

   **c.** What is the theoretical probability of selecting the one-dollar bill?

**6.** At school there are the same number of boys and girls. A student is chosen at random to raise the flag.

   **a.** How many times is it expected that a boy will raise the flag over 42 days of school?

   **b.** The results of a simulation using a coin are shown in the table. How do the results from the simulation compare to the expected number of times?

**Simulation Results**

| Girls (Heads) | Boys (Tails) | Total |
|---|---|---|
| 15 | 27 | 42 |

**7.** **Think About the Process** There are five different colored bean bags in a box.

   **a.** What should be the first step before using the theoretical probability formula?

   **A.** The first step is to count the number of favorable outcomes.

   **B.** The first step is to pick the event.

   **C.** The first step is to count the total number of possible outcomes.

   **D.** The first step is to check that all outcomes are equally likely to occur.

   **b.** What is the probability of pulling the yellow-colored bean bag from the box?

   P(yellow bean bag) = ■

**8. Reasoning** The spinner is divided into eight equal parts.

a. Find the theoretical probability of landing on section(s) *P*(greater than 5) of the spinner.

b. Are you able to use the probability to predict future events? Explain.

**9. Mental Math** There are five cab drivers for a company. When a person calls, a driver is chosen at random to pick the person up.

a. If there are 120 calls during a day, how many calls is Driver 4 expected to take?

b. To simulate the situation, names are put into a hat. The results from pulling a name out of a hat are shown in the table in **Figure 1**. How do the results from the simulation compare to the expected number of calls Driver 4 takes?

**10.** There is a deck of flashcards and each card has a different number ranging from 1 to 40. Find the theoretical probability of the event P(the number is less than 24) when picking from a deck of flashcards.

**11. Challenge** Seven different names were put into a hat. A name is chosen 100 times and the name Grace is chosen 23 times.

a. What is the experimental probability of the name Grace being chosen?

b. What is the theoretical probability of the name Grace being chosen?

c. Explain how each probability would change if the number of names in the hat were different.

**12. Challenge** Noah has eight different pairs of shoes. Each day Noah picks a pair at random to wear.

a. Over 296 days, how many times is it expected that he will wear pairs 2 and 4 combined?

b. The results from the simulation using a spinner with eight spots are in the table in **Figure 2**. How do the results from the simulation compare to the expected number of times he will wear pairs 2 and 4 combined?

A. The result from the simulation is the same as the expected result.

B. The result from the simulation is less than the expected result.

C. The result from the simulation is greater than the expected result.

**(Figure 1)**

**Simulation Results**

| Driver 1 (1) | Driver 2 (2) | Driver 3 (3) | Driver 4 (4) | Driver 5 (5) | Total |
| --- | --- | --- | --- | --- | --- |
| 29 | 31 | 20 | 19 | 21 | 120 |

**(Figure 2)**

**Simulation Results**

| Pair 1 (1) | Pair 2 (2) | Pair 3 (3) | Pair 4 (4) | Pair 5 (5) | Pair 6 (6) | Pair 7 (7) | Pair 8 (8) | Total |
| --- | --- | --- | --- | --- | --- | --- | --- | --- |
| 27 | 37 | 52 | 37 | 42 | 34 | 33 | 34 | 296 |

See your complete lesson at MyMathUniverse.com

**Vocabulary**
probability
model, uniform
probability model

CCSS: 7.SP.C.7a, 7.SP.C.7b, Also 7.SP.C.7

## Key Concept

A **probability model** consists of an action, its sample space, and a list of events with their probabilities. The events and probabilities in the list have these characteristics:

- Each outcome in the sample space is in exactly one event.
- The sum of all of the probabilities must be 1.

**Action:** One spin of the spinner

**Sample space:** red, red, blue, red, blue

**Probabilities:**

$$P(\text{red}) = \frac{3}{5}$$

$$P(\text{blue}) = \frac{2}{5}$$

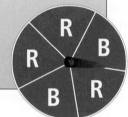

Check: The sum of probabilities is 1.

$$\frac{3}{5} + \frac{2}{5} = \frac{5}{5}$$
$$= 1$$

## Part 1

### Example  Identifying Complete Probability Models

Which list of probabilities does *not* complete a probability model for this action?

**Action:** Choose one card.

**Sample Space:**

continued on next page >

# Part 1

**Example** continued

**List 1**

$P$(fewer than three shapes) $= \frac{1}{3}$

$P$(at least three shapes) $= \frac{2}{3}$

**List 2**

$P$(fish) $= \frac{1}{3}$

$P$(apple) $= \frac{1}{2}$

$P$(leaf) $= \frac{1}{6}$

**List 3**

$P$(even number of apples) $= \frac{1}{3}$

$P$(odd number of apples) $= \frac{1}{6}$

## Solution

For each list, check that each card is in exactly one event and that the sum of the probabilities is 1.

**List 1:**

Fewer than three shapes                    At least three shapes

   Each card is in exactly one event.

$P$(fewer than three shapes) $= \frac{1}{3}$        $P$(at least three shapes) $= \frac{2}{3}$

$$\frac{1}{3} + \frac{2}{3} = \frac{3}{3}$$
$$= 1$$

List 1 completes a probability model.

**List 2:**

Fish                        Apples                        Leaves

Each card is in exactly one event.

$$\frac{1}{3} + \frac{1}{2} + \frac{1}{6} = \frac{2}{6} + \frac{3}{6} + \frac{1}{6}$$

The sum of the probabilities is 1.

$$= \frac{6}{6}$$
$$= 1$$

List 2 completes a probability model.

continued on next page >

# Part 1

## Solution continued

### List 3:

Even Apples

Odd Apples

> Not every card is in an event.

List 3 does not account for all of the cards, so it does not complete a probability model.

# Part 2

## Intro

A probability model based on using the theoretical probability of equally likely outcomes is a **uniform probability model**.

Before setting up a probability model, ask yourself:

"Can I use theoretical probability?"
OR
"Do I need to collect data and use relative frequencies?"

## Example  Using Uniform Probability Models

Tell whether you can use a uniform probability model for each situation. Explain your reasoning.

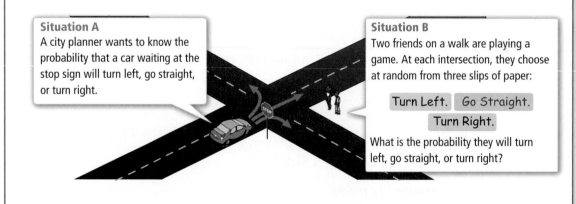

**Situation A**
A city planner wants to know the probability that a car waiting at the stop sign will turn left, go straight, or turn right.

**Situation B**
Two friends on a walk are playing a game. At each intersection, they choose at random from three slips of paper:

Turn Left.  Go Straight.  Turn Right.

What is the probability they will turn left, go straight, or turn right?

continued on next page >

# Part 2

## Example continued

### Solution

**Situation A**

A city planner wants to know the probability that a car waiting at the stop sign will turn left, go straight, or turn right.

You do not know if cars are equally likely to go in each of the three directions. You *cannot* use a uniform probability model.

**Situation B**

Two friends on a walk are playing a game. At each intersection, they choose at random from three slips of paper:

Turn Left. Go Straight. Turn Right.

Each slip of paper is equally likely to be chosen. You *can* use theoretical probability to set up a uniform probability model.

# Part 3

## Example Writing Probability Models

The table shows data collected from four cashiers in a grocery store. Write a probability model to find the probability that a customer will use each type of bag.

**Answers to "What type of bag would you like?"**

| Type of Bag | Number of Customer Requests |
|---|---|
| Plastic | 252 |
| Paper | 21 |
| Customer's own reusable bags | 77 |

### Solution

The three outcomes, paper, plastic, and reusable, are not necessarily equally likely. Use the data in the table to find the experimental probability for each type of bag.

continued on next page >

# Part 3

**Solution** continued

To find the experimental probabilities, you need to know the total number of customers. This gives the number of trials.

$$\text{Total number of trials} = 252 + 21 + 77$$

$$= 350$$

Action: Choose a type of bag.

Sample space: paper, plastic, reusable

Probabilities:

$$P(\text{bag type}) = \frac{\text{number of customers who chose that type}}{\text{total number of customers}}$$

$$P(\text{plastic}) = \frac{252}{350}$$

$$= 0.72$$

$$P(\text{paper}) = \frac{21}{350}$$

$$= 0.06$$

$$P(\text{reusable}) = \frac{77}{350}$$

$$= 0.22$$

**Check** · · · · · · · · · · · · · · · · · · · · · · · · · · · · · · · · · · · · · · · · · · · · · · ·

The sum of the probabilities should be 1.

$$P(\text{plastic}) + P(\text{paper}) + P(\text{reusable}) = 0.72 + 0.06 + 0.22$$

$$= 1$$

1. You are playing a game using this spinner. You get one spin on each turn. Which list shows a complete probability model for the spinner?

   **A.** $P(\text{letter}) = \frac{4}{8}$, $P(\text{even number}) = \frac{2}{8}$

   **B.** $P(\text{letter}) = \frac{4}{8}$, $P(\text{odd number}) = \frac{2}{8}$

   **C.** $P(\text{letter}) = \frac{4}{8}$, $P(\text{number}) = \frac{4}{8}$

   **D.** $P(\text{even number}) = \frac{2}{8}$,
      $P(\text{odd number}) = \frac{2}{8}$

2. A bag contains 17 green, 11 orange, and 19 purple tennis balls. A person chooses a tennis ball without looking. Can you use a uniform probability model for the event of choosing a tennis ball from the bag?

3. A box contains green marbles and blue marbles. Yosef shakes the box and chooses a marble at random. He records the color, then places the marble back into the box. Yosef repeats the process until he chooses 50 marbles. The table shows the count for each color. Write a probability model for choosing a marble. Simplify your answers.

   **Choosing Marbles**

   | Green | Blue |
   |-------|------|
   | 37    | 13   |

4. The table shows the results of a survey where 50 people were asked to pick a number from 1 to 5. Find the

probabilities for a complete probability model for the responses. **(Figure 1)**

5. **a.** **Writing** Determine whether the list $P(1) = \frac{3}{10}$, $P(2) = \frac{1}{2}$, $P(3) = \frac{1}{10}$, and $P(4) = \frac{1}{10}$ is a complete probability model.

   **b.** If the list is not a complete probability model, explain changes that you could make to the list to make it a complete probability model. If the list is a complete probability model, describe an action and sample space that this list could complete.

6. **Reasoning** A bin holds 18 blue T-shirts, 15 green T-shirts, and 17 yellow T-shirts. You choose a T-shirt at random from the bin.

   **a.** Are the outcomes of this event equally likely?

   **b.** Describe how to change this event to make it equally likely if it is not, or not equally likely if it is. Explain.

7. There is a bucket with 10 black pens and 5 blue pens. Each person is going to choose one pen. Decide if you can use a uniform probability model for these situations.

   **Situation 1 Each person flips a coin, with heads indicating the person should pick a black pen.**

   **Situation 2 Each person picks a pen with his or her eyes closed.**

   For which situation(s) can you use a uniform probability model?

   **A.** Only Situation 2

   **B.** Both situations

   **C.** Only Situation 1

   **D.** Neither situation

**(Figure 1)**

| Number | 1 | 2 | 3 | 4 | 5 |
|--------|---|---|---|---|---|
| Number Who Chose | 9 | 5 | 10 | 6 | 20 |

See your complete lesson at MyMathUniverse.com

**8. Estimation** The table shows data from a survey asking people what type of juice they like.

| Type of Juice | Number of People |
| --- | --- |
| Orange | 129 |
| Cranberry | 147 |
| Apple | 56 |

**a.** Write the list of probabilities for a probability model that gives the probability that a person chosen at random likes each type of juice.

**b.** Estimate the number of people who would say they like orange juice in a survey of 500 people.

**9. Think About the Process** These lists are possible probability models for an event with four possible outcomes.

**List 1**  $P(1) = \frac{1}{29}$, $P(2) = \frac{1}{29}$, $P(3) = \frac{1}{29}$, $P(4) = \frac{1}{29}$

**List 2**  $P(1) = \frac{7}{29}$, $P(2) = \frac{12}{29}$, $P(3) = \frac{7}{29}$, $P(4) = \frac{3}{29}$

**List 3**  $P(1) = \frac{4}{29}$, $P(2) = \frac{1}{29}$, $P(3) = \frac{3}{29}$, $P(4) = \frac{2}{29}$

**List 4**  $P(1) = -\frac{112}{29}$, $P(2) = \frac{19}{29}$, $P(3) = \frac{3}{29}$, $P(4) = \frac{7}{29}$

**a.** How can you decide which list is a complete probability model?

**A.** Check that each outcome is in exactly one event and the sum of the probabilities is 1.

**B.** Check that each outcome is in more than one event and the sum of the probabilities is 1.

**C.** Check that each outcome is in exactly one event and the sum of the probabilities is less than 1.

**D.** Check that each outcome is in exactly one event and the sum of the probabilities is greater than 1.

**b.** Which list is a complete probability model?

**10. Think About the Process** You choose 1 of these cards at random.

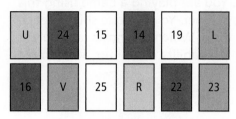

$P(\text{letter}) = \frac{1}{3}$; $P(\text{white}) = \frac{4}{12}$

**a.** How can you find the probability statement that could make a complete probability model?

**A.** Check that each outcome in the sample space is in exactly 1 event and that the sum of all the probabilities is greater than 1.

**B.** Check that each outcome in the sample space is in exactly 1 event and that the sum of all the probabilities is 1.

**C.** Check that each outcome in the sample space is in more than 1 event and that the sum of all the probabilities is 1.

**D.** Check that each outcome in the sample space is in more than 1 event and that the sum of all the probabilities is less than 1.

**b.** Which probability statement could you add to make a complete probability model?

**A.** $P(\text{dark gray}) = \frac{1}{3}$

**B.** $P(\text{light gray}) = \frac{1}{3}$

**C.** $P(\text{odd number}) = \frac{4}{12}$

**11. Challenge** A stocked fishing pond has 496 catfish, 186 perch, and 124 trout in it. Of the fish in the pond, only $\frac{1}{8}$ of the catfish, $\frac{1}{3}$ of the perch, and $\frac{1}{2}$ of the trout will bite a hook. If a man casts a hook into the pond, is he equally likely to catch any of the types of fish?

CCSS: 7.SP.C.7, 7.SP.C.7b, Also 7.SP.C.7a

## Part 1

### Example Comparing Simulations and Uniform Probability Models

When you reach this five-way fork in a computer maze, the game chooses one path at random for you to go down.

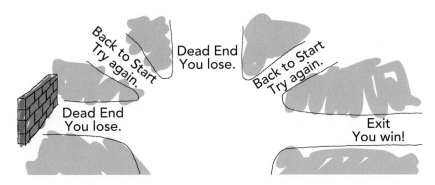

Use a spinner to simulate 250 times what happens when you reach this point in the game. How do your results compare with what a uniform probability model of this situation predicts?

### Solution

**Method 1** Sample: Use colors to represent the outcomes.

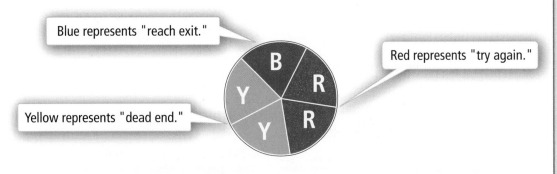

Blue represents "reach exit."

Red represents "try again."

Yellow represents "dead end."

Sample data and answer

**Results of Game**

| Outcomes | Yellow: Dead End | Red: Try Again | Blue: Reach Exit |
|---|---|---|---|
| Frequency | 90 | 113 | 47 |

continued on next page >

**Solution** continued

The sum of the frequencies gives you the total number of attempts.

$$90 + 113 + 47 = 250$$

A uniform probability model predicts these results.

Dead end: $\frac{2}{5}(250) = 100$ times, *or* 100 times in 250 attempts

Try again: $\frac{2}{5}(250) = 100$ times, *or* 100 times in 250 attempts

Reach exit: $\frac{1}{5}(250) = 50$ times, *or* 50 times in 250 attempts

The results of the simulation are fairly close to those predicted by the uniform probability model. The number of "dead ends" was a little lower than expected, as was the number of times that the "exit" was reached. The number of "try agains" was higher than expected.

**Method 2** Sample: Use numbers to represent the outcomes.

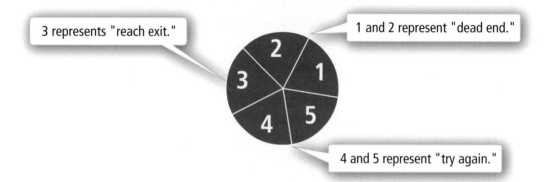

3 represents "reach exit."

1 and 2 represent "dead end."

4 and 5 represent "try again."

Sample data and answer

**Results of Game**

| Outcomes | 1 and 2: Dead End | 4 and 5: Try Again | 3: Reach Exit |
|---|---|---|---|
| Frequency | 90 | 113 | 47 |

The sum of the frequencies gives you the total number of attempts.

$$90 + 113 + 47 = 250$$

continued on next page >

## Part 1

**Solution** continued

A uniform probability model predicts these results.

Dead end: $\frac{2}{5}(250) = 100$ times, *or* 100 times in 250 attempts

Try again: $\frac{2}{5}(250) = 100$ times, *or* 100 times in 250 attempts

Reach exit: $\frac{1}{5}(250) = 50$ times, *or* 50 times in 250 attempts

The results of the simulation are fairly close to those predicted by the uniform probability model. The number of "dead ends" was a little lower than expected, as was the number of times that the "exit" was reached. The number of "try agains" was higher than expected.

## Part 2

### Example  Finding Probabilities to Make Decisions

A city planner wants to know the probability that a car will turn left, go straight, or turn right at an intersection. If the probability that a car will turn left is greater than 50%, then a traffic light will be installed.

The city planner collected the data shown during three one-hour periods. Should she recommend that a traffic light be installed?

If   $P(\text{turn left}) > 50\%$   then      the city planner will recommend a traffic light.

**8:00 A.M – 9:00 A.M.**

| Left | 38 |
|------|----|
| Right | 50 |
| Straight | 22 |

**12:00 P.M – 1:00 P.M.**

| Left | 52 |
|------|----|
| Right | 31 |
| Straight | 18 |

**6:00 P.M – 7:00 P.M.**

| Left | 25 |
|------|----|
| Right | 24 |
| Straight | 10 |

**Solution** · · · · · · · · · · · · · · · · · · · · · · · · · · · · · · · · · · · · · · · · · · · · · · · · · · · · · · · · · · · ·

Find the total number of cars going in each direction.

total number of cars turning left $= 38 + 52 + 25$

$= 115$

continued on next page >

**Solution** continued

total number of cars turning right $= 50 + 31 + 24$

$= 105$

total number of cars going straight $= 22 + 18 + 10$

$= 50$

Find the total number of cars observed.

total number of cars observed $= 115 + 105 + 50$

$= 270$

Use the experimental probability formula.

$$P(\text{turn left}) = \frac{\text{number of cars turning left}}{\text{total number of cars observed}}$$

$$= \frac{115}{270}$$

A probability of $\frac{135}{270}$ would be 50%. Since 115 is less than 135, the probability that a car will turn left is less than 50%.

The city planner should not recommend that a traffic light be installed.

1. In a video game, you reach a four-way fork in a computer maze. The game chooses one path at random for you to go down. One path leads to a dead end, two paths lead you back to the start, and one path leads to the exit. You use a spinner with colors to simulate what happens when you reach this point in the game 240 times. How do your results compare with what a uniform probability model of this situation predicts?

**Spinner**

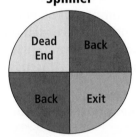

a. Complete the table for what the uniform probability model predicts.

| Outcome | Uniform Model Prediction |
|---|---|
| Dead End | ■ times in 240 attempts |
| Back to Start | ■ times in 240 attempts |
| Exit | ■ times in 240 attempts |

b. Use **Figure 1** shown below. The number of times you reached a dead end was ■ expected. The number of times you went back to the start was ■ expected. The number of times you reached the exit was ■ expected. The results of the simulation are ■ close to those predicted by the uniform probability model.

2. **Think About the Process** A city planner wants to know the probability that a car will turn left, go straight, or turn right at a particular intersection. If the probability that a car will turn left is greater than 50%, the city planner will recommend that a traffic light be installed. The city planner collected the data shown during three one-hour periods.

**Intersection Actions**

| Time Period | Left | Straight | Right |
|---|---|---|---|
| 7:00–8:00 A.M. | 47 | 26 | 33 |
| 1:00–2:00 P.M. | 48 | 24 | 35 |
| 6:00–7:00 P.M. | 34 | 20 | 18 |

a. What is one possible first step in finding the probability?

   **A.** Find the total number of cars in the 7:00–8:00 A.M. time period.

   **B.** Find the total number of cars observed and the number of cars that turned left.

   **C.** Multiply 50% by the total number of cars.

   **D.** Find the percent of cars that turned left in each time period.

b. Should she recommend that a traffic light be installed? Fill in the answer line to complete your choice.

   **A.** No, because the probability that a car will turn left is ■%.

   **B.** Yes, because the probability that a car will turn left is ■%.

**(Figure 1)**

| Simulation Results | | | |
|---|---|---|---|
| Outcome | Yellow = Dead End | Red = Back To Start | Blue = Exit |
| Frequency | 36 | 149 | 55 |

3. **Think About the Process** Meredith's family wants to go on vacation. Both of her parents want to go to Hawaii. She and her brother want to go to California. One of her sisters wants to go to Florida and her other sister wants to go to Texas. She uses a spinner with numbers to simulate their choices 120 times based on the 6 family members. See **Figure 2** below.

**Spinner**

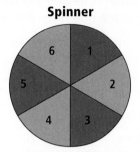

a. Find one possible setup for this simulation.

b. Complete the table for what the uniform probability model predicts.

| Outcome | Uniform Model Prediction |
|---|---|
| Hawaii | ■ times in 120 attempts |
| California | ■ times in 120 attempts |
| Florida | ■ times in 120 attempts |
| Texas | ■ times in 120 attempts |

c. The number of times Hawaii was chosen was ■ expected. The number of times California was chosen was ■ expected. The number of times Florida was chosen was ■ expected. The number of times Texas was chosen was ■ expected. The results of the simulation are ■ close to those predicted by the uniform probability model.

4. A gardener planted 20 pumpkin seeds in each of 10 patches. She recorded the number of seeds that sprouted in each patch. **Figure 7** shows the data. Assume each patch is a random sample of the seeds.

a. Find the probability of a seed sprouting.

b. The seed producer claims that greater than 80% of the seeds will sprout. Does this probability support the seed producer's claim?

c. Describe reasons why the patches may not be random samples.

5. **Challenge** A researcher tested 5 random samples of 50 light bulbs for two brands. He recorded the number of bulbs that burnt out after less than 1,000 hours of use. The table shows the data.

**Number of Bulbs that Burn Out**

| Brand | Sample | | | | |
|---|---|---|---|---|---|
| | 1 | 2 | 3 | 4 | 5 |
| A | 1 | 7 | 4 | 8 | 9 |
| B | 7 | 3 | 6 | 2 | 5 |

a. Find the probability of a light bulb burning out after less than 1,000 hours of use for each brand. Simplify your answers.

b. Which brand of light bulb lasts for the greater amount of time?

**(Figure 2)**

| Simulation Results | | | | | | |
|---|---|---|---|---|---|---|
| Outcome | 1 | 2 | 3 | 4 | 5 | 6 |
| Frequency | 28 | 26 | 15 | 13 | 9 | 29 |

# 17-1 | Compound Events

**Vocabulary**
compound event,
dependent events,
independent
events

CCSS: 7.SP.C.8, 7.SP.C.8b

## Part 1

### Intro

In probability situations, an **action** is a process with an uncertain result. In the previous topic, you worked with actions that involved only one step or choice. Multi-step actions involve more than one step or choice.

Consider an example.

Action: Spin the spinner once. — A one-step action

Action: Spin the spinner twice. — A two-step action

Consider a different type of action.

Action: Choose one person from the group. — A one-step action

Action: Choose four people from the group. — A four-step action

continued on next page >

# Part 1

**Intro** continued

Here is another example.

Action: Roll one number cube. — A one-step action

Action: Roll three number cubes. — A three-step action

Finally, consider an action involving choosing clothes.

Action: Choose one shirt. — A one-step action

Action: Choose one shirt and one pair of pants. — A two-step action

# Part 1

## Example  Counting Choices for Actions

How many steps or choices does each action involve? Choose from the numerals below.

3       8       5       1       6       9       4       7       2

**a.**
Choose one fruit
and one drink

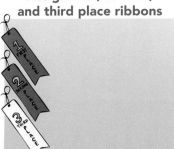

**b.**
Assign first, second,
and third place ribbons

**c.**
Choose a
six-character password

## Solution · · · · · · · · · · · · · · · · · · · · · · · · · · · · · · · · · · · · · · · · · ·

**a.** Choose one fruit and one drink.

> There are five items to pick from, but only two choices to make. The action has 2 steps.

**b.** Assign first, second, and third place ribbons.

> This action has 3 steps

**c.** Choose a six-character password.

> Each character requires a choice. This action has 6 steps.

# Part 2

## Intro

A **compound event** is an event associated with a multi-step action. A compound event is composed of events that are the outcomes of the steps of the action.

A compound event for a two-step action has two parts.

**Action:** Spin the spinner twice.

**Compound event**
Spin red. Then spin green.

(R, G)

> Use parentheses to show the two outcomes are one compound event.

A compound event for a four-step action has four parts.

**Action:** Choose four people from a group.

**Compound event**
boy, girl, girl, boy

(B, G, G, B)

> Parentheses show that the four outcomes are one compound event.

A compound event for a three-step action has three parts.

**Action:** Roll three number cubes.

**Compound event**
blue cube: 2, red cube: 6, green cube: 2

(2, 6, 2)

> Parentheses show that the three outcomes are one compound event.

continued on next page >

# Part 2

### Intro continued

A compound event for a two-step action has two parts.

> **Action:** Choose a shirt and a pair of pants.
>
> **Compound event**
> yellow shirt and light blue jeans
>
> (yellow, light blue)

Parentheses show that the two outcomes are one compound event.

### Example Identifying Compound Events

Choose each group of jewelry on the right that shows a possible compound event for this action.

> **Action:** Choose a necklace, a bracelet, and a ring.
>
>

### Solution

These two groups show a possible outcome for each of the three steps of the action.

These two groups of jewelry are possible outcomes for the action of choosing a necklace, a bracelet, and a ring.

# Part 3

### Intro

Two events are **independent events** if the occurrence of one event does not affect the probability of the other event.

Action: Choose one tile at random and replace it. Then choose a second tile at random.

Compound Event: Choose A. Then choose a B.

> before choosing first tile

$P(B) = \dfrac{2}{11}$ — (A, B)

> after replacing first tile

$P(B) = \dfrac{2}{11}$

> probability of 2nd choice not affected by 1st choice

The events *choose A* and *choose a B* are independent events for this action.

Two events are **dependent events** if the occurrence of the first event affects the probability of the second event.

Action: Choose one tile at random and set it aside. Then choose a second tile at random.

Compound Event: Choose A. Then choose a B.

> before choosing first tile

$P(B) = \dfrac{2}{11}$ — (A, B)

> after setting aside the first tile

$P(B) = \dfrac{2}{10}$, or $\dfrac{1}{5}$

> probability of 2nd choice affected by 1st choice

The events *choose A* and *choose a B* are dependent events for this action.

# Part 3

### Example Classifying Events as Dependent or Independent

Decide if the events that make up each compound event are independent or dependent.

**Action**
Player 1 chooses a game piece.
Player 2 chooses a game piece.

**Compound Event**
Player 1 chooses red.
Player 2 chooses green.

**Action**
Spin the spinner twice.

**Compound Event**
The spinner stops on green twice.

## Solution

**Compound Event**
Player 1 chooses red.
Player 2 chooses green.

Before Player 1 chooses

$P$(choose green) $= \frac{1}{4}$

After Player 1 chooses

$P$(choose green) $= \frac{1}{3}$ ◁ The probability changes.

The outcome of Player 1's choice affects the probability that Player 2 chooses green. The events are dependent.

**Compound Event**
The spinner stops on green twice.

Before first spin

$P$(spin green) $= \frac{1}{4}$

After first spin

$P$(spin green) $= \frac{1}{4}$ ◁ The probability does not change.

The outcome of the first spin does not affect the probability of spinning green on the second spin. The events are independent.

# Key Concept

A compound event is an event associated with a multi-step action.

Events are independent if the occurrence of one event does not affect the probability of the other event.

**Action:** Toss a coin. Roll a number cube.

Step 1 Outcome                                   Step 2 Outcome

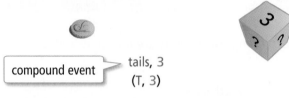

compound event — tails, 3
(T, 3)

The outcomes are independent events because tossing tails does not affect the probability of spinning 3.

Events are dependent if the occurrence of the first event affects the probability of the second event.

**Action:** Choose two people for your group.

Step 1 Outcome                                   Step 2 Outcome

compound event — boy, girl
(B, G)

The outcomes are dependent events because choosing a boy affects the probability of choosing a girl.

1. Roll three number cubes. How many steps or choices does the action involve?

2. Which action involves 2 steps?
   A. Choose four people from a group.
   B. Choose a book from the library.
   C. Choose two books from the library.
   D. Roll three number cubes.

3. Which action involves 3 steps?
   A. Roll two number cubes two times, then roll one number cube one time.
   B. Select one person from three different groups.
   C. Select two six character passwords.
   D. Flip four coins.

4. Roll a number cube two times. Find a compound event for the action.
   A. (1, 5, 3, 5)      B. (1, 1, 1)
   C. (1, 5)            D. 1

5. Roll a number cube four times. Find a compound event for the action.
   A. (4, 4, 4, 4)      B. (2, 2, 2)
   C. (3, 5, 4, 2, 1)   D. (3, 2)

6. Which of the choices shows a compound event for this action?
   Choosing three numbers from 1 to 100.
   A. (79, 79, 79, 79)
   B. 8
   C. (16, 79, 10)
   D. (79, 16)

7. **Think About the Process** You are asked to make a five-character password using the letters R, O, G, B, Y, P, W, and L.
   a. How do you choose a password so that the compound event is composed of dependent events?
      A. Compound events are always independent.

   B. You can choose the same letter five times.
   C. You choose five letters from the list that must be different.
   D. Compound events are always dependent.
   b. Which compound event could be composed of dependent events?
      A. (G, P, B, W, L)
      B. (G, G, W, P, P)
      C. (L, L, L, L, L)
      D. (G, P, B, W, G)

8. Which compound event is composed of independent events?

| Action | Compound Event |
| --- | --- |
| Choosing three numbers from 1 to 10 | (8, 5, 4) |
| Choosing three people from a group of two girls and two boys | (B, B, G) |

   A. (8, 5, 4) and (B, B, G)
   B. (8, 5, 4) only
   C. (B, B, G) only
   D. None of the above

9. Which compound event is composed of dependent events?

| Action | Compound Event |
| --- | --- |
| Choosing any two colored cards from a stack, replacing the card each time you choose. | (Red, Red) |
| Choosing any two colored cards from a stack, without replacing the card each time you choose. | (Red, Green) |

   A. (Red, Red) and (Red, Green)
   B. (Red, Red) only
   C. (Red, Green) only
   D. None of the above

10. **Think About the Process** You are asked to order a pizza with five toppings. Your choices are shown in the table.

| Pizza Toppings | |
|---|---|
| Mushrooms | Broccoli |
| Pepperoni | Pineapple |
| Olives | Tomatoes |
| Peppers | Spinach |

a. What determines the number of parts for a compound event of this action?

A. A compound event always has two steps.

B. The action has five steps so the compound event for this action has five parts.

C. The number of parts for a compound event is one more than the number of steps in the action.

D. The number of parts for a compound event is one less than the number of steps in the action.

b. Which choice shows a compound event for this action?

A. (Spinach, Pepperoni, Broccoli, Peppers, Olives)

B. (Spinach, Pepperoni, Onions, Olives, Broccoli)

C. (Spinach, Broccoli, Olives)

D. (Spinach, Pepperoni, Broccoli, Peppers)

11. **Writing** The number on your soccer jersey is 23. You decide to choose a three-character password by selecting at random two different letters, followed by one number, from the phrase SOCCER 23.

a. Which choice shows a compound event for this action?

A. (O, R, 2, 3)  B. (2, O, R)

C. (O, R, 3)  D. (O, 2, R)

b. Write your own multi-step action. Then write a possible compound event for that action.

12. a. **Reasoning** Are the events that make up the following compound event independent or dependent?

**Action:**

**Spin the spinner. Then spin again.**

**Compound Event:**

**The spinner lands on green. The spinner then lands on yellow.**

b. Is it possible to have the same outcome for both parts of a two-step dependent compound event? Explain.

13. **Error Analysis** On a recent math test students were asked to find the number of steps in rolling three number cubes three times. Fausto gave an incorrect answer, 3.

a. Find the number of steps in the action.

b. Which error might Fausto have made?

A. Fausto should have added the number of rolls to the number of number cubes to get the correct answer. He instead used the number of rolls as the number of steps.

B. Fausto should have subtracted the number of rolls from the number of number cubes to get the correct answer. He instead used the number of rolls as the number of steps.

C. Fausto should have subtracted the number of rolls from the number of number cubes to get the correct answer. He instead used the number of number of cubes as the number of steps.

D. Fausto should have multiplied the number of rolls by the number of number cubes to get the correct answer. He instead used the number of number cubes as the number of steps.

CCSS: 7.SP.C.8, 7.SP.C.8b

## Part 1

### Intro

To write the sample space of a multi-step action, use an organized approach to list all possible outcomes of the action.

Action: Toss a coin twice.

Start with one outcome of the first toss, heads, and pair it with each possible outcome of the second toss, heads and tails.

1st Toss     2nd Toss

Sample space: Possible outcomes
(Heads, Heads)          (H, H)
(Heads, Tails)          (H, T)

Then, use the other outcome of the first toss, tails, and pair it with each possible outcome of the second toss, heads and tails.

1st Toss     2nd Toss

Sample space: Possible outcomes
(Tails, Heads)          (T, H)
(Tails, Tails)          (T, T)

### Example  Using Organized Lists for Sample Spaces

For each condition, use an organized list to show all possible flavor combinations for Scoop 1 and Scoop 2.

**a.** Scoop 1 and Scoop 2 can be either the same flavor or different flavors.

**b.** Scoop 1 and Scoop 2 must be different flavors.

FROZEN YOGURT

Scoop 2?

Scoop 1?

**Flavors**

Peach
Strawberry
Banana

continued on next page >

**Solution** · · · · · · · · · · · · · · · · · · · · · · · · · · · · · · · · · · · · · · · · · · · · · · · · · · · · · · · · · · · · · · · ·

**a.** The scoops can be the same or different flavors, so pair each flavor for Scoop 1 with each flavor to Scoop 2.

| | Scoop 1 | Scoop 2 | |
|---|---|---|---|
| 1st flavor | peach<br>peach<br>peach | peach<br>strawberry<br>banana | Each flavor |
| 2nd flavor | strawberry<br>strawberry<br>strawberry | peach<br>strawberry<br>banana | Each flavor |
| 3rd flavor | banana<br>banana<br>banana | peach<br>strawberry<br>banana | Each flavor |

You can also write the organized list of the sample space using a capital letter for each flavor.

P = peach, S = strawberry, B = banana

Sample Space (Scoop 1, Scoop 2)

(P, P)  (S, P)  (B, P)
(P, S)  (S, S)  (B, S)
(P, B)  (S, B)  (B, B)

**b.** The scoops must be different flavors, so pair each flavor for Scoop 1 with the other two flavors for Scoop 2.

| | Scoop 1 | Scoop 2 | |
|---|---|---|---|
| 1st flavor | peach<br>peach | strawberry<br>banana | Other 2 flavors |
| 2nd flavor | strawberry<br>strawberry | peach<br>banana | Other 2 flavors |
| 3rd flavor | banana<br>banana | peach<br>strawberry | Other 2 flavors |

You can also write the organized list of the sample space using a capital letter for each flavor.

P = peach, S = strawberry, B = banana

Sample Space (Scoop 1, Scoop 2)

(P, S)  (S, P)  (B, P)
(P, B)  (S, B)  (B, S)

# Part 2

### Intro

You can use a table to display the sample space of a two-step action.

**Action**
Spin the spinner once.
Toss the coin once.

|   | R | G | Y | B |
|---|---|---|---|---|
| **H** | R, H | G, H | Y, H | B, H |
| **T** | R, T | G, T | Y, T | B, T |

Outcomes of Step 1

Outcomes of Step 2

Sample space has eight outcomes.

Compound event:
spin red, toss tails

### Example Using Tables for Sample Spaces

On a scavenger hunt, a clue leads you to a locker with a note on it. Use a table to show all possible combinations of the lock. How many combinations are possible?

Open the locker to find your next clue. The combination is a number XY. The digit X is 7, 8, or 9. The digit Y is from 0 to 4.

### Solution

There are 15 possible lock combinations.

**Possible Lock Combinations**

|   | 7 | 8 | 9 |
|---|---|---|---|
| **0** | 70 | 80 | 90 |
| **1** | 71 | 81 | 91 |
| **2** | 72 | 82 | 92 |
| **3** | 73 | 83 | 93 |
| **4** | 74 | 84 | 94 |

The first digit is 7, 8, or 9.

The second digit is from 0 to 4.

See your complete lesson at MyMathUniverse.com

# Part 3

## Intro

You can use a tree diagram to display the sample space of a multi-step action.

Action: Make a snack.

**Step 1**
Choose crackers (C) or pretzels (P).

**Step 2**
Choose apple (A) or orange (O).

**Step 3**
Choose milk (M), juice (J), or water (W).

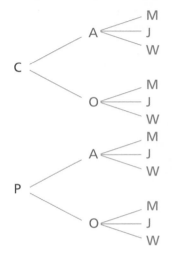

| Step 1 | Step 2 | Step 3 | Outcome |
|---|---|---|---|
| | A | M | crackers, apple, milk |
| | | J | crackers, apple, juice |
| | | W | crackers, apple, water |
| C | O | M | crackers, orange, milk |
| | | J | crackers, orange, juice |
| | | W | crackers, orange, water |
| | A | M | pretzels, apple, milk |
| | | J | pretzels, apple, juice |
| | | W | pretzels, apple, water |
| P | O | M | pretzels, orange, milk |
| | | J | pretzels, orange, juice |
| | | W | pretzels, orange, water |

## Example  Using Tree Diagrams for Sample Spaces

Complete the tree diagram to show all possible ways boys and girls can be born into a family with three children. Then complete the list of outcomes.

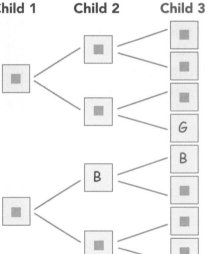

| Child 1 | Child 2 | Child 3 | Outcome |
|---|---|---|---|
| | | ■ | ■ |
| | ■ | ■ | boy, boy, girl |
| | ■ | ■ | ■ |
| ■ | | G | ■ |
| | | B | ■ |
| | B | ■ | ■ |
| | ■ | ■ | ■ |
| | ■ | ■ | girl, girl, girl |

## Solution

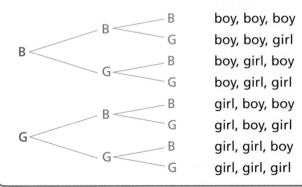

| Child 1 | Child 2 | Child 3 | Outcomes |
|---|---|---|---|
| | B | B | boy, boy, boy |
| | | G | boy, boy, girl |
| B | | B | boy, girl, boy |
| | G | G | boy, girl, girl |
| | B | B | girl, boy, boy |
| | | G | girl, boy, girl |
| G | | B | girl, girl, boy |
| | G | G | girl, girl, girl |

# Key Concept

These displays show three ways to represent the sample space for tossing two coins.

**Organized List**

(H, H) (T, H)
(H, T) (T, T)

**Table**

|        | Heads | Tails |
|--------|-------|-------|
| **Heads** | H, H  | T, H  |
| **Tails** | H, T  | T, T  |

**Tree Diagram**

1. Three friends at a restaurant each order a different flavored fruit drink. The available flavors are strawberry (S), peach (P), and orange (O). Which list represents the sample space of the friends' fruit drinks? The lists are written in the format (Friend 1, Friend 2, Friend 3).

   **A.** (S, P, O)
   (S, O, P)
   (P, S, O)
   (P, O, S)
   (O, S, P)
   (O, P, S)

   **B.** (S, S)
   (S, P)
   (S, O)
   (P, S)
   (P, P)
   (P, O)
   (O, S)
   (O, P)
   (O, O)

   **C.** (S, P, O)
   (S, O, P)
   (S, S, S)
   (P, S, O)
   (P, O, S)
   (P, P, P)
   (O, S, P)
   (O, P, S)
   (O, O, O)

   **D.** (S, P, O)
   (P, O, S)
   (O, S, P)

2. Two friends each choose a slice of pizza with one topping. The toppings to choose from are tomatoes (T), ham (H), onions (O), and eggplant (E). Write an organized list using the format (Friend 1, Friend 2) to represent the sample space of topping combinations.

3. Draw a tree diagram that displays the sample space for selecting two different letters from w, u, r, v, e. The order in which the members are selected is important. For example, wu is not the same selection as uw.

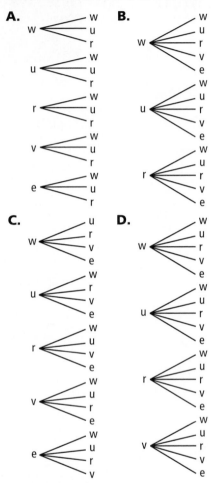

4. Use a table to show the sample space of two-digit numbers using the digits 8, 3, 2, 4. Use the column label as the tens digit and the row label as the ones digit.

5. **a.** Use a table to show the sample space of number-letter combinations using the digits in the number 9,825 and the letters in the word GAME. Use the column label as the digit and the row label as the letter.

   **b.** Find the number of possible outcomes.

**6. Think About the Process** A probability experiment consists of spinning a spinner with 3 colored sections and then a spinner with 8 numbered sections. The numbers are 1 to 8. The colors are green (G), white (W), and red (R).

a. What is the first step in order to draw a tree diagram that displays the sample space for the experiment?

b. Which tree diagram below displays the sample space for the experiment?

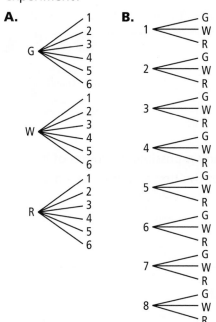

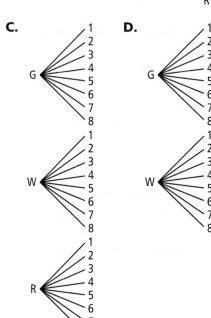

c. How many different outcomes does the experiment have?

**7. Think About the Process** You can use a table with 3 rows and 6 columns to show the sample space of combinations of a number followed by a letter using 3 numbers and 6 letters.

a. What other table could you use to show the sample space?

   **A.** A table with 6 rows and 6 columns

   **B.** A table with 3 rows and 3 columns

   **C.** A table with 6 rows and 3 columns

   **D.** A table with 9 rows and 2 columns

b. Use a table to show the sample space of number-letter combinations. Use the column label as the letter and the row label as the number.

c. There are ■ possible outcomes in the sample space.

**8. Reasoning** A soccer tournament assigns a unique two-color uniform to each team using the colors yellow (Y), green (G), orange (O), and purple (P). Each uniform is mostly one color with a different colored stripe.

a. Write a list that represents the sample space in the format (main color, stripe color).

b. Does it matter what order you list the different ways to assign the uniform colors? Explain your reasoning.

**9. Error Analysis** A clothing store sells shirts with long, short, or no sleeves. Each style is available in gray, blue, or pink. A clerk incorrectly states the sample space for the possible color and sleeve styles as (gray, long), (gray, short), (blue, long), (blue, short), (pink, long), and (pink, short).

a. Use a table to show the sample space of color and sleeve styles combinations. Use the column label as the color and the row label as the sleeve style.

b. What error did the clerk make? Consider the possible outcomes the clerk left out.

See your complete lesson at MyMathUniverse.com

| **Counting Outcomes**

**Vocabulary**
counting principle

CCSS: 7.SP.C.8a, 7.SP.C.8b, Also 7.SP.C.8

## Key Concept

The tree diagram of the sample space for this action illustrates the Counting Principle.

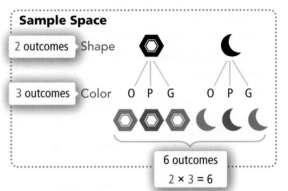

The Counting Principle

If there are *m* possible outcomes of one action and *n* possible outcomes of a second action, then there are $m \times n$ outcomes of the first action followed by the second action.

## Part 1

### Example  Using the Counting Principle

Use the Counting Principle to find the number of possible outcomes of the class election. Then check your result by writing out the sample space for the election.

**Ballot for Class Election**

| | | |
|---|---|---|
| **President** | Marta | ☐ |
| | Ethan | ☐ |
| **Secretary** | Ben | ☐ |
| | Rosa | ☐ |
| | Zack | ☐ |
| **Treasurer** | Andi | ☐ |
| | Theo | ☐ |

continued on next page >

**Example** continued

### Solution · · · · · · · · · · · · · · · · · · · · · · · · · · · · · · · · · · · · · · · · · · · · · · · ·

You can extend the Counting Principle to three or more actions.

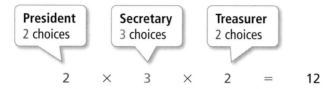

| President | Secretary | Treasurer |
| 2 choices | 3 choices | 2 choices |

$$2 \times 3 \times 2 = 12$$

There are 12 possible outcomes for the election.

### Check · · · · · · · · · · · · · · · · · · · · · · · · · · · · · · · · · · · · · · · · · · · · · · · · · · ·

Use an organized list to show the 12 possible outcomes in the sample space.

|    | President | Secretary | Treasurer |
|----|-----------|-----------|-----------|
| 1  | Marta     | Ben       | Andi      |
| 2  | Marta     | Ben       | Theo      |
| 3  | Marta     | Rosa      | Andi      |
| 4  | Marta     | Rosa      | Theo      |
| 5  | Marta     | Zack      | Andi      |
| 6  | Marta     | Zack      | Theo      |
| 7  | Ethan     | Ben       | Andi      |
| 8  | Ethan     | Ben       | Theo      |
| 9  | Ethan     | Rosa      | Andi      |
| 10 | Ethan     | Rosa      | Theo      |
| 11 | Ethan     | Zack      | Andi      |
| 12 | Ethan     | Zack      | Theo      |

### Intro

Given the sample space of an action, you can identify outcomes that have particular characteristics. These outcomes compose an event in the sample space.

Action
Toss a coin and roll a standard number cube.

Sample space
(H, 1)  (H, 2)  (H, 3)
(H, 4)  (H, 5)  (H, 6)
(T, 1)  (T, 2)  (T, 3)
(T, 4)  (T, 5)  (T, 6)

"Or" means outcomes can include a T, an odd number, or both.

Event
Toss tails or roll an odd number.

(T, 1)  (T, 2)  (T, 3)
(T, 4)  (T, 5)  (T, 6)
(H, 1)  (H, 3)  (H, 5)

9 outcomes in the event

### Example  Counting Outcomes with Tree Diagrams

Use the tree diagram that shows all possible ways boys (B) and girls (G) can be born into a family with three children. Complete the table.

**Child 1    Child 2    Child 3**

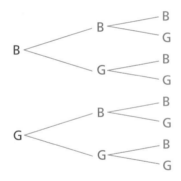

| Event | Outcomes in Event | Number of Outcomes |
|---|---|---|
| Get exactly 2 boys | ▪ | ▪ |
| Get at least 2 girls | ▪ | ▪ |

### Solution

Event: Get exactly two boys.

**Child 1    Child 2    Child 3**    Outcomes in Event: 3

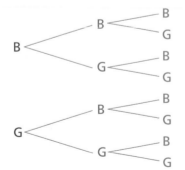

(boy, boy, girl)
(boy, girl, boy)

(girl, boy, boy)

continued on next page >

## Part 2

**Solution** continued

Event: Get at least two girls.

**Child 1    Child 2    Child 3**     Outcomes in Event: 4

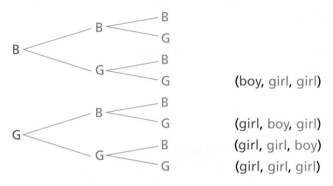

(boy, girl, girl)

(girl, boy, girl)
(girl, girl, boy)
(girl, girl, girl)

| Event | Outcomes in Events | Number of Outcomes |
|-------|-------------------|--------------------|
| Get exactly 2 boys | (boy, boy, girl), (boy, girl, boy), (girl, boy, boy) | 3 |
| Get at least 2 girls | (boy, girl, girl), (girl, boy, girl), (girl, girl, boy), (girl, girl, girl) | 4 |

## Part 3

### Example  Counting Outcomes in Events

In how many different ways can Alice, Becky, Carl, and David place first, second, and third in a race? In how many different ways can Alice finish ahead of David?

continued on next page >

### Solution

You can use the Counting Principle to find the number of ways the four runners can place first, second, and third.

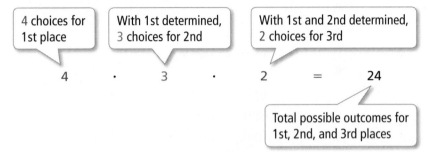

4 choices for 1st place

With 1st determined, 3 choices for 2nd

With 1st and 2nd determined, 2 choices for 3rd

$$4 \cdot 3 \cdot 2 = 24$$

Total possible outcomes for 1st, 2nd, and 3rd places

You can make an organized list of the possible outcomes for the first three places. Use the list to find and count all possible outcomes in which A (Alice) comes before D (David), or A appears and D does not.

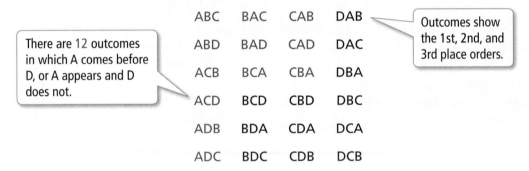

There are 12 outcomes in which A comes before D, or A appears and D does not.

Outcomes show the 1st, 2nd, and 3rd place orders.

| ABC | BAC | CAB | DAB |
| ABD | BAD | CAD | DAC |
| ACB | BCA | CBA | DBA |
| ACD | BCD | CBD | DBC |
| ADB | BDA | CDA | DCA |
| ADC | BDC | CDB | DCB |

There are 24 different ways the runners can place first, second, and third in the race. There are 12 different ways Alice can finish ahead of David.

1. Think About the Process You are going to order a new bike. The bike seat comes in 3 different colors and the frame of the bike comes in 7 different colors.

   a. How can you find the number of ways a new bike can be ordered?

      A. Divide the number of colors possible for the bike frame by the number of possible colors for the bike seat.

      B. Subtract the number of colors possible for the bike seat from the number of possible colors for the bike frame.

      C. Multiply the number of colors possible for the bike frame by the number of possible colors for the bike seat.

      D. Add the number of colors possible for the bike frame to the number of possible colors for the bike seat.

   b. How many ways can a new bike be ordered?

   c. Which list below shows the possible ways a bike can be ordered? Use S and a number to represent a seat color and F and a number to represent a frame color.

      A. {S1F1, S1F2, S1F3, S1F4, S1F5, S2F1, S2F2, S2F3, S2F4, S2F5}

      B. {S1F1, S1F2, S1F3, S1F4, S1F5, S1F6, S1F7, S2F1, S2F2, S2F3, S2F4, S2F5, S2F6, S2F7, S3F1, S3F2, S3F3, S3F4, S3F5, S3F6, S3F7}

      C. {S1F1, S1F2, S1F3, S1F4, S1F5, S1F6, S1F7, S2F1, S2F2, S2F3, S2F4, S2F5, S2F6, S2F7}

2. A sales representative can take one of 2 different routes from City C to City F and any one of 3 different routes from City F to City H.

   a. How many different routes can he take from City C to City H, going through City F?

   b. Use F and a number to represent a route from City C to City F and use H and a number to represent a route from City F to City H. Which list below shows the possible routes?

      A. {F1H1, F1H2, F1H3, F1H4, F1H5, F1H6, F2H1, F2H2, F2H3, F2H4, F2H5, F2H6}

      B. {F1H1, F1H2, F1H3, F2H1, F2H2, F2H3, F3H1, F3H2, F3H3}

      C. {F1H1, F1H2, F1H3, F2H1, F2H2, F2H3}

3. A restaurant offers 5 appetizers and 10 main courses. How many ways can a person order a two-course meal?

4. A person can order a new car with a choice of 15 possible colors, with or without air conditioning, with or without automatic transmission, with or without power windows, and with or without a CD player. In how many different ways can a new car be ordered with regard to these options?

5. You have been asked to flip a coin for heads or tails and then select a golf ball from a bucket that contains 3 yellow golf balls and 4 white golf balls.

   a. Use Y and a number to represent a yellow golf ball and W and a number to represent a white golf ball. Which list below shows the sample space?

      A. {HW1, HW2, HW3, HY1, HY2, HY3, HY4, TW1, TW2, TW3, TY1, TY2, TY3, TY4}

      B. {HY1, HY2, HY3, HW1, HW2, HW3, HW4, TY1, TY2, TY3, TW1, TW2, TW3, TW4}

      C. {HY, HW, TY, TW}

   b. How many ways can you expect to get heads and select a yellow golf ball?

See your complete lesson at MyMathUniverse.com

6. At a restaurant you are going to order an appetizer and a main course. In how many different ways can you order a two-course meal that includes lasagna as the main course?

**Restaurant Menus**

| Appetizers | Main Course |
|---|---|
| Barbecue Wings | Hamburger |
| Chips and Salsa | Quesadilla |
| Mozzarella Sticks | Steak Tips |
| Mild Wings | Cheeseburger |
| Hot Wings | Lasagna |
| | Pizza |

7. **Think About the Process** Without repeating letters and digits, create three-character passwords using the letters and digits S, 2, T, or 9.

a. Which list below shows the sample space?

A. {SSS, SS2, SST, SS9, S2S, S22, S2T, S29, STS, ST2, STT, ST9, S9S, S92, S9T, S99, 2SS, 2S2, 2ST, 2S9, 22S, 222, 22T, 229, 2TS, 2T2, 2TT, 2T9, 29S, 292, 29T, T29, TTS, TT2, TTT, TT9, T9S, T92, T9T, 299, TSS, TS2, TST, TS9, T2S, T22, T2T, T99, 9SS, 9S2, 9ST, 9S9, 92S, 92T, 929, 9TS, 9T2, 9TT, 9T9, 99S, 992, 99T, 999}

B. {S2T, S29, ST9, SSS, 2T9, 222, TTT, 999}

C. {S2T, S29, ST2, ST9, S92, S9T, 2ST, 2S9, 2TS, 2T9, 29S, 29T, TS2, TS9, T2S, T29, T9S, T92, 9S2, 9ST, 92S, 92T, 9TS, 9T2}

b. How can you find the number of those passwords that begin with T?

A. Count the number of passwords in the sample space.

B. Use the counting principle to find the number of passwords in the sample space.

C. Count the number of passwords in the sample space that begin with T.

c. How many of those passwords begin with T?

8. Without repeating digits, form three-digit numbers using the digits 2, 3, 4, and 7.

a. Which list shows the sample space?

A. {222, 223, 224, 227, 232, 233, 234, 237, 242, 243, 244, 247, 272, 273, 274, 277, 322, 323, 324, 327, 332, 333, 334, 337, 342, 343, 344, 347, 372, 373, 374, 377, 422, 423, 424, 427, 432, 433, 434, 437, 442, 443, 444, 447, 472, 473, 474, 477, 722, 723, 724, 727, 732, 734, 737, 742, 743, 744, 747, 772, 773, 774, 777}

B. {234, 237, 247, 222, 347, 333, 444, 777}

C. {234, 237, 243, 247, 273, 274, 324, 327, 342, 347, 372, 374, 423, 427, 432, 437, 472, 473, 723, 724, 732, 734, 742, 743}

b. How many of those three-digit numbers contain 4?

9. In a bag of marbles there are 9 blue marbles and 6 red marbles. You pick one marble out of the bag and then, without replacing the first marble, you pick another marble out of the bag. How many ways can you pick two blue marbles?

10. **Writing** You are going to pick a marble from a bag with 2 red marbles and 4 blue marbles. Then you are going to flip a coin for heads or tails.

a. Use R and a number to represent a red marble and B and a number to represent a blue marble. Make a list that shows the sample space.

b. How many ways can you pick a blue marble and get heads?

c. How would changing the number of blue marbles in the bag change the number of ways you can pick a blue marble and then get heads?

# Finding Theoretical Probabilities

CCSS: 7.SP.C.8, 7.SP.C.8a, Also 7.SP.C.6

## Key Concept

When all outcomes of an action are equally likely, you can use the theoretical probability formula to find the probability of an event.

$$P(\text{event}) = \frac{\text{number of favorable outcomes}}{\text{number of possible outcomes}}$$

$P(\text{same color twice}) = \frac{3}{9}$ ← 3 favorable outcomes

$= \frac{1}{3}$ ← 9 possible outcomes

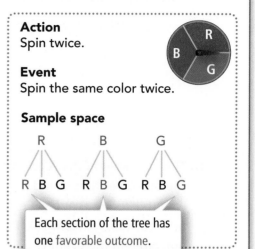

**Action**
Spin twice.

**Event**
Spin the same color twice.

**Sample space**

```
   R        B        G
  /|\      /|\      /|\
 R B G    R B G    R B G
```

Each section of the tree has one favorable outcome.

## Part 1

### Example  Finding Theoretical Probabilities of Compound Events

The table shows the possible outcomes of choosing one card from the group shown, replacing it, and then choosing a second card. Find each probability.

a. $P(\text{at least one apple})$
b. $P(\text{exactly one apple})$
c. $P(\text{exactly one apple and one fish})$
d. $P(\text{at least one apple or fish})$

|     | F    | S    | A    | K    | L    |
| --- | ---- | ---- | ---- | ---- | ---- |
| F   | F, F | S, F | A, F | K, F | L, F |
| S   | F, S | S, S | A, S | K, S | L, S |
| A   | F, A | S, A | A, A | K, A | L, A |
| K   | F, K | S, K | A, K | K, K | L, K |
| L   | F, L | S, L | A, L | K, L | L, L |

## Solution

Because you replace the card after the first choice, there are 5 ways to make each choice. So, there are 5 · 5, or 25, possible outcomes, as shown in the table.

continued on next page >

See your complete lesson at MyMathUniverse.com

# Part 1

### Solution continued

**a.** The outcomes in the A column and A row are the outcomes that include apples. There are nine outcomes in the event *choose at least one apple*.

$$P(\text{at least one apple}) = \frac{9}{25}, \text{ or } 36\%$$

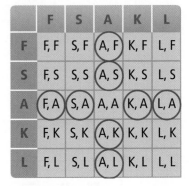

**b.** The outcomes in the A column and A row are the outcomes that includes apples. Because you want outcomes that have exactly one apple, do not count the outcome (A, A). There are eight outcomes in the event *choose exactly one apple*.

$$P(\text{exactly one apple}) = \frac{8}{25}, \text{ or } 32\%$$

**c.** Outcomes in the event *choose one apple and one fish* must include both A and F. There are two outcomes in this event.

$$P(\text{one apple and one fish}) = \frac{2}{25}, \text{ or } 8\%$$

**d.** The outcomes in the F column, F row, A column, and A row are the outcomes that include at least one fish or one apple. There are 16 outcomes in this event.

$$P(\text{at least one apple or fish}) = \frac{16}{25}, \text{ or } 64\%$$

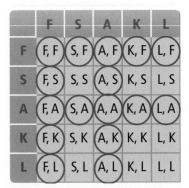

See your complete lesson at MyMathUniverse.com

# Part 2

## Example Counting Outcomes to Find Theoretical Probabilities

In a certain book, you can arrange the eyes, noses, and mouths of the three people in various combinations. The people are Dana, Jay, and Sara.

You choose a combination at random. Use an organized list, a table, or a tree diagram to find the probability that your combination shows exactly two parts of the same person.

## Solution

Sample: Use a tree diagram and find all of the outcomes that include exactly two parts of the same person.

| Eyes | Nose | Mouth | Outcome | |
|------|------|-------|---------|---|
| | | Dana | Dana, Dana, Dana | |
| | Dana | Jay | Dana, Dana, Jay | ✓ |
| | | Sara | Dana, Dana, Sara | ✓ |
| | | Dana | Dana, Jay, Dana | ✓ |
| Dana | Jay | Jay | Dana, Jay, Jay | ✓ |
| | | Sara | Dana, Jay, Sara | |
| | | Dana | Dana, Sara, Dana | ✓ |
| | Sara | Jay | Dana, Sara, Jay | |
| | | Sara | Dana, Sara, Sara | ✓ |
| | | Dana | Jay, Dana, Dana | ✓ |
| | Dana | Jay | Jay, Dana, Jay | ✓ |
| | | Sara | Jay, Dana, Sara | |
| | | Dana | Jay, Jay, Dana | ✓ |
| Jay | Jay | Jay | Jay, Jay, Jay | |
| | | Sara | Jay, Jay, Sara | ✓ |
| | | Dana | Jay, Sara, Dana | |
| | Sara | Jay | Jay, Sara, Jay | ✓ |
| | | Sara | Jay, Sara, Sara | ✓ |
| | | Dana | Sara, Dana, Dana | ✓ |
| | Dana | Jay | Sara, Dana, Jay | |
| | | Sara | Sara, Dana, Sara | ✓ |
| | | Dana | Sara, Jay, Dana | |
| Sara | Jay | Jay | Sara, Jay, Jay | ✓ |
| | | Sara | Sara, Jay, Sara | ✓ |
| | | Dana | Sara, Sara, Dana | ✓ |
| | Sara | Jay | Sara, Sara, Jay | ✓ |
| | | Sara | Sara, Sara, Sara | |

The sample space shows 27 outcomes, of which 18 include exactly two parts of the same person. The probability is $\frac{18}{27}$, or $66\frac{2}{3}\%$.

### Intro

You can run trials of a two-step action and compare experimental probabilities to theoretical probabilities.

To find an experimental probability, use this formula.

$$P(\text{event}) = \frac{\text{number of times event occurs}}{\text{total number of trials}}$$

### Example  Comparing Experimental and Theoretical Probabilities

A class ran 330 trials of this two-step action.

**Action:** Toss once. Spin once.

Complete the table. For which compound event is the count closest to the expected count?

| Event | Count | Experimental Probability | Expected Count | Theoretical Probability |
|-------|-------|-------------------------|----------------|-------------------------|
| (H, R) | 45 | ▣ | ▣ | ▣ |
| (H, B) | 59 | ▣ | ▣ | ▣ |
| (H, G) | 64 | ▣ | ▣ | ▣ |
| (T, R) | 45 | ▣ | ▣ | ▣ |
| (T, B) | 58 | ▣ | ▣ | ▣ |
| (T, G) | 59 | ▣ | ▣ | ▣ |

continued on next page >

# Part 3

**Example** continued

**Solution** · · · · · · · · · · · · · · · · · · · · · · · · · · · · · · · · · · · · · · · · · · · · · · · · · · · · · · · ·

$P(\text{event}) = \dfrac{\text{count}}{330}$

$330 \times \dfrac{1}{6} = 55$

$P(\text{event}) = \dfrac{1}{6}$

| Event | Count | Experimental Probability | Expected Count | Theoretical Probability |
|-------|-------|-------------------------|----------------|------------------------|
| (H, R) | 45 | 0.1364 | 55 | 0.1667 |
| (H, B) | 59 | 0.1788 | 55 | 0.1667 |
| (H, G) | 64 | 0.1939 | 55 | 0.1667 |
| (T, R) | 45 | 0.1364 | 55 | 0.1667 |
| (T, B) | 58 | 0.1758 | 55 | 0.1667 |
| (T, G) | 59 | 0.1788 | 55 | 0.1667 |

The count for (toss tails, spin blue) is closest to its expected count.

1. A fair coin is tossed two times in succession. The sample space is shown, where *H* represents a head and *T* represents a tail. Find the probability of getting exactly one tail.

**Sample Space**

| (Toss 1, Toss 2) | |
|---|---|
| (H, H) | (T, H) |
| (H, T) | (T, T) |

2. **a.** Draw a tree diagram that displays the sample space for selecting two different letters from $S = \{B, C, D, E, F\}$.

   **b.** What is the probability of choosing a combination with one *B*?

3. Three fair coins are tossed with possible outcomes of heads, *H*, and tails, *T*.

**Sample Space**

| Toss 1 | Toss 2 | Toss 3 |
|---|---|---|
| H | H | H |
| H | H | T |
| H | T | T |
| T | T | T |
| T | T | H |
| T | H | H |
| H | T | ■ |
| T | H | ■ |

   **a.** Complete the table.

   **b.** Find the probability of tossing at least 2 heads.

4. The table shows the result of spinning the wheel once and tossing a coin 44 times.

**Results of 44 Trials**

| Event | Count |
|---|---|
| (1, H) | 6 |
| (1, T) | 10 |
| (2, H) | 6 |
| (2, T) | 7 |
| (3, H) | 8 |
| (3, T) | 7 |

   **a.** Find the theoretical probability of spinning a three and tossing a tail. Simplify your answer.

   **b.** Find the experimental probability of spinning a three and tossing a tail. Simplify your answer.

5. **Figure 1** below shows the results of rolling a number cube and tossing a coin 120 times. The numbers 1 through 6 represent the numbers on a standard number cube. The letter *H* represents a coin landing on a head and the letter *T* represents the coin landing on a tail.

   **a.** The theoretical probability of $P(4, T)$ is ■.

   **b.** The experimental probability of $P(4, T)$ is ■.

   **c.** How does the experimental probability compare with the theoretical probability for $P(4, T)$?

**(Figure 1)**

| Results of 120 Trials | | | | | | | | | | | |
|---|---|---|---|---|---|---|---|---|---|---|---|
| Event | Count | Event | Count | Event | Count | Event | Count | Event | Count | Event | Count |
| (1, H) | 6 | (2, H) | 8 | (3, H) | 10 | (4, H) | 4 | (5, H) | 15 | (6, H) | 14 |
| (1, T) | 7 | (2, T) | 6 | (3, T) | 12 | (4, T) | 13 | (5, T) | 17 | (6, T) | 8 |

See your complete lesson at MyMathUniverse.com

**6. Think About the Process** A single number cube is rolled twice. The 36 equally likely outcomes are shown below.

| | | | Second Roll | | | |
|---|---|---|---|---|---|---|
| | **1** | **2** | **3** | **4** | **5** | **6** |
| **1** | (1, 1) | (1, 2) | (1, 3) | (1, 4) | (1, 5) | (1, 6) |
| **2** | (2, 1) | (2, 2) | (2, 3) | (2, 4) | (2, 5) | (2, 6) |
| **3** | (3, 1) | (3, 2) | (3, 3) | (3, 4) | (3, 5) | (3, 6) |
| **4** | (4, 1) | (4, 2) | (4, 3) | (4, 4) | (4, 5) | (4, 6) |
| **5** | (5, 1) | (5, 2) | (5, 3) | (5, 4) | (5, 5) | (5, 6) |
| **6** | (6, 1) | (6, 2) | (6, 3) | (6, 4) | (6, 5) | (6, 6) |

(First Roll labels the rows)

**a.** What is the first step in finding the probability of getting two numbers whose sum is 10?

  **A.** Find the number of combinations that will give a sum of 10 using the numbers 1 through 36.

  **B.** Find the number of combinations that will give a sum of 10 using the numbers 1 through 6.

  **C.** Divide 10 by 36.

  **D.** Divide 10 by 6.

**b.** Find the probability of getting two numbers whose sum is 10.

**7. Think About the Process** A bag contains six different colored marbles. You choose a marble at random and do not replace it. Then you select another marble. The different colors are shown in the table. A table that shows the sample space is useful in finding probabilities.

| Colors | |
|---|---|
| Red (R) | Yellow (Y) |
| Orange (O) | Purple (P) |
| Green (G) | Blue (B) |

**a.** How do you find the number of possible outcomes to make a table?

  **A.** There are 6 possibilities for the first pick. There are 6 possibilities for the second pick. Add 6 + 6 to find the number of possible outcomes.

  **B.** There are 6 possibilities for the first pick. There are 5 possibilities for the second pick. Multiply 6 × 5 to find the number of possible outcomes.

  **C.** There are 6 possibilities for the first pick. There are 5 possibilities for the second pick. Add 6 + 5 to find the number of possible outcomes.

  **D.** There are 6 possibilities for the first pick. There are 6 possibilities for the second pick. Multiply 6 × 6 to find the number of possible outcomes.

**b.** Complete the table in **Figure 2**.

**c.** Find the probability of picking one green and one yellow marble.

**(Figure 2)**

| Possible Combinations | | | | | |
|---|---|---|---|---|---|
| (Y, O) | (O, R) | (R, G) | (G, P) | (P, B) | (B, Y) |
| (Y, R) | (O, G) | (R, P) | (G, B) | (P, Y) | (B, O) |
| (■, G) | (O, P) | (R, B) | (G, Y) | (P, O) | (B, R) |
| (Y, P) | (O, B) | (R, Y) | (G, O) | (P, ■) | (B, G) |
| (Y, B) | (■, Y) | (R, O) | (G, R) | (P, G) | (B, P) |

See your complete lesson at MyMathUniverse.com

CCSS: 7.SP.C.8, 7.SP.C.8c

## Key Concept

Random numbers may be used to simulate probabilities.

A quarterback usually completes 60% of his passes.

Action: Quarterback throws a pass.

Sample space: complete pass    incomplete pass

Use any known probabilities to assign numbers to represent each outcome.

Probabilities:

> The sum of the probabilities is 1.

$$P(\text{complete}) = 0.6 \qquad P(\text{incomplete}) = 1 - 0.6$$
$$= 0.4$$

Assign digits from 0 to 9:

> 6 of 10 digits → $\underbrace{1, 2, 3, 4, 5, 6}_{\text{complete}}$     $\underbrace{7, 8, 9, 0}_{\text{incomplete}}$ ← 4 of 10 digits

Generate a list of $n$ random numbers to stimulate $n$ possible outcomes of the action.

Use random numbers to simulate future passes.

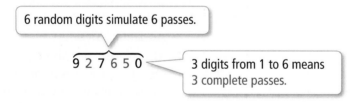

> 6 random digits simulate 6 passes.
>
> 9 2 7 6 5 0
>
> 3 digits from 1 to 6 means 3 complete passes.

# Part 1

### Example  Understanding Simulations with Numbers

A quiz has multiple-choice questions with four answer choices. Only one answer choice is correct.

Which ways of assigning numbers to outcomes can you use to simulate guessing an answer at random? Identify each way that you CANNOT use.

Use numbers from
1 to 4.
correct: 1
incorrect: 2, 3, 4

Use numbers from
1 to 10.
correct: 1–4
incorrect: 5–10

Use numbers from
1 to 100.
correct: 1–25
incorrect: 26–100

### Solution

Because one out of four answer choices is correct, you know these probabilities:

$$P(\text{correct}) = \frac{1}{4}, \text{ or } 25\%$$

$$P(\text{incorrect}) = \frac{3}{4}, \text{ or } 75\%$$

You can use any group of numbers for which $\frac{1}{4}$ of the numbers can be assigned to correct and $\frac{3}{4}$ of the numbers can be assigned to incorrect. This is true for the first and third ways shown to assign numbers:

Use numbers 1 to 4.

correct: 1 —————— $\frac{1}{4}$ of numbers 1 to 4

incorrect: 2, 3, 4 —————— $\frac{3}{4}$ of numbers 1 to 4

Use numbers 1 to 100.

correct: 1 − 25 —————— 25 numbers, or $\frac{1}{4}$ of numbers 1 to 100

incorrect: 26 − 100 —————— 75 numbers, or $\frac{3}{4}$ of numbers 1 to 100

The second way shown to assign numbers does not work.

Use numbers 1 to 10.

correct: 1 − 4 —————— 4 numbers is *not* $\frac{1}{4}$ of numbers 1 to 10.

incorrect: 5 − 10 —————— 6 numbers is *not* $\frac{3}{4}$ of numbers 1 to 10.

# Part 2

### Example  Using Simulations with Numbers

A quarterback usually completes 60% of his passes. Use numbers to represent possible outcomes of one pass:

Complete:        1, 2, 3, 4, 5, 6
Incomplete:     7, 8, 9, 0

Each list of random numbers shows outcomes of ten passes. Match each list to every event that it satisfies.

4 9 4 3 9 8 6 3 5 0          1 8 5 9 4 4 4 6 3 9

6 6 8 4 6 1 4 9 6 8          2 7 8 2 2 4 9 9 8 0

**a.** Event: Completes exactly 3 passes in a row
**b.** Event: Completes at least 6 passes

### Solution

For each list of random numbers, count the number of digits from 1 to 6, and find the greatest number of these that occur in a row.

4 9 4 3 9 8 [6 3 5] 0 — 6 complete; 3 in a row

6 6 8 [4 6 1 4] 9 6 8 — 7 complete; 4 in a row

1 8 5 9 [4 4 4 6 3] 9 — 7 complete; 5 in a row

2 7 8 [2 2 4] 9 9 8 0 — 4 complete; 3 in a row

**a.** Completes exactly 3 passes in a row:

4 9 4 3 9 8 6 3 5 0
2 7 8 2 2 4 9 9 8 0

**b.** Completes at least 6 passes:

4 9 4 3 9 8 6 3 5 0
6 6 8 4 6 1 4 9 6 8
1 8 5 9 4 4 4 6 3 9

## Part 3

### Example Designing Simulations with Numbers

A gardener plants several seeds in each hole. Each seed has a 30% chance of sprouting.

Use random numbers to simulate planting 5 seeds in each of 24 holes. How many simulated seeds sprout in each hole? Make a frequency table of your results.

**Solution**

**Step 1** Find the probabilities of possible outcomes.

$$P(\text{sprout}) = 0.3 \qquad\qquad P(\text{no sprout}) = 1 - 0.3$$
$$= 0.7$$

**Step 2** Assign numbers from 0 to 9 to the outcomes *sprout* and *no sprout*.

| 3 of 10 numbers | → 1, 2, 3 | 4, 5, 6, 7, 8, 9, 0 ← | 7 of 10 numbers |

sprout          no sprout

**Step 3** Use random numbers to simulate planting the seeds.

To simulate planting 5 seeds, generate 5 random numbers from 0 to 9. Do this 24 times to simulate planting seeds in 24 holes. Sample simulation data:

> Each group of 5 digits represents one hole.

```
37283   31260   54608   53038  ← Two seeds sprouted.
05175   88421   95709   06172
57863   78646   33535   61110  ← Three seeds sprouted.
34483   56408   19877   32441
91439   12944   62186   54680  ← No seeds sprouted.
84603   67177   46314   92591
```

Note the number of simulated seeds that sprout in each hole. For example, the five boxed groups of digits represent the five holes in which one seed sprouted.

**Step 4** Make a frequency table of the results.

**Planting Five Seeds per Hole**

| Number of seeds that sprouted | 0 | 1 | 2 | 3 | 4 | 5 |
|---|---|---|---|---|---|---|
| Frequency | 5 | 5 | 8 | 6 | 0 | 0 |

See your complete lesson at MyMathUniverse.com

1. Suppose that when the weather conditions are a certain way, it rains 80% of the time. Which of these ways of assigning numbers will simulate the possible outcomes?

   **A.** Use numbers from 1 to 10.
   Rain: 1, 2, 3, 4, 5, 6, 7, 8
   No Rain: 9, 10

   **B.** Use numbers from 0 to 10.
   Rain: All numbers except 8
   No Rain: 8

   **C.** Use numbers from 1 to 10.
   Rain: 9, 10
   No rain: 1, 2, 3, 4, 5, 6, 7, 8

   **D.** Use numbers from 0 to 10.
   Rain: 8, 9
   No Rain: 0, 1, 2, 3, 4, 5, 6, 7

2. A factory makes notebooks. For a simulation, a manager at the factory assigns the numbers 0–26 to the outcome that the cover is red and the numbers 27–49 to the outcome that the cover is not red. What action could the manager use these numbers to simulate? Select all that apply.

   **A.** If 46% of the notebooks the factory produces have red covers, these numbers could simulate choosing a notebook at random.

   **B.** If $\frac{27}{50}$ of the notebooks the factory produces do not have red covers, these numbers could simulate choosing a notebook at random.

   **C.** If 46% of the notebooks the factory produces do not have red covers, these numbers could simulate choosing a notebook at random.

   **D.** If $\frac{27}{50}$ of the notebooks the factory produces have red covers, these numbers could simulate choosing a notebook at random.

3. **Think About the Process** You use a number cube to simulate an outcome that has $\frac{1}{6}$ probability of occurring. The number 1 represents the desired outcome. The numbers 2, 3, 4, 5, and

6 represent other outcomes. You want to simulate 10 outcomes.

   **a.** How can you find a list that represents the outcome occurring exactly two times?

   **A.** Find a list of 10 of the assigned numbers with 2 numbers that are 1.

   **B.** Find a list of 10 of the assigned numbers with 2 numbers that are 2, 3, 4, 5, or 6.

   **C.** Find a list of 2 of the assigned numbers with 1 number that is 2, 3, 4, 5, or 6.

   **D.** Find a list of 2 of the assigned numbers with 1 number that is 1.

   **b.** Which of these lists simulates the desired outcome occurring exactly two times?

   **A.** 6 3 6 1 2 5 6 3 1 2

   **B.** 3 6 6 3 6 1 2 5 6 3

   **C.** 1 6 6 3 6 1 2 5 1 3

   **D.** 1 6 3 6 2 6 5 3 3 3

4. **Think About the Process** In a survey at a restaurant, 70% of the diners prefer the new menu. A simulation uses the numbers 0–6 to represent diners that prefer the new menu. The numbers 7–9 represent diners that do not prefer the new menu. The lists below show 10 trials asking 5 diners about menu preference.

   | 8 1 4 3 5 | 6 8 1 9 3 | 8 4 9 2 4 |
   |-----------|-----------|-----------|
   | 9 9 7 9 8 | 2 1 8 8 9 | |
   | 3 1 4 8 9 | 5 5 5 1 3 | 5 5 3 1 8 |
   | 4 0 3 4 4 | 1 8 2 0 2 | |

   **a.** How can you find whether 2 diners out of 5 in a trial prefer the new menu?

   **A.** Count the outcomes in the trial that are 6.

   **B.** Count the trials that have outcomes that are 6.

   **C.** Count the outcomes in the trial that are 0 to 6.

   **D.** Count the trials that have outcomes that are 0 to 6.

   **b.** In ■ of the 10 trials, 2 of the 5 diners prefer the new menu.

**5.** In a sporting event, Team A and Team B are evenly matched. A tied game is not possible. Team A wins: 0, 1, 2, 3, 4. Team B wins: 5, 6, 7, 8, 9. Which of these lists of random numbers shows a simulated outcome that Team B wins 4 games out of 6 games played?

**A.** 7 6 8 7      **B.** 7 6 3 8 7 3

**C.** 7 6 3 2 7 3    **D.** 7 3 2 1 7 3

**6.** A boy wins a carnival game 50% of the time. He uses random numbers from 0 to 9 to simulate playing the game. The numbers 0–4 represent winning. The numbers 5–9 represent losing. The results show 10 simulations of playing the game 3 times. How many of these trials simulate the boy winning all 3 games?

| | |
|---|---|
| 4 1 2 | 7 5 0 |
| 2 3 0 | 8 0 8 |
| 1 0 4 | 2 3 7 |
| 4 2 4 | 6 4 8 |
| 1 2 1 | 2 0 8 |

**7. Writing** In a small town, 80% of people bike to work.

**a.** Which way of assigning numbers to outcomes can you use to simulate the probability that someone chosen at random bikes to work? Select all that apply.

**A.** Use numbers from 0 to 9.
Bike: 0, 1, 2, 3, 4, 5, 6, 7
Do not bike: 8, 9

**B.** Use numbers from 0 to 9.
Bike: 8
Do not bike: 0, 1, 2, 3, 4, 5, 6, 7

**C.** Use numbers from 1 to 10.
Bike: 1, 2, 3, 4, 5, 6, 7, 8
Do not bike: 9, 10

**D.** Use numbers from 0 to 10.
Bike: 9, 10
Do not bike: 0, 1, 2, 3, 4, 5, 6, 7, 8

**b.** Describe how to use the assigned numbers to do a study of how people in the town get to work.

**8.** An artist usually sells 4 of her works each month. She sells 50% of her works to tourists. A simulation uses the numbers 0–4 to represent selling a work to a tourist and 5–9 to represent selling a work to someone who is not a tourist. The lists of random numbers below simulate selling 4 paintings a month for 10 months. Make a frequency table of the number of months with each number of sales to tourists.

| | | |
|---|---|---|
| 3 5 8 3 | 2 7 8 2 | 4 0 3 7 |
| 8 9 6 4 | 5 2 2 7 | |
| 7 2 9 7 | 6 5 5 1 | 7 8 3 7 |
| 4 2 3 1 | 7 3 8 5 | |

| Sales to Tourists Each Month | | | | | |
|---|---|---|---|---|---|
| **Number** | 0 | 1 | 2 | 3 | 4 |
| **Frequency** | ■ | ■ | ■ | ■ | ■ |

**9. Challenge** Suppose you have an 80% chance of winning a game. For a simulation, the numbers 0 to 7 represent a win. The numbers 8 and 9 represent a loss.

**a.** Which of these lists simulate the outcomes of 10 games with 5 wins in a row? Select all that apply.

**A.** 5 9 7 9 6 8 3 1 7 9

**B.** 5 7 6 9 3 1 7 9 8 7

**C.** 5 7 6 3 1 8 7 7 9 9

**D.** 7 7 8 9 5 7 6 3 1 9

**b.** Write three different lists that also show 5 wins in a row.

CCSS: 7.SP.C.8

## Key Concept

You can investigate probability using a simulation.

About 15% of people in the United States are left-handed. What is the probability that exactly one of the next two people you meet is left-handed?

**Set up a simulation model.** Identify the action to simulate. Use known probabilities to choose a simulation model for the outcomes.

Action: Ask two people at random if they are left-handed.

Simulated outcomes: Use numbers from 1 to 100.

left-handed: 1–15          not left-handed: 16–100

Simulation (one trial): Choose two numbers from 1 to 100 at random.

Generate 25 pairs of random numbers from 1 to 100.

**Carry out the simulation.** Conduct many trials of the simulated action, and record the results.

(2, 30) (65, 39) (13, 21) (12, 84) (19, 71)
(25, 9) (13, 83) (36, 93) (92, 85) (44, 37)
(99, 50) (67, 37) (66, 99) (84, 1) (22, 82)
(54, 59) (29, 73) (52, 66) (18, 73) (10, 2)
(37, 73) (48, 36) (31, 29) (29, 37) (100, 59)

**Analyze the data.** Identify and tally the favorable outcomes.

There are 6 favorable outcomes.

(2, 30) (65, 39) (13, 21) (12, 84) (19, 71)
(25, 9) (13, 83) (36, 93) (92, 85) (44, 37)
(99, 50) (67, 37) (66, 99) (84, 1) (22, 82)
(54, 59) (29, 73) (52, 66) (18, 73) (10, 2)
(37, 73) (48, 36) (31, 29) (29, 37) (100, 59)

Two left-handed people is not a favorable outcome.

continued on next page >

# Key Concept

continued

**Find an experimental probability.** Use the experimental probability formula.

The results of the 25 trials included six favorable outcomes

$$P(\text{exactly one left-handed}) = \frac{\text{number of favorable outcomes}}{\text{total number of trials}}$$
$$= \frac{6}{25}$$

Based on the simulation, the experimental probability that exactly one of the next two people you meet is left-handed is $\frac{6}{25}$, or 24%.

# Part 1

## Example  Using Simulations to Estimate Probabilities

About 42% of people in the United States have type A blood. Use this simulation to estimate the probability that each of the next two blood donors at a hospital has type A blood.

Action: Test two people for type A blood.

Simulated outcomes: Use numbers from 1 to 100.

  type A: 1 to 42      not type A: 43 to 100

Simulation (one trial): Choose two numbers from 1 to 100 at random.

Results of 24 trials

| (67, 52) | (85, 53) | (21, 1) | (55, 2) |
| (72, 89) | (99, 2) | (25, 76) | (51, 47) |
| (31, 35) | (31, 94) | (63, 53) | (60, 55) |
| (88, 6) | (58, 52) | (62, 29) | (50, 44) |
| (74, 68) | (8, 15) | (55, 61) | (46, 20) |
| (28, 90) | (29, 30) | (88, 51) | (63, 56) |

## Solution · · · · · · · · · · · · · · · · · · · · · · · · · · · · · · · · · · · · · · · · · · · · · · · · · · · · · · · · · ·

Use numbers from 1 to 100 to represent the outcomes.

  type A: 1 to 42      not type A: 43 to 100

Outcomes that satisfy the event *two Type A donors* are those with both numbers from 1 to 42. Identify and tally these outcomes.

continued on next page >

## Part 1

### Solution continued

Results of 24 trials

| | | | |
|---|---|---|---|
| (67, 52) | (85, 53) | (21, 1) | (55, 5) |
| (72, 89) | (99, 2) | (25, 76) | (51, 47) |
| (31, 35) | (31, 94) | (63, 53) | (60, 55) |
| (88, 6) | (58, 52) | (62, 29) | (50, 44) |
| (74, 68) | (8, 15) | (55, 61) | (46, 20) |
| (28, 90) | (29, 30) | (88, 51) | (63, 56) |

There are 4 favorable outcomes.

The results of the 24 trials included 4 favorable outcomes.

$$P(\text{two type A}) = \frac{\text{number of favorable outcomes}}{\text{total number of trials}}$$

$$= \frac{4}{24}$$

$$= \frac{1}{6}$$

The experimental probability that each of the next two blood donors at the hospital has type A blood is $\frac{1}{6}$.

## Part 2

### Example Designing Simulations to Estimate Probabilities

About 44% of people in the United States have type O blood. Use a simulation to estimate the probability that exactly two of the next three blood donors at a hospital have type O blood.

### Solution

Set up and carry out a simulation model, and analyze the results.

Sample:

**Step 1** Identify the action.

You are looking for exactly two out of three donors having type O blood, so use this action.

Action: Test three people at random for type O blood.

**Step 2** Assign numbers to outcomes.

$P(\text{type O}) = 0.44$, so $P(\text{not type O}) = 1 - 0.44$, or 0.56.

Simulated outcomes: Use numbers from 1 to 100.

type O: 1 to 44          not type O: 45 to 100

continued on next page >

# Part 2

**Solution** continued

**Step 3** Describe one trial.

One trial is testing three people.

Simulation (one trial): Choose three numbers from 1 to 100 at random.

**Step 4** Run many trials.

To run 30 trials, generate 90 random numbers from 1 to 100 and look at them in groups of three. See the list in Step 5.

**Step 5** Analyze the results.

Outcomes that satisfy the events *exactly two type O* are those with exactly two numbers from 1 to 44. Identify and count these outcomes.

### Results of 30 Trials

| | | | | |
|---|---|---|---|---|
| (47, 82, 2) | (40, 75, 72) | (26, 97, 28) | (76, 84, 33) | (19, 74, 64) |
| (73, 21, 86) | (80, 82, 26) | (95, 37, 65) | (95, 24, 38) | (49, 77, 86) |
| (14, 58, 43) | (17, 49, 14) | (2, 39, 38) | (15, 14, 3) | (13, 42, 64) |
| (85, 52, 68) | (39, 59, 72) | (84, 60, 56) | (17, 6, 69) | (88, 50, 87) |
| (7, 21, 59) | (86, 34, 3) | (81, 81, 61) | (40, 26, 90) | (67, 33, 73) |
| (47, 88, 96) | (4, 56 80) | (89, 81, 26) | (90, 6, 79) | (8, 29, 59) |

There are 10 favorable outcomes.

**Step 6** Find an experimental probability.

The results of 30 trials included 10 favorable outcomes.

$$P(\text{exactly two type O}) = \frac{\text{number of favorable outcomes}}{\text{total number of trials}}$$

$$= \frac{10}{30}$$

$$= \frac{1}{3}$$

The experimental probability that exactly two of the next three blood donors have type O blood is $\frac{1}{3}$.

1. **Estimation** The chance that a person gets a horseshoe to encircle the stake in a game of horseshoes is 70%. Let the numbers 0 to 6 represent a horseshoe that encircles the stake, and let 7 to 9 represent a horseshoe that does not.

   (7,0) (1,1) (3,4) (4,9) (2,1) (5,9) (1,4) (8,1) (2,9) (0,3)

   **a.** What is the experimental probability that a person gets two horseshoes to encircle the stake?

   **b.** Without doing any calculations, how would you expect the estimate to change if the chance a horseshoe encircles the stake were 60%?

   **A.** The probability would be less than the probability found.

   **B.** The probability would be greater than the probability found.

   **C.** The probability would be the same.

2. Dylan is playing a game that has a 60% chance of a person winning. Set up a simulation to estimate the probability of Dylan winning exactly one game.

   (5,6) (6,5) (9,3) (6,4) (0,8) (3,1) (7,5) (5,1) (6,3) (0,3)

   (3,2) (4,7) (8,9) (8,6) (4,7) (2,1) (4,1) (0,2) (7,2) (3,9)

   **a.** Which of the following assigned numbers, for a win and a loss, can be used for the simulation model?

   **A.** Win: 0 to 6   Loss: 7 to 9

   **B.** Win: 0 to 7   Loss: 7 to 9

   **C.** Win: 0 to 5   Loss: 6 to 10

   **D.** Win: 0 to 5   Loss: 6 to 9

   **b.** What is the experimental probability that Dylan will win exactly one game?

3. **Writing** At a startup company there is a 50% chance an item is defective. The random numbers (8, 8), (9, 2),

(8, 7), (7, 0), (4, 9), (4, 4), (4, 3), (5, 5), (3, 2), and (3, 2) represent 10 trials for a simulation. You must design a simulation to estimate the probability that the next two items that are checked are defective.

   **a.** Which of the following assigned numbers, for defective and not defective items, can be used for the simulation model?

   **A.** Defective: 0 to 6
   Not Defective: 7 to 9

   **B.** Defective: 0 to 5
   Not Defective: 6 to 9

   **C.** Defective: 0 to 4
   Not Defective: 5 to 9

   **D.** Defective: 0 to 4
   Not Defective: 5 to 10

   **b.** Use this simulation to estimate the probability. Explain when it would be appropriate to use a simulation to find the probability of a compound event.

4. **Think About the Process** A baseball team wins about 70% of its games. There are 20 trials. Let the numbers 0 to 6 represent a win for the team and 7 to 9 represent a loss.

   (1,1,9,9)  (4,6,8,6)  (1,3,3,6)  (7,1,6,0)
   (9,7,0,1)  (8,3,3,2)  (1,0,8,4)  (4,9,1,4)
   (9,6,0,3)  (6,1,5,8)  (9,7,7,6)  (5,6,2,2)
   (8,5,7,7)  (6,2,4,4)  (5,8,2,3)  (8,8,5,9)
   (9,1,0,0)  (7,2,2,3)  (8,6,7,4)  (6,8,7,8)

   **a.** Which of the following statements is considered a favorable outcome?

   **A.** Each trial has four numbers that are greater than or equal to 6.

   **B.** Each trial has four numbers that are greater than 6.

   **C.** Each trial has four numbers that are less than or equal to 6.

   **D.** Each trial has two numbers that are less than or equal to 6.

   **b.** What is the experimental probability that the team wins the next four games?

5. **Error Analysis** A problem on a test says that 80% of people enjoy the beach. The students are asked to use the simulation numbers (8, 6), (5, 4), (2, 2), (0, 9), (4, 0), (5, 8), (0, 7), (6, 5), (5, 6), and (1, 5) to estimate the probability that exactly one person says he or she enjoys the beach. Let the numbers 0–7 represent a person who enjoys going to the beach and let 8–9 represent a person who does not. One student says that the probability is about 100%.

a. Estimate the probability that exactly one person enjoys the beach.

b. What error might the student have made?

   **A.** The student found the probability that at least one person enjoys the beach.

   **B.** The student found the probability that both people enjoy the beach.

   **C.** The student found the probability that neither person enjoys the beach.

6. **Think About the Process** About 50% of the people in a state work for a small business. Use a simulation to estimate the probability that at least one of the next four people work for a small business.

(6,4,1,1)  (0,5,0,1)  (7,5,8,2)  (0,4,0,3)
(3,0,7,4)  (7,3,8,3)  (5,2,5,0)  (2,2,3,5)
(0,8,0,3)  (3,7,5,0)  (7,6,9,4)  (9,2,2,5)
(7,1,2,1)  (4,4,9,3)  (7,5,9,6)  (8,2,2,3)
(1,2,8,8)  (8,1,2,1)  (7,6,5,2)  (3,1,5,4)

a. Which of the following is the correct action to simulate the event?

   **A.** Two people are tested at random to see if they work for a small business.

   **B.** One person is tested at random to see if he or she works for a small business.

   **C.** Three people are tested at random to see if they work for a small business.

   **D.** Four people are tested at random to see if they work for a small business.

b. Which of the following assigned numbers, for people who work for a small business and those who don't, can be used for the simulation model?

   **A.** Work for a Small Business: 0 to 4
   Don't Work for a Small Business: 5 to 9

   **B.** Work for a Small Business: 0 to 4
   Don't Work for a Small Business: 5 to 10

   **C.** Work for a Small Business: 0 to 5
   Don't Work for a Small Business: 6 to 9

   **D.** Work for a Small Business: 0 to 3
   Don't Work for a Small Business: 4 to 9

c. What is the experimental probability that at least one of the next four people work for a small business?

7. **Challenge** Pierre plants six flower bulbs. Each bulb has a 50% chance of growing. The random numbers below represent a simulation with 20 trials. Let the numbers 0 to 4 represent a bulb that grows and 5 to 9 represent a bulb that does not. Estimate the chance that all six flower bulbs will grow. How should the estimate change if the number of bulbs changes? Verify the answer using the results from the simulation.

(6, 8, 8, 6, 0, 5)  (7, 3, 7, 2, 7, 8)
(5, 0, 4, 4, 9, 6)  (7, 9, 1, 2, 8, 5)
(4, 8, 6, 6, 6, 8)  (7, 9, 2, 9, 7, 2)
(0, 2, 2, 5, 8, 3)  (9, 7, 0, 4, 6, 1)
(9, 8, 7, 9, 5, 3)  (6, 8, 2, 7, 5, 7)
(0, 6, 9, 8, 0, 1)  (9, 4, 2, 0, 1, 3)
(8, 2, 6, 1, 2, 8)  (5, 5, 2, 7, 8, 0)
(5, 8, 8, 2, 0, 0)  (9, 8, 8, 3, 6, 6)
(2, 7, 7, 9, 7, 5)  (0, 3, 4, 2, 0, 0)
(0, 9, 8, 8, 9, 6)  (4, 9, 5, 3, 8, 6)

CCSS: 7.SP.C.7, 7.SP.C.8

## Part 1

### Example Comparing Expected Results with Experiments

Suppose you roll two standard number cubes 500 times.

**a.** How many times do you expect to get a sum of 9?

**b.** Suppose you run the experiment and get the sample results shown. Compare the result to your prediction in part (a).

**Sample Results**

| Event | Count |
|-------|-------|
| (3, 6) | 19 |
| (4, 5) | 13 |
| (5, 4) | 15 |
| (6, 3) | 16 |

### Solution

**a.** There are 36 possible outcomes for rolling two number cubes, four of which give a sum of 9.

$$P(\text{sum of 9}) = \frac{\text{number of favorable outcomes}}{\text{number of possible outcomes}}$$

$$= \frac{4}{36}$$

$$= \frac{1}{9}$$

|   | 1 | 2 | 3 | 4 | 5 | 6 |
|---|---|---|---|---|---|---|
| **1** | 1, 1 | 2, 1 | 3, 1 | 4, 1 | 5, 1 | 6, 1 |
| **2** | 1, 2 | 2, 2 | 3, 2 | 4, 2 | 5, 2 | 6, 2 |
| **3** | 1, 3 | 2, 3 | 3, 3 | 4, 3 | 5, 3 | (6, 3) |
| **4** | 1, 4 | 2, 4 | 3, 4 | 4, 4 | (5, 4) | 6, 4 |
| **5** | 1, 5 | 2, 5 | 3, 5 | (4, 5) | 5, 5 | 6, 5 |
| **6** | 1, 6 | 2, 6 | (3, 6) | 4, 6 | 5, 6 | 6, 6 |

Because $P(\text{sum of 9})$ is $\frac{1}{9}$, the number of times you expect to get a sum of 9 in 500 rolls is $\frac{1}{9}$ of 500.

$$\frac{1}{9} \cdot 500 = 55.\overline{5}$$

You can expect to get a sum of 9 about 56 times in 500 rolls of two number cubes.

continued on next page >

## Part 1

**Solution** continued

**b.** Run the experiment with a probability tool. A sample table of results is shown below.

**Sample Results**

| Event | Count |
|-------|-------|
| (3, 6) | 19 |
| (4, 5) | 13 |
| (5, 4) | 15 |
| (6, 3) | 16 |

The total number of times the experiment produced a sum of 9 is:

19 + 13 + 15 + 16, or 63 times

This experimental count is greater than the number of times predicted by theoretical probability, which is about 56.

## Part 2

### Example   Finding Probabilities of Compound Events

A hamster can run from Nest to Food through a system of tunnels in his cage, as shown in the diagram. At each numbered point there is a 50% chance that a gate closes off the tunnel at any given moment.

What is the probability that there is an open path from Nest to Food at any given moment?

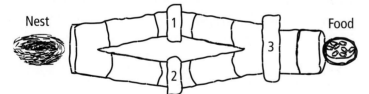

continued on next page >

# Part 2

**Example** continued

**Solution** · · · · · · · · · · · · · · · · · · · · · · · · · · · · · · · · · · · · · · · · · · · · · · · · · ·

**Method 1** Use theoretical probability.

Make an organized list showing all possible combinations of gates 1, 2, and 3 being open (O) or closed (C). There is an open path from Nest to Food only if gate 3 is open and either gate 1 or gate 2 is also open.

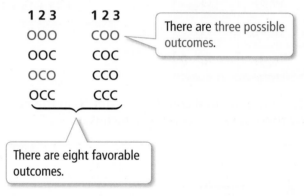

| 1 2 3 | 1 2 3 |
|-------|-------|
| OOO   | COO   |
| OOC   | COC   |
| OCO   | CCO   |
| OCC   | CCC   |

There are three possible outcomes.

There are eight favorable outcomes.

At any given moment, the probability of each gate being open is 50%, so all eight outcomes in the list are equally likely.

$$P(\text{open path}) = \frac{\text{number of favorable outcomes}}{\text{number of possible outcomes}}$$

$$= \frac{3}{8}$$

The theoretical probability that there is an open path from Nest to Food at any given moment is $\frac{3}{8}$, or 37.5%.

continued on next page >

# Part 2

**Solution** continued

Method 2 Use simulation.

Use a coin toss to simulate each gate being open (H) or closed (T).

**Simulated action:** Toss three coins to determine one outcome in the form (gate 1, gate 2, gate 3).

Sample set of 50 trials of the simulation:

| 123 | 123 | 123 | 123 | 123 | 123 | 123 | 123 | 123 | 123 |
|-----|-----|-----|-----|-----|-----|-----|-----|-----|-----|
| HTT | THH | THH | THT | HTT | THT | HTH | THH | TTH | HHH |
| THT | TTT | TTH | TTH | HHT | TTT | HTH | HTH | THT | HTT |
| HHT | HHH | HHT | HTH | HTH | TTH | TTT | THT | TTT | HHH |
| HHH | HHT | THH | HHH | HTT | THT | HTT | HTT | TTH | HHH |
| HTT | HTH | THT | HHH | HHT | THT | HHT | HHT | HHT | HHT |

A favorable outcome must have H (open) for gate 3 and at least one H (open) at gate 1 or gate 2. For the sample data, this occurs 17 times out of 50.

Find an experimental probability.

$$P(\text{open path}) = \frac{\text{number of favorable outcomes}}{\text{total number of trials}}$$

$$= \frac{17}{50}$$

The experimental probability that there is an open path from Nest to Food at any given moment is $\frac{17}{50}$, or 34%.

**1.** You use a simulation to flip two coins, a quarter and a dime, 600 times.

**a.** How many times would you expect to get tails on exactly one coin?

**b.** Suppose the results of the simulation are as shown in the table, where the first letter represents the quarter and the second letter represents the dime. Compare them to your prediction.

**Simulation Results**

| Event | Count |
|-------|-------|
| (H, T) | 159 |
| (T, H) | 164 |

**2.** A rat can run from his nest to his food dish through a system of tunnels in his cage, as shown in the diagram. At each numbered point there is a 50% chance that a gate closes off the tunnel at any given moment. What is the theoretical probability that there is an open path from the rat's nest to his food dish at any given moment?

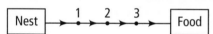

**3.** A certain airline offers different ways to get from City 1 to City 2, as shown in the figure. The points *K, L, M,* and *N* represent layovers along the way. There is a 50% chance of a delay during each layover. What is the theoretical probability that there is a route without any delays? Explain how you can use this result to find the theoretical probability that each possible route has at least one delay.

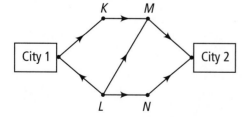

**4. Think About the Process** Charlotte is an experienced air traveler. She has taken many trips that require changing planes. She typically has a 70% chance of making it from one flight to the next. She uses a random-digit generator to produce this simulation of ten trips that would each require her to change planes twice.

**Simulation Results**

| | |
|------|------|
| (5, 2) | (0, 2) |
| (5, 1) | (8, 3) |
| (3, 0) | (0, 0) |
| (5, 5) | (4, 2) |
| (6, 3) | (9, 9) |

**a.** How should Charlotte assign digits to the outcomes?

**A.** Let 0, 1, 2, 3, 4, and 5 represent making it from one flight to the next. Let 6, 7, 8, and 9 represent not making it from one flight to the next.

**B.** Let 0, 1, 2, 3, 4, 5, and 6 represent making it from one flight to the next. Let 7, 8, and 9 represent not making it from one flight to the next.

**C.** Let 7 represent making it from one flight to the next. Let 0, 1, 2, 3, 4, 5, 6, 8, and 9 represent not making it from one flight to the next.

**D.** Let 6 represent making it from one flight to the next. Let 0, 1, 2, 3, 4, 6, 7, 8, and 9 represent not making it from one flight to the next.

**b.** For this simulation, what is the experimental probability that she makes it to both the second and the third planes?

5. **Think About the Process** You use a simulation to flip two coins, a quarter and a dime, 400 times. You want to find how many times to expect no more than one coin to show heads.

**Simulation Results**

| Event | Count |
|-------|-------|
| (H, T) | 96 |
| (T, H) | 92 |
| (T, T) | 90 |

a. Which of these expressions should you simplify to find how many times to expect no more than one coin to show heads?

A. $\frac{1}{2} \cdot (96 + 92 + 90)$

B. $\frac{1}{4} \cdot (96 + 92 + 90)$

C. $\frac{1}{4} \cdot 400$

D. $\frac{3}{4} \cdot (96 + 92 + 90)$

E. $\frac{1}{2} \cdot 400$

F. $\frac{3}{4} \cdot 400$

b. How many times would you expect no more than one coin to show heads?

c. Suppose the results of the simulation are as shown in the table. Compare them to your prediction.

The total number of times the simulation produced no more than one coin showing heads is ■ the number of times predicted by theoretical probability.

6. You use a simulation to roll two standard number cubes 500 times.

**Simulation Results**

| Event | Count |
|-------|-------|
| (2, 6) | 13 |
| (3, 5) | 12 |
| (4, 4) | 7 |
| (5, 3) | 15 |
| (6, 2) | 11 |

a. How many times would you expect to get a sum of 8?

b. Suppose the results of the simulation are as shown in the table. Compare them to your prediction.

The total number of times the simulation produced a sum of 8 is ■ the number of times predicted by theoretical probability.

7. The diagram shows the routes Yossi can take to get to work in the morning. The points *P*, *Q*, *R*, and *S* correspond to places where there is a 50% chance a traffic jam will delay Yossi. To find the theoretical probability that there is a route without any delays, he counted the favorable outcomes. Yossi incorrectly claimed that because there are 2 favorable outcomes, the theoretical probability is 12.5%.

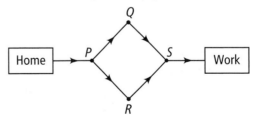

a. What is the correct theoretical probability?

b. What mistake might Yossi have made?

# English/Spanish Glossary

## A

**Absolute deviation from the mean** Absolute deviation measures the distance that the data value is from the mean. You find the absolute deviation by taking the absolute value of the deviation of a data value. Absolute deviations are always nonnegative.

**Desviación absoluta de la media** La desviación absoluta mide la distancia a la que un valor se encuentra de la media. Para hallar la desviación absoluta, tomas el valor absoluto de la desviación de un valor. Las desviaciones absolutas siempre son no negativas.

**Absolute value** The absolute value of a number $a$ is the distance between $a$ and zero on a number line. The absolute value of $a$ is written as $|a|$.

**Valor absoluto** El valor absoluto de un número $a$ es la distancia entre a y cero en la recta numérica. El valor absoluto de $a$ se escribe como $|a|$.

**Accuracy** The accuracy of an estimate or measurement is the degree to which it agrees with an accepted or actual value of that measurement.

**Exactitud** La exactitud de una estimación o medición es el grado de concordancia con un valor aceptado o real de esa medición.

**Action** In a probability situation, an action is a process with an uncertain result.

**Acción** En una situación de probabilidad, una acción es el proceso con un resultado incierto.

**Acute angle** An acute angle is an angle with a measure between 0° and 90°.

**Ángulo agudo** Un ángulo agudo es un ángulo que mide entre 0° y 90°.

**Acute triangle** An acute triangle is a triangle with three acute angles.

**Triángulo acutángulo** Un triángulo acutángulo es un triángulo que tiene tres ángulos agudos.

**Addend** Addends are the numbers that are added together to find a sum.

**Sumando** Los sumandos son los números que se suman para hallar un total.

# English/Spanish Glossary

**Additive inverses** Two numbers that have a sum of 0.

**Inversos de suma** Dos números cuya suma es 0.

**Adjacent angles** Two angles are adjacent angles if they share a vertex and a side, but have no interior points in common.

**Ángulos adyacentes** Dos ángulos son adyacentes si tienen un vértice y un lado en común, pero no comparten puntos internos.

**Algebraic expression** An algebraic expression is a mathematical phrase that consists of variables, numbers, and operation symbols.

**Expresión algebraica** Una expresión algebraica es una frase matemática que consiste en variables, números y símbolos de operaciones.

**Analyze** To analyze is to think about and understand facts and details about a given set of information. Analyzing can involve providing a written summary supported by factual information, diagrams, charts, tables, or any combination of these.

**Analizar** Analizar es pensar en los datos y detalles de cierta información y comprenderlos. El análisis puede incluir la presentación de un resumen escrito sustentado por información objetiva, diagramas, tablas o una combinación de esos elementos.

**Angle** An angle is a figure formed by two rays with a common endpoint.

**Ángulo** Un ángulo es una figura formada por dos semirrectas que tienen un extremo en común.

**Angle of rotation** The angle of rotation is the number of degrees a figure is rotated.

**Ángulo de rotación** El ángulo de rotación es el número de grados que se rota una figura.

**Annual salary** The amount of money earned at a job in one year.

**Salario annual** La cantidad de dinero ganó en un trabajo en un año.

**Area** The area of a figure is the number of square units the figure encloses.

**Área** El área de una figura es el número de unidades cuadradas que ocupa.

# English/Spanish Glossary

**Area of a circle** The formula for the area of a circle is $A = \pi r^2$, where $A$ represents the area and $r$ represents the radius of the circle.

**Área de un círculo** La fórmula del área de un círculo es $A = \pi r^2$, donde $A$ representa el área y $r$ representa el radio del círculo.

**Area of a parallelogram** The formula for the area of a parallelogram is $A = bh$, where $A$ represents the area, $b$ represents a base, and $h$ is the corresponding height.

**Área de un paralelogramo** La fórmula del área de un paralelogramo es $A = bh$, donde $A$ representa el área, $b$ representa una base y $h$ es la altura correspondiente.

**Area of a rectangle** The formula for the area of a rectangle is $A = bh$, where $A$ represents the area, $b$ represents the base, and $h$ represents the height of the rectangle.

**Área de un rectángulo** La fórmula del área de un rectángulo es $A = bh$, donde $A$ representa el área, $b$ representa la base y $h$ representa la altura del rectángulo.

**Area of a square** The formula for the area of a square is $A = s^2$, where $A$ represents the area and $s$ represents a side length.

**Área de un cuadrado** La fórmula del área de un cuadrado es $A = s^2$, donde $A$ representa el área y $l$ representa la longitud de un lado.

**Area of a trapezoid** The formula for the area of a trapezoid is $A = \frac{1}{2}h(b_1 + b_2)$, where $A$ represents the area, $b_1$ and $b_2$ represent the bases, and $h$ represents the height between the bases.

**El área de un trapezoide** La fórmula para el área de un trapezoide es $A = \frac{1}{2}h(b_1 + b_2)$, donde $A$ representa el área, $b_1$ y $b_2$ representan las bases, y $h$ representa la altura entre las bases.

**Area of a triangle** The formula for the area of a triangle is $A = \frac{1}{2}bh$, where $A$ represents the area, $b$ represents the length of a base, and $h$ represents the corresponding height.

**Área de un triángulo** La fórmula del área de un triángulo es $A = \frac{1}{2}bh$, donde $A$ representa el área, $b$ representa la longitud de una base y $h$ representa la altura correspondiente.

**Asset** An asset is money you have or property of value that you own.

**Ventaja** Una ventaja es dinero que tiene o la propiedad de valor que usted posee.

# English/Spanish Glossary

**Associative Property of Addition** For any numbers $a$, $b$, and $c$:
$(a + b) + c = a + (b + c)$

**Propiedad asociativa de la suma** Para los números cualesquiera $a$, $b$ y $c$:
$(a + b) + c = a + (b + c)$

**Associative Property of Multiplication** For any numbers $a$, $b$, and $c$:
$(a \cdot b) \cdot c = a \cdot (b \cdot c)$

**Propiedad asociativa de la multiplicación** Para los números cualesquiera $a$, $b$ y $c$:
$(a \cdot b) \cdot c = a \cdot (b \cdot c)$

**Average of two numbers** The average of two numbers is the value that represents the middle of two numbers. It is found by adding the two numbers together and dividing by 2.

**Promedio de dos números** El promedio de dos números es el valor que está justo en el medio de esos dos números. Se halla sumando los dos números y dividiendo el resultado por 2.

## B

**Balance** The balance in an account is the principal amount plus the interest earned.

**Saldo** El saldo de una cuenta es el capital más el interés ganado.

**Balance of a checking Account** The balance of a checking account is the amount of money in the checking account.

**El equilibrio de una Cuenta Corriente Bancaria** El equilibrio de una cuenta corriente bancaria es la cantidad de dinero en la cuenta corriente bancaria.

**Balance of a loan** The balance of a loan is the remaining unpaid principal.

**El equilibrio de un préstamo** El equilibrio de un préstamo es el director impagado restante.

**Bar diagram** A bar diagram is a way to represent part to whole relationships.

**Diagrama de barras** Un diagrama de barras es una forma de representar una relación de parte a entero.

**Base** The base is the repeated factor of a number written in exponential form.

**Base** La base es el factor repetido de un número escrito en forma exponencial.

# English/Spanish Glossary

**Base area of a cone** The base area of a cone is the area of a circle. Base Area = $\pi r^2$.

**Área de la base de un cono** El área de la base de un cono es el área de un círculo. El área de la base = $\pi r^2$.

**Base of a cone** The base of a cone is a circle with radius $r$.

**Base de un cono** La base de un cono es un círculo con radio $r$.

**Base of a cylinder** A base of a cylinder is one of a pair of parallel circular faces that are the same size.

**Base de un cilindro** Una base de un cilindro es una de dos caras circulares paralelas que tienen el mismo tamaño.

**Base of a parallelogram** A base of a parallelogram is any side of the parallelogram.

**Base de un paralelogramo** La base de un paralelogramo es cualquiera de los lados del paralelogramo.

**Base of a prism** A base of a prism is one of a pair of parallel polygonal faces that are the same size and shape. A prism is named for the shape of its bases.

**Base de un prisma** La base de un prisma es una de las dos caras poligonales paralelas que tienen el mismo tamaño y la misma forma. El nombre de un prisma depende de la forma de sus bases.

**Base of a pyramid** A base of a pyramid is a polygonal face that does not connect to the vertex.

**Base de una pirámide** La base de una pirámide es una cara poligonal que no se conecta con el vértice.

**Base of a triangle** The base of a triangle is any side of the triangle.

**Base de un triángulo** La base de un triángulo es cualquiera de los lados del triángulo.

**Benchmark** A benchmark is a number you can use as a reference point for other numbers.

**Referencia** Una referencia es un número que usted puede utilizar como un punto de referencia para otros números.

# English/Spanish Glossary

**Bias** A bias is a tendency toward a particular perspective that is different from the overall perspective of the population.

**Sesgo** Un sesgo es una tendencia hacia una perspectiva particular que es diferente de la perspectiva general de la población.

**Biased sample** In a biased sample, the number of subjects in the sample with the trait that you are studying is not proportional to the number of members in the population with that trait. A biased sample does not accurately represent the population.

**Muestra sesgada** En una muestra sesgada, el número de sujetos de la muestra que tiene la característica que se está estudiando no es proporcional al número de miembros de la población que tienen esa característica. Una muestra sesgada no representa con exactitud la población.

**Bivariate categorical data** Bivariate categorical data pairs categorical data collected about two variables of the same population.

**Datos bivariados por categorías** Los datos bivariados por categorías agrupan pares de datos obtenidos acerca de dos variables de la misma población.

**Bivariate data** Bivariate data is comprised of pairs of linked observations about a population.

**Datos bivariados** Los datos bivariados se forman a partir de pares de observaciones relacionadas sobre una población.

**Box plot** A box plot is a statistical graph that shows the distribution of a data set by marking five boundary points where data occur along a number line. Unlike a dot plot or a histogram, a box plot does not show frequency.

**Diagrama de cajas** Un diagrama de cajas es un diagrama de estadísticas que muestra la distribución de un conjunto de datos al marcar cinco puntos de frontera donde se hallan los datos sobre una recta numérica. A diferencia del diagrama de puntos o el histograma, el diagrama de cajas no muestra la frecuencia.

**Budget** A budget is a plan for how you will spend your money.

**Presupuesto** Un presupuesto es un plan para cómo gastará su dinero.

# English/Spanish Glossary

## C

**Categorical data** Categorical data consist of data that fall into categories.

**Datos por categorías** Los datos por categorías son datos que se pueden clasificar en categorías.

**Center of a circle** The center of a circle is the point inside the circle that is the same distance from all points on the circle. Name a circle by its center.

**Centro de un círculo** El centro de un círculo es el punto dentro del círculo que está a la misma distancia de todos los puntos del círculo. Un círculo se identifica por su centro.

**Center of a regular polygon** The center of a regular polygon is the point that is equidistant from its vertices.

**Centro de un polígono regular** El centro de un polígono regular es el punto equidistante de todos sus vértices.

**Center of rotation** The center of rotation is a fixed point about which a figure is rotated.

**Centro de rotación** El centro de rotación es el punto fijo alrededor del cual se rota una figura.

**Check register** A record that shows all of the transactions for a bank account, including withdrawals, deposits, and transfers. It also shows the balance of the account after each transaction.

**Verifique registro** Un registro que muestra todas las transacciones para una cuenta bancaria, inclusive retiradas, los depósitos, y las transferencias. También muestra el equilibrio de la cuenta después de cada transacción.

**Circle** A circle is the set of all points in a plane that are the same distance from a given point, called the center.

**Círculo** Un círculo es el conjunto de todos los puntos de un plano que están a la misma distancia de un punto dado, llamado centro.

**Circle graph** A circle graph is a graph that represents a whole divided into parts.

**Gráfica circular** Una gráfica circular es una gráfica que representa un todo dividido en partes.

# English/Spanish Glossary

**Circumference of a circle** The circumference of a circle is the distance around the circle. The formula for the circumference of a circle is $C = \pi d$, where $C$ represents the circumference and $d$ represents the diameter of the circle.

**Circunferencia de un círculo** La circunferencia de un círculo es la distancia alrededor del círculo. La fórmula de la circunferencia de un círculo es $C = \pi d$, donde $C$ representa la circunferencia y $d$ representa el diámetro del círculo.

**Cluster** A cluster is a group of points that lie close together on a scatter plot.

**Grupo** Un grupo es un conjunto de puntos que están agrupados en un diagrama de dispersión.

**Coefficient** A coefficient is the number part of a term that contains a variable.

**Coeficiente** Un coeficiente es la parte numérica de un término que contiene una variable.

**Common denominator** A common denominator is a number that is the denominator of two or more fractions.

**Común denominador** Un común denominador es un número que es el denominador de dos o más fracciones.

**Common multiple** A common multiple is a multiple that two or more numbers share.

**Múltiplo común** Un múltiplo común es un múltiplo que comparten dos o más números.

**Commutative Property of Addition** For any numbers $a$ and $b$: $a + b = b + a$

**Propiedad conmutativa de la suma** Para los números cualesquiera $a$ y $b$: $a + b = b + a$

**Commutative Property of Multiplication** For any numbers $a$ and $b$: $a \cdot b = b \cdot a$

**Propiedad conmutativa de la multiplicación** Para los números cualesquiera $a$ y $b$: $a \cdot b = b \cdot a$

**Comparative inference** A comparative inference is an inference made by interpreting and comparing two sets of data.

**Inferencia comparativa** Una inferencia comparativa es una inferencia que se hace al interpretar y comparar dos conjuntos de datos.

# English/Spanish Glossary

**Compare** To compare is to tell or show how two things are alike or different.

**Comparar** Comparar es describir o mostrar en qué se parecen o en qué se diferencian dos cosas.

**Compatible numbers** Compatible numbers are numbers that are easy to compute mentally.

**Números compatibles** Los números compatibles son números fáciles de calcular mentalmente.

**Complementary angles** Two angles are complementary angles if the sum of their measures is 90°. Complementary angles that are adjacent form a right angle.

**Ángulos complementarios** Dos ángulos son complementarios si la suma de sus medidas es 90°. Los ángulos complementarios que son adyacentes forman un ángulo recto.

**Complex fraction** A complex fraction is a fraction $\frac{A}{B}$ where $A$ and/or $B$ are fractions and $B$ is not zero.

**Fracción compleja** Una fracción compleja es una fracción $\frac{A}{B}$ donde $A$ y/o $B$ son fracciones y $B$ es distinto de cero.

**Compose a shape** To compose a shape, join two (or more) shapes so that there is no gap or overlap.

**Componer una figura** Para componer una figura, debes unir dos (o más) figuras de modo que entre ellas no queden espacios ni superposiciones.

**Composite figure** A composite figure is the combination of two or more figures into one object.

**Figura compuesta** Una figura compuesta es la combinación de dos o más figuras en un objeto.

**Composite number** A composite number is a whole number greater than 1 with more than two factors.

**Número compuesto** Un número compuesto es un número entero mayor que 1 con más de dos factores.

**Compound event** A compound event is an event associated with a multi-step action. A compound event is composed of events that are the outcomes of the steps of the action.

**Evento compuesto** Un evento compuesto es un evento que se relaciona con una acción de varios pasos. Un evento compuesto se compone de eventos que son los resultados de los pasos de una acción.

# English/Spanish Glossary

**Compound interest** Compound interest is interest paid on both the principal and the interest earned in previous interest periods. To calculate compound interest, use the formula $B = p(1 + r)^n$, where $B$ is the balance in the account, $p$ is the principal, $r$ is the annual interest rate, and $n$ is the time in years that the account earns interest.

**Interés compuesto** El interés compuesto es el interés que se paga sobre el capital y el interés obtenido en períodos de interés anteriores. Para calcular el interés compuesto, usa la fórmula $B = c(1 + r)^n$ donde $B$ es el saldo de la cuenta, $c$ es el capital, $r$ es la tasa de interés anual y $n$ es el tiempo en años en que la cuenta obtiene un interés.

**Cone** A cone is a three-dimensional figure with one circular base and one vertex.

**Cono** Un cono es una figura tridimensional con una base circular y un vértice.

**Congruent figures** Two two-dimensional figures are congruent $\cong$ if the second can be obtained from the first by a sequence of rotations, reflections, and translations.

**Figuras congruentes** Dos figuras bidimensionales son congruentes $\cong$ si la segunda puede obtenerse a partir de la primera mediante una secuencia de rotaciones, reflexiones y traslaciones.

**Conjecture** A conjecture is a statement that you believe to be true but have not yet proved to be true.

**Conjetura** Una conjetura es un enunciado que crees que es verdadero, pero que todavía no has comprobado que sea verdadero.

**Constant** A constant is a term that only contains a number.

**Constante** Una constante es un término que solamente contiene un número.

**Constant of proportionality** In a proportional relationship, one quantity $y$ is a constant multiple of the other quantity $x$. The constant multiple is called the constant of proportionality. The constant of proportionality is equal to the ratio $\frac{y}{x}$.

**Constante de proporcionalidad** En una relación proporcional, una cantidad $y$ es un múltiplo constante de la otra cantidad $x$. El múltiplo constante se llama constante de proporcionalidad. La constante de proporcionalidad es igual a la razón $\frac{y}{x}$.

# English/Spanish Glossary

**Construct** To construct is to make something, such as an argument, by organizing ideas. Constructing an argument can involve a written response, equations, diagrams, charts, tables, or a combination of these.

**Construir** Construir es hacer o crear algo, como se construye un argumento al organizar ideas. Para construir un argumento puede usarse una respuesta escrita, ecuaciones, diagramas, tablas o una combinación de esos elementos.

**Convenience sampling** Convenience sampling is a sampling method in which a researcher chooses members of the population that are convenient and available. Many researchers use this sampling technique because it is fast and inexpensive. It does not require the researcher to keep track of everyone in the population.

**Muestra de conveniencia** Una muestra de conveniencia es un método de muestreo en el que un investigador escoge miembros de la población que están convenientemente disponibles. Muchos investigadores usan esta técnica de muestreo porque es rápida y no es costosa. No requiere que el investigador lleve un registro de cada miembro de la población.

**Cost of attendance** The cost of attendance of one year of college is the sum of all of your expenses during the year.

**El costo de asistencia** El costo de asistencia de un año del colegio es la suma de todos sus gastos durante el año.

**Cost of credit** The cost of credit for a loan is the difference between the total cost and the principal.

**El costo de crédito** El costo de crédito para un préstamo es la diferencia entre el coste total y el director.

**Converse of the Pythagorean Theorem** If the sum of the squares of the lengths of two sides of a triangle equals the square of the length of the third side, then the triangle is a right triangle. If $a^2 + b^2 = c^2$, then the triangle is a right triangle.

**Expresión recíproca del Teorema de Pitágoras** Si la suma del cuadrado de la longitud de dos lados de un triángulo es igual al cuadrado de la longitud del tercer lado, entonces el triángulo es un triángulo rectángulo. $a^2 + b^2 = c^2$, entonces el triángulo es un triángulo rectángulo.

**Conversion factor** A conversion factor is a rate that equals 1.

**Factor de conversión** Un factor de conversión es una tasa que es igual a 1.

# English/Spanish Glossary

**Coordinate plane** A coordinate plane is formed by a horizontal number line called the *x*-axis and a vertical number line called the *y*-axis.

**Plano de coordenadas** Un plano de coordenadas está formado por una recta numérica horizontal llamada eje de las *x* y una recta numérica vertical llamada eje de las *y*.

**Corresponding angles** Corresponding angles lie on the same side of a transversal and in corresponding positions.

**Ángulos correspondientes** Los ángulos correspondientes se ubican al mismo lado de una secante y en posiciones correspondientes.

**Counterexample** A counterexample is a specific example that shows that a conjecture is false.

**Contraejemplo** Un contraejemplo es un ejemplo específico que muestra que una conjetura es falsa.

**Counting Principle** If there are *m* possible outcomes of one action and *n* possible outcomes of a second action, then there are $m \cdot n$ outcomes of the first action followed by the second action.

**Principio de conteo** Si hay *m* resultados posibles de una acción y *n* resultados posibles de una segunda acción, entonces hay $m \cdot n$ resultados de la primera acción seguida de la segunda acción.

**Coupon** A coupon is part of a printed or online advertisement entitling the holder to a discount at checkout.

**Cupón** Un cupón forma parte de un anuncio impreso o en línea que permite al poseedor a un descuento en comprueba.

**Credit card** A credit card is a card issued by a lender that can be used to borrow money or make purchases on credit.

**Tarjeta de crédito** Una tarjeta de crédito es una tarjeta publicada por un prestamista que puede ser utilizado para pedir dinero prestado o compras de marca a cuenta.

**Credit history** A credit history shows how a consumer has managed credit in the past.

**Acredite la historia** Una historia del crédito muestra cómo un consumidor ha manejado crédito en el pasado.

# English/Spanish Glossary

**Credit report** A report that shows personal information about a consumer and details about the consumer's credit history.

**Acredite reporte** Un reporte que muestra información personal sobre un consumidor y detalles acerca de la historia del crédito del consumidor.

**Critique** A critique is a careful judgment in which you give your opinion about the good and bad parts of something, such as how a problem was solved.

**Crítica** Una crítica es una evaluación cuidadosa en la que das tu opinión acerca de las partes positivas y negativas de algo, como la manera en la que se resolvió un problema.

**Cross section** A cross section is the intersection of a three-dimensional figure and a plane.

**Corte transversal** Un corte transversal es la intersección de una figura tridimensional y un plano.

**Cube** A cube is a rectangular prism whose faces are all squares.

**Cubo** Un cubo es un prisma rectangular cuyas caras son todas cuadrados.

**Cube root** The cube root of a number, $n$, is a number whose cube equals $n$.

**Raíz cúbica** La raíz cúbica de un número, $n$, es un número que elevado al cubo es igual a $n$.

**Cubic unit** A cubic unit is the volume of a cube that measures 1 unit on each edge.

**Unidad cúbica** Una unidad cúbica es el volumen de un cubo en el que cada arista mide 1 unidad.

**Cylinder** A cylinder is a three-dimensional figure with two parallel circular bases that are the same size.

**Cilindro** Un cilindro es una figura tridimensional con dos bases circulares paralelas que tienen el mismo tamaño.

## D

**Data** Data are pieces of information collected by asking questions, measuring, or making observations about the real world.

**Datos** Los datos son información reunida mediante preguntas, mediciones u observaciones sobre la vida diaria.

# English/Spanish Glossary

**Debit card** A debit card is a card issued by a bank that is linked a customer's bank account, normally a checking account. A debit card can normally be used to withdraw money from an ATM or to make a purchase.

**Tarjeta de débito** Una tarjeta de débito es una tarjeta publicada por un banco que es ligado la cuenta bancaria de un cliente, normalmente una cuenta corriente bancaria. Una tarjeta de débito puede ser utilizada normalmente retirar dinero de una ATM o para hacer una compra.

**Decimal** A decimal is a number with one or more places to the right of a decimal point.

**Decimal** Un decimal es un número que tiene uno o más lugares a la derecha del punto decimal.

**Decimal places** The digits after the decimal point are called decimal places.

**Lugares decimales** Los dígitos que están después del punto decimal se llaman lugares decimales.

**Decompose a shape** To decompose a shape, break it up to form other shapes.

**Descomponer una figura** Para descomponer una figura, debes separarla para formar otras figuras.

**Deductive reasoning** Deductive reasoning is a process of reasoning logically from given facts to a conclusion.

**Razonamiento deductivo** El razonamiento deductivo es un proceso de razonamiento lógico que parte de hechos dados hasta llegar a una conclusión.

**Denominator** The denominator is the number below the fraction bar in a fraction.

**Denominador** El denominador es el número que está debajo de la barra de fracción en una fracción.

**Dependent events** Two events are dependent events if the occurrence of the first event affects the probability of the second event.

**Eventos dependientes** Dos eventos son dependientes si el resultado del primer evento afecta la probabilidad del segundo evento.

**Deposit** A transaction that adds money to a bank account is a deposit.

**Depósito** Una transacción que agrega dinero a una cuenta bancaria es un depósito.

# English/Spanish Glossary

**Dependent variable** A dependent variable is a variable whose value changes in response to another (independent) variable.

**Variable dependiente** Una variable dependiente es una variable cuyo valor cambia en respuesta a otra variable (independiente).

**Describe** To describe is to explain or tell in detail. A written description can contain facts and other information needed to communicate your answer. A diagram or a graph may also be included.

**Describir** Describir es explicar o indicar algo en detalle. Una descripción escrita puede incluir hechos y otra información necesaria para comunicar tu respuesta. También puede incluir un diagrama o una gráfica.

**Design** To design is to make using specific criteria.

**Diseñar** Diseñar es crear algo a partir de criterios específicos.

**Determine** To determine is to use the given information and any related facts to find a value or make a decision.

**Determinar** Determinar es usar la información dada y cualquier otro dato relacionado para hallar un valor o tomar una decisión.

**Deviation from the mean** Deviation indicates how far away and in which direction a data value is from the mean. Data values that are less than the mean have a negative deviation. Data values that are greater than the mean have a positive deviation.

**Desviación de la media** La desviación indica a qué distancia y en qué dirección un valor se aleja de la media. Los valores menores que la media tienen una desviación negativa. Los valores mayores que la media tienen una desviación positiva.

**Diagonal** A diagonal of a figure is a segment that connects two nonconsecutive vertices of the figure.

**Diagonal** La diagonal de una figura es un segmento que conecta dos vértices no consecutivos de la figura.

**Diameter** A diameter is a segment that passes through the center of a circle and has both endpoints on the circle. The term diameter can also mean the length of this segment.

**Diámetro** Un diámetro es un segmento que atraviesa el centro de un círculo y tiene sus dos extremos en el círculo. El término diámetro también puede referirse a la longitud de este segmento.

# English/Spanish Glossary

**Difference** The difference is the answer you get when subtracting two numbers.

**Diferencia** La diferencia es la respuesta que obtienes cuando restas dos números.

**Dilation** A dilation is a transformation that moves each point along the ray through the point, starting from a fixed center, and multiplies distances from the center by a common scale factor. If a vertex of a figure is the center of dilation, then the vertex and its image after the dilation are the same point.

**Dilatación** Una dilatación es una transformación que mueve cada punto a lo largo de la semirrecta a través del punto, a partir de un centro fijo, y multiplica las distancias desde el centro por un factor de escala común. Si un vértice de una figura es el centro de dilatación, entonces el vértice y su imagen después de la dilatación son el mismo punto.

**Direct variation** A linear relationship that can be represented by an equation in the form $y = kx$, where $x \neq 0$.

**Dirija variación** Una relación lineal que puede ser representada por una ecuación en la forma $y = kx$, donde $x$ no iguale 0.

**Distribution (of a data set)** The distribution of a data set describes the way that its data values are spread out over all possible values. This includes describing the frequencies of each data value. The shape of a data display shows the distribution of a data set.

**Distribución (de un conjunto de datos)** La distribución de un conjunto de datos describe la manera en que sus valores se esparcen sobre todos los valores posibles. Eso incluye la descripción de las frecuencias de cada valor. La forma de una exhibición de datos muestra la distribución de un conjunto de datos.

**Distributive Property** Multiplying a number by a sum or difference gives the same result as multiplying that number by each term in the sum or difference and then adding or subtracting the corresponding products.
$a \cdot (b + c) = a \cdot b + a \cdot c$ and
$a \cdot (b - c) = a \cdot b - a \cdot c$

**Propiedad distributiva** Multiplicar un número por una suma o una diferencia da el mismo resultado que multiplicar ese mismo número por cada uno de los términos de la suma o la diferencia y después sumar o restar los productos obtenidos.
$a \cdot (b + c) = a \cdot b + a \cdot c$ and
$a \cdot (b - c) = a \cdot b - a \cdot c$

**Dividend** The dividend is the number to be divided.

**Dividendo** El dividendo es el número que se divide.

# English/Spanish Glossary

**Divisible** A number is divisible by another number if there is no remainder after dividing.

**Divisible** Un número es divisible por otro número si no hay residuo después de dividir.

**Divisor** The divisor is the number used to divide another number.

**Divisor** El divisor es el número por el cual se divide otro número.

**Dot plot** A dot plot is a statistical graph that shows the shape of a data set with stacked dots above each data value on a number line. Each dot represents one data value.

**Diagrama de puntos** Un diagrama de puntos es una gráfica estadística que muestra la forma de un conjunto de datos con puntos marcados sobre cada valor de una recta numérica. Cada punto representa un valor.

## E

**Earned wages** Earned wages are the income you receive from an employer for doing a job. Earned wages are also called gross pay.

**Sueldos ganados** Los sueldos ganados son los ingresos que usted recibe de un empleador para hacer un trabajo. Los sueldos ganados también son llamados la paga bruta.

**Easy-access loan** The term easy-access loan refers to a wide variety of loans with a streamlined application process. Many easy-access loans are short-term loans of relatively small amounts of money. They often have high interest rates.

**Préstamo de fácil-acceso** El préstamo del fácil-acceso del término se refiere a una gran variedad de préstamos con un proceso simplificado de aplicación. Muchos préstamos del fácil-acceso son préstamos a corto plazo de cantidades relativamente pequeñas de dinero. Ellos a menudo tienen los tipos de interés altos.

**Edge of a three-dimensional figure** An edge of a three-dimensional figure is a segment formed by the intersection of two faces.

**Arista de una figura tridimensional** Una arista de una figura tridimensional es un segmento formado por la intersección de dos caras.

# English/Spanish Glossary

**Enlargement** An enlargement is a dilation with a scale factor greater than 1. After an enlargement, the image is bigger than the original figure.

**Aumento** Un aumento es una dilatación con un factor de escala mayor que 1. Después de un aumento, la imagen es más grande que la figura original.

**Equation** An equation is a mathematical sentence that includes an equals sign to compare two expressions.

**Ecuación** Una ecuación es una oración matemática que incluye un signo igual para comparar dos expresiones.

**Equilateral triangle** An equilateral triangle is a triangle whose sides are all the same length.

**Triángulo equilátero** Un triángulo equilátero es un triángulo que tiene todos sus lados de la misma longitud.

**Equivalent equations** Equivalent equations are equations that have exactly the same solutions.

**Ecuaciones equivalentes** Las ecuaciones equivalentes son ecuaciones que tienen exactamente la misma solución.

**Equivalent expressions** Equivalent expressions are expressions that always have the same value.

**Expresiones equivalentes** Las expresiones equivalentes son expresiones que siempre tienen el mismo valor.

**Equivalent fractions** Equivalent fractions are fractions that name the same number.

**Fracciones equivalentes** Las fracciones equivalentes son fracciones que representan el mismo número.

**Equivalent inequalities** Equivalent inequalities are inequalities that have the same solution.

**Desigualdades equivalentes** Las desigualdades equivalentes son desigualdades que tienen la misma solución.

**Equivalent ratios** Equivalent ratios are ratios that express the same relationship.

**Razones equivalentes** Las razones equivalentes son razones que expresan la misma relación.

**Estimate** To estimate is to find a number that is close to an exact answer.

**Estimar** Estimar es hallar un número cercano a una respuesta exacta.

# English/Spanish Glossary

**Evaluate a numerical expression** To evaluate a numerical expression is to follow the order of operations.

**Evaluar una expresión numérica** Evaluar una expresión numérica es seguir el orden de las operaciones.

**Evaluate an algebraic expression** To evaluate an algebraic expression, replace each variable with a number, and then follow the order of operations.

**Evaluar una expresión algebraica** Para evaluar una expresión algebraica, reemplaza cada variable con un número y luego sigue el orden de las operaciones.

**Event** An event is a single outcome or group of outcomes from a sample space.

**Evento** Un evento es un resultado simple o un grupo de resultados de un espacio muestral.

**Expand an algebraic expression** To expand an algebraic expression, use the Distributive Property to rewrite a product as a sum or difference of terms.

**Desarrollar una expresión algebraica** Para desarrollar una expresión algebraica, usa la propiedad distributiva para reescribir el producto como una suma o diferencia de términos.

**Expected family contribution** The amount of money a student's family is expected to contribute towards the student's cost of attendance for school.

**Contribución familiar esperado** La cantidad de dinero que la familia de un estudiante es esperada contribuir hacia el estudiante es costado de asistencia para la escuela.

**Expense** Money that a business or a person needs to spend to pay for or buy something.

**Gasto** El dinero que un negocio o una persona debe gastar para pagar por o comprar algo.

**Experiment** To experiment is to try to gather information in several ways.

**Experimentar** Experimentar es intentar reunir información de varias maneras.

# English/Spanish Glossary

**Experimental probability** You find the experimental probability of an event by repeating an experiment many times and using this ratio: $P(\text{event}) =$

$$\frac{\text{number of times event occurs}}{\text{total number of trials}}$$

**Probabilidad experimental** Para hallar la probabilidad experimental de un evento, debes repetir un experimento muchas veces y usar esta razón: $P(\text{evento}) =$

$$\frac{\text{número de veces que sucede el evento}}{\text{número total de pruebas}}$$

**Explain** To explain is to give facts and details that make an idea easier to understand. Explaining can involve a written summary supported by a diagram, chart, table, or a combination of these.

**Explicar** Explicar es brindar datos y detalles para que una idea sea más fácil de comprender. Para explicar algo se puede usar un resumen escrito sustentado por un diagrama, una tabla o una combinación de esos elementos.

**Exponent** An exponent is a number that shows how many times a base is used as a factor.

**Exponente** Un exponente es un número que muestra cuántas veces se usa una base como factor.

**Expression** An expression is a mathematical phrase that can involve variables, numbers, and operations. See algebraic expression or numerical expression.

**Expresión** Una expresión es una frase matemática que puede tener variables, números y operaciones. Ver expresión algebraica o expresión numérica.

**Exterior angle of a triangle** An exterior angle of a triangle is an angle formed by a side and an extension of an adjacent side.

**Ángulo externo de un triángulo** Un ángulo externo de un triángulo es un ángulo formado por un lado y una extensión de un lado adyacente.

## F

**Face of a three-dimensional figure** A face of a three-dimensional figure is a flat surface shaped like a polygon.

**Cara de una figura tridimensional** La cara de una figura tridimensional es una superficie plana con forma de polígono.

# English/Spanish Glossary

**Factor an algebraic expression** To factor an algebraic expression, write the expression as a product.

**Descomponer una expresión algebraica en factores** Para descomponer una expresión algebraica en factores, escribe la expresión como un producto.

**Factors** Factors are numbers that are multiplied to give a product.

**Factores** Los factores son los números que se multiplican para obtener un producto.

**False equation** A false equation has values that do not equal each other on each side of the equals sign.

**Ecuación falsa** Una ecuación falsa tiene valores a cada lado del signo igual que no son iguales entre sí.

**Financial aid** Financial aid is any money offered to a student to assist with the cost of attendance.

**Ayuda financiera** La ayuda financiera es cualquier dinero ofreció a un estudiante para ayudar con el costo de asistencia.

**Financial need** A student's financial need is the difference between the student's cost of attendance and the student's expected family contribution.

**Necesidad financiera** Una necesidad financiera del estudiante es la diferencia entre el estudiante es costada de asistencia y la contribución esperado de familia de estudiante.

**Find** To find is to calculate or determine.

**Hallar** Hallar es calcular o determinar.

**First quartile** For an ordered set of data, the first quartile is the median of the lower half of the data set.

**Primer cuartil** Para un conjunto ordenado de datos, el primer cuartil es la mediana de la mitad inferior del conjunto de datos.

**Fixed expenses** Fixed expenses are expenses that do not change from one budget period to the next.

**Gastos fijos** Los gastos fijos son los gastos que no cambian de un período económico al próximo.

# English/Spanish Glossary

**Fraction** A fraction is a number that can be written in the form $\frac{a}{b}$, where $a$ is a whole number and $b$ is a positive whole number. A fraction is formed by $a$ parts of size $\frac{1}{b}$.

**Fracción** Una fracción es un número que puede expresarse de forma $\frac{a}{b}$, donde $a$ es un entero y $b$ es un número entero positivo. La fracción está formada por $a$ partes de tamaño $\frac{1}{b}$.

**Frequency** Frequency describes the number of times a specific value occurs in a data set.

**Frecuencia** La frecuencia describe el número de veces que aparece un valor específico en un conjunto de datos.

**Function** A function is a rule for taking each input value and producing exactly one output value.

**Función** Una función es una regla por la cual se toma cada valor de entrada y se produce exactamente un valor de salida.

## G

**Gap** A gap is an area of a graph that contains no data points.

**Espacio vacío o brecha** Un espacio vacío o brecha es un área de una gráfica que no contiene ningún valor.

**Grant** A type of monetary award a student can use to pay for his or her education. The student does not need to repay this money.

**Grant** Un tipo de premio monetario que un estudiante puede utilizar para pagar por su educación. El estudiante no debe devolver este dinero.

**Greater than** > The greater-than symbol shows a comparison of two numbers with the number of greater value shown first, or on the left.

**Mayor que** > El símbolo de mayor que muestra una comparación de dos números con el número de mayor valor que aparece primero, o a la izquierda.

**Greatest common factor** The greatest common factor (GCF) of two or more whole numbers is the greatest number that is a factor of all of the numbers.

**Máximo común divisor** El máximo común divisor (M.C.D.) de dos o más números enteros no negativos es el número mayor que es un factor de todos los números.

# English/Spanish Glossary

## H

**Height of a cone** The height of a cone, *h*, is the length of a segment perpendicular to the base that joins the vertex and the base.

**Altura de un cono** La altura de un cono, *h*, es la longitud de un segmento perpendicular a la base que une el vértice y la base.

**Height of a cylinder** The height of a cylinder is the length of a perpendicular segment that joins the planes of the bases.

**Altura de un cilindro** La altura de un cilindro es la longitud de un segmento perpendicular que une los planos de las bases.

**Height of a parallelogram** A height of a parallelogram is the perpendicular distance between opposite bases.

**Altura de un paralelogramo** La altura de un paralelogramo es la distancia perpendicular que existe entre las bases opuestas.

**Height of a prism** The height of a prism is the length of a perpendicular segment that joins the bases.

**Altura de un prisma** La altura de un prisma es la longitud de un segmento perpendicular que une a las bases.

**Height of a pyramid** The height of a pyramid is the length of a segment perpendicular to the base that joins the vertex and the base.

**Altura de una pirámide** La altura de una pirámide es la longitud de un segmento perpendicular a la base que une al vértice con la base.

**Height of a triangle** The height of a triangle is the length of the perpendicular segment from a vertex to the base opposite that vertex.

**Altura de un triángulo** La altura de un triángulo es la longitud del segmento perpendicular desde un vértice hasta la base opuesta a ese vértice.

**Hexagon** A hexagon is a polygon with six sides.

**Hexágono** Un hexágono es un polígono de seis lados.

# English/Spanish Glossary

**Histogram** A histogram is a statistical graph that shows the shape of a data set with vertical bars above intervals of values on a number line. The intervals are equal in size and do not overlap. The height of each bar shows the frequency of data within that interval.

**Histograma** Un histograma es una gráfica de estadísticas que muestra la forma de un conjunto de datos con barras verticales encima de intervalos de valores en una recta numérica. Los intervalos tienen el mismo tamaño y no se superponen. La altura de cada barra muestra la frecuencia de los datos dentro de ese intervalo.

**Hundredths** One hundredth is one part of 100 equal parts of a whole.

**Centésima** Una centésima es 1 de las 100 partes iguales de un todo.

**Hypotenuse** In a right triangle, the longest side, which is opposite the right angle, is the hypotenuse.

**Hipotenusa** En un triángulo rectángulo, el lado más largo, que es opuesto al ángulo recto, es la hipotenusa.

## I

**Identify** To identify is to match a definition or description to an object or to recognize something and be able to name it.

**Identificar** Identificar es unir una definición o una descripción con un objeto, o reconocer algo y poder nombrarlo.

**Identity Property of Addition** The sum of 0 and any number is that number. For any number $n$, $n + 0 = n$ and $0 + n = n$.

**Propiedad de identidad de la suma** La suma de 0 y cualquier número es ese número. Para cualquier número $n$, $n + 0 = n$ and $0 + n = n$.

**Identity Property of Multiplication** The product of 1 and any number is that number. For any number $n$, $n \cdot 1 = n$ and $1 \cdot n = n$.

**Propiedad de identidad de la multiplicación** El producto de 1 y cualquier número es ese número. Para cualquier número $n$, $n \cdot 1 = n$ and $1 \cdot n = n$.

**Illustrate** To illustrate is to show or present information, usually as a drawing or a diagram. You can also illustrate a point using a written explanation.

**Ilustrar** Ilustrar es mostrar o presentar información, generalmente en forma de dibujo o diagrama. También puedes usar una explicación escrita para ilustrar un punto.

# English/Spanish Glossary

**Image** An image is the result of a transformation of a point, line, or figure.

**Imagen** Una imagen es el resultado de una transformación de un punto, una recta o una figura.

**Improper fraction** An improper fraction is a fraction in which the numerator is greater than or equal to its denominator.

**Fracción impropia** Una fracción impropia es una fracción en la cual el numerador es mayor que o igual a su denominador.

**Included angle** An included angle is an angle that is between two sides.

**Ángulo incluido** Un ángulo incluido es un ángulo que está entre dos lados.

**Included side** An included side is a side that is between two angles.

**Lado incluido** Un lado incluido es un lado que está entre dos ángulos.

**Income** Money that a business receives. The money that a person earns from working is also called income.

**Ingresos** El dinero que un negocio recibe. El dinero que una persona gana de trabajar también es llamado los ingresos.

**Income tax** Income tax is money collected by the government based on how much you earn.

**Impuesto de renta** El impuesto de renta es dinero completo por el gobierno basado en cuánto gana.

**Independent events** Two events are independent events if the occurrence of one event does not affect the probability of the other event.

**Eventos independientes** Dos eventos son eventos independientes cuando el resultado de un evento no altera la probabilidad del otro.

**Independent variable** An independent variable is a variable whose value determines the value of another (dependent) variable.

**Variable independiente** Una variable independiente es una variable cuyo valor determina el valor de otra variable (dependiente).

**Indicate** To indicate is to point out or show.

**Indicar** Indicar es señalar o mostrar.

# English/Spanish Glossary

**Indirect measurement** Indirect measurement uses proportions and similar triangles to measure distances that would be difficult to measure directly.

**Medición indirecta** La medición indirecta usa proporciones y triángulos semejantes para medir distancias que serían difíciles de medir de forma directa.

**Inequality** An inequality is a mathematical sentence that uses $<$, $\leq$, $>$, $\geq$, or $\neq$ to compare two quantities.

**Desigualdad** Una desigualdad es una oración matemática que usa $<$, $\leq$, $>$, $\geq$, o $\neq$ para comparar dos cantidades.

**Inference** An inference is a judgment made by interpreting data.

**Inferencia** Una inferencia es una opinión que se forma al interpretar datos.

**Infinitely many solutions** A linear equation in one variable has infinitely many solutions if any value of the variable makes the two sides of the equation equal.

**Número infinito de soluciones** Una ecuación lineal en una variable tiene un número infinito de soluciones si cualquier valor de la variable hace que los dos lados de la ecuación sean iguales.

**Initial value** The initial value of a linear function is the value of the output when the input is 0.

**Valor inicial** El valor inicial de una función lineal es el valor de salida cuando el valor de entrada es 0.

**Integers** Integers are the set of positive whole numbers, their opposites, and 0.

**Enteros** Los enteros son el conjunto de los números enteros positivos, sus opuestos y 0.

**Interest** When you deposit money in a bank account, the bank pays you interest for the right to use your money for a period of time.

**Interés** Cuando depositas dinero en una cuenta bancaria, el banco te paga un interés por el derecho a usar tu dinero por un período de tiempo.

**Interest period** The length of time on which compound interest is based. The total number of interest periods that you keep the money in the account is represented by the variable $n$.

**Período de interés** La cantidad de tiempo sobre la que se calcula el interés compuesto. El número total de períodos de interés que mantienes el dinero en la cuenta se representa con la variable $n$.

# English/Spanish Glossary

**Interest rate** Interest is calculated based on a percent of the principal. That percent is called the interest rate ($r$).

**Tasa de interés** El interés se calcula con base en un porcentaje del capital. Ese porcentaje se llama tasa de interés, ($r$).

**Interest rate for an interest period** The interest rate for an interest period is the annual interest rate divided by the number of interest periods per year.

**El tipo de interés por un período de interés** El tipo de interés por un período de interés es el tipo de interés anual dividido por el número de períodos de interés por año.

**Interquartile range** The interquartile range (IQR) is the distance between the first and third quartiles of the data set. It represents the spread of the middle 50% of the data values.

**Rango intercuartil** El rango intercuartil es la distancia entre el primer y el tercer cuartil del conjunto de datos. Representa la ubicación del 50% del medio de los valores.

**Interval** An interval is a period of time between two points of time or events.

**Intervalo** Un intervalo es un período de tiempo entre dos puntos en el tiempo o entre dos sucesos.

**Invalid inference** An invalid inference is false about the population, or does not follow from the available data. A biased sample can lead to invalid inferences.

**Inferencia inválida** Una inferencia inválida es una inferencia falsa acerca de una población, o no se deduce a partir de los datos disponibles. Una muestra sesgada puede llevar a inferencias inválidas.

**Inverse operations** Inverse operations are operations that undo each other.

**Operaciones inversas** Las operaciones inversas son operaciones que se cancelan entre sí.

**Inverse property of addition** Every number has an additive inverse. The sum of a number and its additive inverse is zero.

**Propiedad inversa de la suma** Todos los números tienen un inverso de suma. La suma de un número y su inverso de suma es cero.

# English/Spanish Glossary

**Irrational numbers** An irrational number is a number that cannot be written in the form $\frac{a}{b}$, where $a$ and $b$ are integers and $b \neq 0$. In decimal form, an irrational number cannot be written as a terminating or repeating decimal.

**Números irracionales** Un número irracional es un número que no se puede escribir en la forma $\frac{a}{b}$ donde $a$ y $b$, son enteros y $b \neq 0$. Los números racionales en forma decimal no son finitos y no son periódicos.

**Isolate a variable** When solving equations, to isolate a variable means to get a variable with a coefficient of 1 alone on one side of an equation. Use the properties of equality and inverse operations to isolate a variable.

**Aislar una variable** Cuando resuelves ecuaciones, aislar una variable significa poner una variable con un coeficiente de 1 sola a un lado de la ecuación. Usa las propiedades de igualdad y las operaciones inversas para aislar una variable.

**Isosceles triangle** An isosceles triangle is a triangle with at least two sides that are the same length.

**Triángulo isósceles** Un triángulo isósceles es un triángulo que tiene al menos dos lados de la misma longitud.

## J

**Justify** To justify is to support your answer with reasons or examples. A justification may include a written response, diagrams, charts, tables, or a combination of these.

**Justificar** Justificar es apoyar tu respuesta con razones o ejemplos. Una justificación puede incluir una respuesta escrita, diagramas, tablas o una combinación de esos elementos.

## L

**Lateral area of a cone** The lateral area of a cone is the area of its lateral surface. The formula for the lateral area of a cone is L.A. $= \pi r \ell$, where $r$ represents the radius of the base and $\ell$ represents the slant height of the cone.

**Área lateral de un cono** El área lateral de un cono es el área de su superficie lateral. La fórmula del área lateral de un cono es A.L. $= \pi r \ell$, donde $r$ representa el radio de la base y $\ell$ representa la altura inclinada del cono.

# English/Spanish Glossary

**Lateral area of a cylinder** The lateral area of a cylinder is the area of its lateral surface. The formula for the lateral area of a cylinder is L.A. = $2\pi rh$, where $r$ represents the radius of a base and $h$ represents the height of the cylinder.

**Área lateral de un cilindro** El área lateral de un cilindro es el área de su superficie lateral. La fórmula del área lateral de un cilindro es A.L. = $2\pi rh$, donde $r$ representa el radio de una base y $h$ representa la altura del cilindro.

**Lateral area of a prism** The lateral area of a prism is the sum of the areas of the lateral faces of the prism. The formula for the lateral area, L.A., of a prism is L.A. = $ph$, where $p$ represents the perimeter of the base and $h$ represents the height of the prism.

**Área lateral de un prisma** El área lateral de un prisma es la suma de las áreas de las caras laterales del prisma. La fórmula del área lateral, A.L., de un prisma es A.L. = $ph$, donde $p$ representa el perímetro de la base y $h$ representa la altura del prisma.

**Lateral area of a pyramid** The lateral area of a pyramid is the sum of the areas of the lateral faces of the pyramid. The formula for the lateral area, L.A., of a pyramid is L.A. = $\frac{1}{2}p\ell$ where $p$ represents the perimeter of the base and $\ell$ represents the slant height of the pyramid.

**Área lateral de una pirámide** El área lateral de una pirámide es la suma de las áreas de las caras laterales de la pirámide. La fórmula del área lateral, A.L., de una pirámide es A.L. = $\frac{1}{2}p\ell$ donde $p$ representa el perímetro de la base y $\ell$ representa la altura inclinada de la pirámide.

**Lateral face of a prism** A lateral face of a prism is a face that joins the bases of the prism.

**Cara lateral de un prisma** La cara lateral de un prisma es la cara que une a las bases del prisma.

**Lateral face of a pyramid** A lateral face of a pyramid is a triangular face that joins the base and the vertex.

**Cara lateral de una pirámide** La cara lateral de una pirámide es una cara lateral que une a la base con el vértice.

**Lateral surface of a cone** The lateral surface of a cone is the curved surface that is not included in the base.

**Superficie lateral de un cono** La superficie lateral de un cono es la superficie curva que no está incluida en la base.

# English/Spanish Glossary

**Lateral surface of a cylinder** The lateral surface of a cylinder is the curved surface that is not included in the bases.

**Superficie lateral de un cilindro** La superficie lateral de un cilindro es la superficie curva que no está incluida en las bases.

**Least common multiple** The least common multiple (LCM) of two or more numbers is the least multiple shared by all of the numbers.

**Mínimo común múltiplo** El mínimo común múltiplo (MCM) de dos o más números es el múltiplo menor compartido por todos los números.

**Leg of a right triangle** In a right triangle, the two shortest sides are legs.

**Cateto de un triángulo rectángulo** En un triángulo rectángulo, los dos lados más cortos son los catetos.

**Less than** $<$ The less-than symbol shows a comparison of two numbers with the number of lesser value shown first, or on the left.

**Menor que** $<$ El símbolo de menor que muestra una comparación de dos números con el número de menor valor que aparece primero, o a la izquierda.

**Liability** A liability is money that you owe.

**Obligación** Una obligación es dinero que usted debe.

**Lifetime income** The amount of money earned over a lifetime of working.

**Ingresos para toda la vida** La cantidad de dinero ganó sobre una vida de trabajar.

**Like terms** Terms that have identical variable parts are like terms.

**Términos semejantes** Los términos que tienen partes variables idénticas son términos semejantes.

**Line of reflection** A line of reflection is a line across which a figure is reflected.

**Eje de reflexión** Un eje de reflexión es una línea a través de la cual se refleja una figura.

**Linear equation** An equation is a linear equation if the graph of all of its solutions is a line.

**Ecuación lineal** Una ecuación es lineal si la gráfica de todas sus soluciones es una línea recta.

# English/Spanish Glossary

**Linear function** A linear function is a function whose graph is a straight line. The rate of change for a linear function is constant.

**Función lineal** Una función lineal es una función cuya gráfica es una línea recta. La tasa de cambio en una función lineal es constante.

**Linear function rule** A linear function rule is an equation that describes a linear function.

**Regla de la función lineal** La ecuación que describe una función lineal es la regla de la función lineal.

**Loan** A loan is an amount of money borrowed for a period of time with the promise of paying it back.

**Préstamo** Un préstamo es una cantidad de dinero pedido prestaddo por un espacio de tiempo con la promesa de pagarlo apoya.

**Loan length** Loan length is the period of time set to repay a loan.

**Preste longitud** La longitud del préstamo es el conjunto de espacio de tiempo de devolver un préstamo.

**Loan term** The term of a loan is the period of time set to repay the loan.

**Preste término** El término de un préstamo es el conjunto de espacio de tiempo de devolver el préstamo.

**Locate** To locate is to find or identify a value, usually on a number line or coordinate graph.

**Ubicar** Ubicar es hallar o identificar un valor, generalmente en una recta numérica o en una gráfica de coordenadas.

**Loss** When a business's expenses are greater than the business's income, there is a loss.

**Pérdida** Cuando los gastos de un negocio son más que los ingresos del negocio, hay una pérdida.

**Mapping diagram** A mapping diagram describes a relation by linking the input values to the corresponding output values using arrows.

**Diagrama de correspondencia** Un diagrama de correspondencia describe una relación uniendo con flechas los valores de entrada con sus correspondientes valores de salida.

**Markdown** Markdown is the amount of decrease from the selling price to the sale price. The markdown as a percent decrease of the original selling price is called the percent markdown.

**Rebaja** La rebaja es la cantidad de disminución de un precio de venta a un precio rebajado. La rebaja como una disminución porcentual del precio de venta original se llama porcentaje de rebaja.

**Markup** Markup is the amount of increase from the cost to the selling price. The markup as a percent increase of the original cost is called the percent markup.

**Margen de ganancia** El margen de ganancia es la cantidad de aumento del costo al precio de venta. El margen de ganancia como un aumento porcentual del costo original se llama porcentaje del margen de ganancia.

**Mean** The mean represents the center of a numerical data set. To find the mean, sum the data values and then divide by the number of values in the data set.

**Media** La media representa el centro de un conjunto de datos numéricos. Para hallar la media, suma los valores y luego divide por el número de valores del conjunto de datos.

**Mean absolute deviation** The mean absolute deviation is a measure of variability that describes how much the data values are spread out from the mean of a data set. The mean absolute deviation is the average distance that the data values are spread around the mean.

$$\text{mean absolute deviation} = \frac{\text{sum of the absolute deviations of the data values}}{\text{total number of data values}}$$

**Desviación absoluta media** La desviación absoluta media es una medida de variabilidad que describe cuánto se alejan los valores de la media de un conjunto de datos. La desviación absoluta media es la distancia promedio que los valores se alejan de la media.

$$\text{desviación absoluta media} = \frac{\text{suma de las desviaciones absolutas de los valores}}{\text{número total de valores}}$$

# English/Spanish Glossary

**Measure of variability** A measure of variability describes the spread of values in a data set. There may be more than one measure of variability for a data set.

**Medida de variabilidad** Una medida de variabilidad describe la distribución de los valores de un conjunto de datos. Puede haber más de una medida de variabilidad para un conjunto de datos.

**Measurement data** Measurement data consist of data that are measures.

**Datos de mediciones** Los datos de mediciones son datos que son medidas.

**Measures of center** A measure of center is a value that represents the middle of a data set. There may be more than one measure of center for a data set.

**Medida de tendencia central** Una medida de tendencia central es un valor que representa el centro de un conjunto de datos. Puede haber más de una medida de tendencia central para un conjunto de datos.

**Median** The median represents the center of a numerical data set. For an odd number of data values, the median is the middle value when the data values are arranged in numerical order. For an even number of data values, the median is the average of the two middle values when the data values are arranged in numerical order.

**Mediana** La mediana representa el centro de un conjunto de datos numéricos. Para un número impar de valores, la mediana es el valor del medio cuando los valores están organizados en orden numérico. Para un número par de valores, la mediana es el promedio de los dos valores del medio cuando los valores están organizados en orden numérico.

**Median-median line** The median-median line, or median trend line, is a method of finding a fit line for a scatter plot that suggests a linear association. This method involves dividing the data into three subgroups and using medians to find a summary point for each subgroup. The summary points are used to find the equation of the fit line.

**Recta mediana-mediana** La recta mediana-mediana es un método que se usa para hallar una línea de ajuste para un diagrama de dispersión que sugiere una asociación lineal. Este método implica dividir los datos en tres subgrupos y usar medianas para hallar un punto medio para cada subgrupo. Los puntos medios se usan para hallar la ecuación de la línea de ajuste.

**Million** Whole numbers in the millions have 7, 8, or 9 digits.

**Millón** Los números enteros no negativos que están en los millones tienen 7, 8 ó 9 dígitos.

# English/Spanish Glossary

**Mixed number** A mixed number combines a whole number and a fraction.

**Número mixto** Un número mixto combina un número entero no negativo con una fracción.

**Mode** The item, or items, in a data set that occurs most frequently.

**Modo** El artículo, o los artículos, en un conjunto de datos que ocurre normalmente.

**Model** To model is to represent a situation using pictures, diagrams, or number sentences.

**Demostrar** Demostrar es usar ilustraciones, diagramas o enunciados numéricos para representar una situación.

**Monetary incentive** A monetary incentive is an offer that might encourage customers to buy a product.

**Estímulo monetario** Un estímulo monetario es una oferta que quizás favorezca a clientes para comprar un producto.

**Multiple** A multiple of a number is the product of the number and a whole number.

**Múltiplo** El múltiplo de un número es el producto del número y un número entero no negativo.

## N

**Natural numbers** The natural numbers are the counting numbers.

**Números naturales** Los números naturales son los números que se usan para contar.

**Negative exponent property** For every nonzero number $a$ and integer $n$, $a^{-n} = \frac{1}{a^n}$.

**Propiedad del exponente negativo** Para todo número distinto de cero $a$ y entero $n$, $a^{-n} = \frac{1}{a^n}$.

**Negative numbers** Negative numbers are numbers less than zero.

**Números negativos** Los números negativos son números menores que cero.

# English/Spanish Glossary

**Net** A net is a two-dimensional pattern that you can fold to form a three-dimensional figure. A net of a figure shows all of the surfaces of that figure in one view.

**Modelo plano** Un modelo plano es un diseño bidimensional que puedes doblar para formar una figura tridimensional. Un modelo plano de una figura muestra todas las superficies de la figura en una vista.

**Net worth** Net worth is the total value of all assets minus the total value of all liabilities.

**Patrimonio neto** El patrimonio neto es el valor total de todas las ventajas menos el valor total de todas las obligaciones.

**Net worth statement** Net worth is the total value of all assets minus the total value of all liabilities.

**Declaración de patrimonio neto** El patrimonio neto es el valor total de todas las ventajas menos el valor total de todas las obligaciones.

**No solution** A linear equation in one variable has no solution if no value of the variable makes the two sides of the equation equal.

**Sin solución** Una ecuación lineal en una variable no tiene solución si ningún valor de la variable hace que los dos lados de la ecuación sean iguales.

**Nonlinear function** A nonlinear function is a function that does not have a constant rate of change.

**Función no lineal** Una función no lineal es una función que no tiene una tasa de cambio constante.

**Numerator** The numerator is the number above the fraction bar in a fraction.

**Numerador** El numerador es el número que está arriba de la barra de fracción en una fracción.

**Numerical expression** A numerical expression is a mathematical phrase that consists of numbers and operation symbols.

**Expresión numérica** Una expresión numérica es una frase matemática que contiene números y símbolos de operaciones.

# English/Spanish Glossary

O

**Obtuse angle** An obtuse angle is an angle with a measure greater than 90° and less than 180°.

**Ángulo obtuso** Un ángulo obtuso es un ángulo con una medida mayor que 90° y menor que 180°.

**Obtuse triangle** An obtuse triangle is a triangle with one obtuse angle.

**Triángulo obtusángulo** Un triángulo obtusángulo es un triángulo que tiene un ángulo obtuso.

**Octagon** An octagon is a polygon with eight sides.

**Octágono** Un octágono es un polígono de ocho lados.

**Online payment system** An online payment system allows money to be exchanged electronically between buyer and seller, usually using credit card or bank account information.

**Sistema en línea de pago** Un sistema en línea del pago permite dinero para ser cambiado electrónicamente entre comprador y vendedor, utilizando generalmente información de tarjeta de crédito o cuenta bancaria.

**Open sentence** An open sentence is an equation with one or more variables.

**Enunciado abierto** Un enunciado abierto es una ecuación con una o más variables.

**Opposites** Opposites are two numbers that are the same distance from 0 on a number line, but in opposite directions.

**Opuestos** Los opuestos son dos números que están a la misma distancia de 0 en la recta numérica, pero en direcciones opuestas.

**Order of operations** The order of operations is the order in which operations should be performed in an expression. Operations inside parentheses are done first, followed by exponents. Then, multiplication and division are done in order from left to right, and finally addition and subtraction are done in order from left to right.

**Orden de las operaciones** El orden de las operaciones es el orden en el que se deben resolver las operaciones de una expresión. Las operaciones que están entre paréntesis se resuelven primero, seguidas de los exponentes. Luego, se multiplica y se divide en orden de izquierda a derecha, y finalmente se suma y se resta en orden de izquierda a derecha.

# English/Spanish Glossary

**Ordered pair** An ordered pair identifies the location of a point in the coordinate plane. The *x*-coordinate shows a point's position left or right of the *y*-axis. The *y*-coordinate shows a point's position up or down from the *x*-axis.

**Par ordenado** Un par ordenado identifica la ubicación de un punto en el plano de coordenadas. La coordenada *x* muestra la posición de un punto a la izquierda o a la derecha del eje de las *y*. La coordenada *y* muestra la posición de un punto arriba o abajo del eje de las *x*.

**Origin** The origin is the point of intersection of the *x*- and *y*-axes on a coordinate plane.

**Origen** El origen es el punto de intersección del eje de las *x* y el eje de las *y* en un plano de coordenadas.

**Outcome** An outcome is a possible result of an action.

**Resultado** Un resultado es un desenlace posible de una acción.

**Outlier** An outlier is a piece of data that doesn't seem to fit with the rest of a data set.

**Valor extremo** Un valor extremo es un valor que parece no ajustarse al resto de los datos de un conjunto.

## P

**Parallel lines** Parallel lines are lines in the same plane that never intersect.

**Rectas paralelas** Las rectas paralelas son rectas que están en el mismo plano y nunca se intersecan.

**Parallelogram** A parallelogram is a quadrilateral with both pairs of opposite sides parallel.

**Paralelogramo** Un paralelogramo es un cuadrilátero en el cual los dos pares de lados opuestos son paralelos.

**Partial product** A partial product is part of the total product. A product is the sum of the partial products.

**Producto parcial** Un producto parcial es una parte del producto total. Un producto es la suma de los productos parciales.

# English/Spanish Glossary

**Pay period** Wages for many jobs are paid at regular intervals, such a weekly, biweekly, semimonthly, or monthly. The interval of time is called a pay period.

**Pague el período** Los sueldos para muchos trabajos son pagados con regularidad, tal semanal, quincenal, quincenal, o mensual. El intervalo de tiempo es llamado un período de la paga.

**Payroll deductions** Your employer can deduct your income taxes from your wages before you receive your paycheck. The amounts deducted are called payroll deductions.

**Deducciones de nómina** Su empleador puede descontar sus impuestos de renta de sus sueldos antes que reciba su cheque de pago. Las cantidades descontadas son llamadas nómina deducciones.

**Percent** A percent is a ratio that compares a number to 100.

**Porcentaje** Un porcentaje es una razón que compara un número con 100.

**Percent bar graph** A percent bar graph is a bar graph that shows each category as a percent of the total number of data items.

**Gráfico de barras de por ciento** Un gráfico de barras del por ciento es un gráfico de barras que muestra cada categoría como un por ciento del número total de artículos de datos.

**Percent decrease** When a quantity decreases, the percent of change is called a percent decrease. percent decrease = $\dfrac{\text{amount of decrease}}{\text{original quantity}}$

**Disminución porcentual** Cuando una cantidad disminuye, el porcentaje de cambio se llama disminución porcentual. disminución porcentual = $\dfrac{\text{cantidad de disminución}}{\text{cantidad original}}$

**Percent equation** The percent equation describes the relationship between a part and a whole. You can use the percent equation to solve percent problems. part = percent · whole

**Ecuación de porcentaje** La ecuación de porcentaje describe la relación entre una parte y un todo. Puedes usar la ecuación de porcentaje para resolver problemas de porcentaje. parte = por ciento · todo

**Percent error** Percent error describes the accuracy of a measured or estimated value compared to an actual or accepted value.

**Error porcentual** El error porcentual describe la exactitud de un valor medido o estimado en comparación con un valor real o aceptado.

# English/Spanish Glossary

**Percent increase** When a quantity increases, the percent of change is called a percent increase.

**Aumento porcentual** Cuando una cantidad aumenta, el porcentaje de cambio se llama aumento porcentual.

**Percent of change** Percent of change is the percent something increases or decreases from its original measure or amount. You can find the percent of change by using the equation: percent of change = amount of change original quantity

**Porcentaje de cambio** El porcentaje de cambio es el porcentaje en que algo aumenta o disminuye en relación a la medida o cantidad original. Puedes hallar el porcentaje de cambio con la siguiente ecuación: porcentaje de cambio = cantidad de cambio cantidad original

**Perfect cube** A perfect cube is the cube of an integer.

**Cubo perfecto** Un cubo perfecto es el cubo de un entero.

**Perfect square** A perfect square is a number that is the square of an integer.

**Cuadrado perfecto** Un cuadrado perfecto es un número que es el cuadrado de un entero.

**Perimeter** Perimeter is the distance around a figure.

**Perímetro** El perímetro es la distancia alrededor de una figura.

**Period** A period is a group of 3 digits in a number. Periods are separated by a comma and start from the right of a number.

**Período** Un período es un grupo de 3 dígitos en un número. Los períodos están separados por una coma y empiezan a la derecha del número.

**Periodic savings plan** A periodic savings plan is a method of saving that involves making deposits on a regular basis.

**Plan de ahorros periódico** Un plan de ahorros periódico es un método de guardar que implica depósitos que hace con regularidad.

**Perpendicular lines** Perpendicular lines intersect to form right angles.

**Rectas perpendiculares** Las rectas perpendiculares se intersecan para formar ángulos rectos.

# English/Spanish Glossary

**Pi** Pi ($\pi$) is the ratio of a circle's circumference, *C*, to its diameter, *d*.

**Pi** Pi ($\pi$) es la razón de la circunferencia de un círculo, *C*, a su diámetro, *d*.

**Place value** Place value is the value given to an individual digit based on its position within a number.

**Valor posicional** El valor posicional es el valor asignado a determinado dígito según su posición en un número.

**Plane** A plane is a flat surface that extends indefinitely in all directions.

**Plano** Un plano es una superficie plana que se extiende indefinidamente en todas direcciones.

**Polygon** A polygon is a closed figure formed by three or more line segments that do not cross.

**Polígono** Un polígono es una figura cerrada compuesta por tres o más segmentos que no se cruzan.

**Population** A population is the complete set of items being studied.

**Población** Una población es todo el conjunto de elementos que se estudian.

**Positive numbers** Positive numbers are numbers greater than zero.

**Números positivos** Los números positivos son números mayores que cero.

**Power** A power is a number expressed using an exponent.

**Potencia** Una potencia es un número expresado con un exponente.

**Predict** To predict is to make an educated guess based on the analysis of real data.

**Predecir** Predecir es hacer una estimación informada según el análisis de datos reales.

**Prime factorization** The prime factorization of a composite number is the expression of the number as a product of its prime factors.

**Descomposición en factores primos** La descomposición en factores primos de un número compuesto es la expresión del número como un producto de sus factores primos.

# English/Spanish Glossary

**Prime number** A prime number is a whole number greater than 1 with exactly two factors, 1 and the number itself.

**Número primo** Un número primo es un número entero mayor que 1 con exactamente dos factores, 1 y el número mismo.

**Principal** The original amount of money deposited or borrowed in an account.

**Capital** La cantidad original de dinero que se deposita o se pide prestada en una cuenta.

**Prism** A prism is a three-dimensional figure with two parallel polygonal faces that are the same size and shape.

**Prisma** Un prisma es una figura tridimensional con dos caras poligonales paralelas que tienen el mismo tamaño y la misma forma.

**Probability model** A probability model consists of an action, its sample space, and a list of events with their probabilities. The events and probabilities in the list have these characteristics: each outcome in the sample space is in exactly one event, and the sum of all of the probabilities must be 1.

**Modelo de probabilidad** Un modelo de probabilidad consiste en una acción, su espacio muestral y una lista de eventos con sus probabilidades. Los eventos y las probabilidades de la lista tienen estas características: cada resultado del espacio muestral está exactamente en un evento, y la suma de todas las probabilidades debe ser 1.

**Probability of an event** The probability of an event is a number from 0 to 1 that measures the likelihood that the event will occur. The closer the probability is to 0, the less likely it is that the event will happen. The closer the probability is to 1, the more likely it is that the event will happen. You can express probability as a fraction, decimal, or percent.

**Probabilidad de un evento** La probabilidad de un evento es un número de 0 a 1 que mide la probabilidad de que suceda el evento. Cuanto más se acerca la probabilidad a 0, menos probable es que suceda el evento. Cuanto más se acerca la probabilidad a 1, más probable es que suceda el evento. Puedes expresar la probabilidad como una fracción, un decimal o un porcentaje.

**Product** A product is the value of a multiplication or an expression showing multiplication.

**Producto** Un producto es el valor de una multiplicación o una expresión que representa la multiplicación.

# English/Spanish Glossary

**Profit** When a business's expenses are less than the business's income, there is a profit.

**Ganancia** Cuando los gastos de un negocio son menos que los ingresos del negocio, hay una ganancia.

**Proof** A proof is a logical, deductive argument in which every statement of fact is supported by a reason.

**Comprobación** Una comprobación es un argumento lógico y deductivo en el que cada enunciado de un hecho está apoyado por una razón.

**Proper fraction** A proper fraction has a numerator that is less than its denominator.

**Fracción propia** Una fracción propia tiene un numerador que es menor que su denominador.

**Proportion** A proportion is an equation stating that two ratios are equal.

**Proporción** Una proporción es una ecuación que establece que dos razones son iguales.

**Proportional relationship** Two quantities $x$ and $y$ have a proportional relationship if $y$ is always a constant multiple of $x$. A relationship is proportional if it can be described by equivalent ratios.

**Relación de proporción** Dos cantidades $x$ y $y$ tienen una relación de proporción si $y$ es siempre un múltiplo constante de $x$. Una relación es de proporción si se puede describir con razones equivalentes.

**Pyramid** A pyramid is a three-dimensional figure with a base that is a polygon and triangular faces that meet at a vertex. A pyramid is named for the shape of its base.

**Pirámide** Una pirámide es una figura tridimensional con una base que es un polígono y caras triangulares que se unen en un vértice. El nombre de la pirámide depende de la forma de su base.

# English/Spanish Glossary

**Pythagorean Theorem** In any right triangle, the sum of the squares of the lengths of the legs equals the square of the length of the hypotenuse. If a triangle is a right triangle, then $a^2 + b^2 = c^2$, where $a$ and $b$ represent the lengths of the legs, and $c$ represents the length of the hypotenuse.

**Teorema de Pitágoras** En cualquier triángulo rectángulo, la suma del cuadrado de la longitud de los catetos es igual al cuadrado de la longitud de la hipotenusa. Si un triángulo es un triángulo rectángulo, entonces $a^2 + b^2 = c^2$, donde $a$ y $b$ representan la longitud de los catetos, y $c$ representa la longitud de la hipotenusa.

## Q

**Quadrant** The $x$- and $y$-axes divide the coordinate plane into four regions called quadrants.

**Cuadrante** Los ejes de las $x$ y de las $y$ dividen el plano de coordenadas en cuatro regiones llamadas cuadrantes.

**Quadrilateral** A quadrilateral is a polygon with four sides.

**Cuadrilátero** Un cuadrilátero es un polígono de cuatro lados.

**Quarter circle** A quarter circle is one fourth of a circle.

**Círculo cuarto** Un círculo cuarto es la cuarta parte de un círculo.

**Quartile** The quartiles of a data set divide the data set into four parts with the same number of data values in each part.

**Cuartil** Los cuartiles de un conjunto de datos dividen el conjunto de datos en cuatro partes que tienen el mismo número de valores cada una.

**Quotient** The quotient is the answer to a division problem. When there is a remainder, "quotient" sometimes refers to the whole-number portion of the answer.

**Cociente** El cociente es el resultado de una división. Cuando queda un residuo, "cociente" a veces se refiere a la parte de la solución que es un número entero.

# English/Spanish Glossary

## R

**Radius** A radius of a circle is a segment that has one endpoint at the center and the other endpoint on the circle. The term radius can also mean the length of this segment.

**Radio** Un radio de un círculo es un segmento que tiene un extremo en el centro y el otro extremo en el círculo. El término radio también puede referirse a la longitud de este segmento.

**Radius of a sphere** The radius of a sphere, *r*, is a segment that has one endpoint at the center and the other endpoint on the sphere.

**Radio de una esfera** El radio de una esfera, *r*, es un segmento que tiene un extremo en el centro y el otro extremo en la esfera.

**Random sample** In a random sample, each member in the population has an equal chance of being selected.

**Muestra aleatoria** En una muestra aleatoria, cada miembro en la población tiene una oportunidad igual de ser seleccionado.

**Range** The range is a measure of variability of a numerical data set. The range of a data set is the difference between the greatest and least values in a data set.

**Rango** El rango es una medida de la variabilidad de un conjunto de datos numéricos. El rango de un conjunto de datos es la diferencia que existe entre el mayor y el menor valor del conjunto.

**Rate** A rate is a ratio involving two quantities measured in different units.

**Tasa** Una tasa es una razón que relaciona dos cantidades medidas con unidades diferentes.

**Rate of change** The rate of change of a linear function is the ratio vertical change horizontal change between any two points on the graph of the function.

**Tasa de cambio** La tasa de cambio de una función lineal es la razón del cambio vertical cambio horizontal que existe entre dos puntos cualesquiera de la gráfica de la función.

**Ratio** A ratio is a relationship in which for every *x* units of one quantity there are *y* units of another quantity.

**Razón** Una razón es una relación en la cual por cada *x* unidades de una cantidad hay *y* unidades de otra cantidad.

# English/Spanish Glossary

**Rational numbers** A rational number is a number that can be written in the form $\frac{a}{b}$ or $-\frac{a}{b}$, where $a$ is a whole number and $b$ is a positive whole number. The rational numbers include the integers.

**Números racionales** Un número racional es un número que se puede escribir como $\frac{a}{b}$ or $-\frac{a}{b}$, donde $a$ es un número entero no negativo y $b$ es un número entero positivo. Los números racionales incluyen los enteros.

**Real numbers** The real numbers are the set of rational and irrational numbers.

**Números reales** Los números reales son el conjunto de los números racionales e irracionales.

**Reason** To reason is to think through a problem using facts and information.

**Razonar** Razonar es usar hechos e información para estudiar detenidamente un problema.

**Rebate** A rebate returns part of the purchase price of an item after the buyer provides proof of purchase through a mail-in or online form.

**Reembolso** Un reembolso regresa la parte del precio de compra de un artículo después de que el comprador proporcione comprobante de compra por un correo-en o forma en línea.

**Recall** To recall is to remember a fact quickly.

**Recordar** Recordar es traer a la memoria un hecho rápidamente.

**Reciprocals** Two numbers are reciprocals if their product is 1. If a nonzero number is named as a fraction, $\frac{a}{b}$, then its reciprocal is $\frac{b}{a}$.

**Recíprocos** Dos números son recíprocos si su producto es 1. Si un número distinto de cero se expresa como una fracción, $\frac{a}{b}$, entonces su recíproco es $\frac{b}{a}$.

**Rectangle** A rectangle is a quadrilateral with four right angles.

**Rectángulo** Un rectángulo es un cuadrilátero que tiene cuatro ángulos rectos.

**Rectangular prism** A rectangular prism is a prism with bases in the shape of a rectangle.

**Prisma rectangular** Un prisma rectangular es un prisma cuyas bases tienen la forma de un rectángulo.

# English/Spanish Glossary

**Reduction** A reduction is a dilation with a scale factor less than 1. After a reduction, the image is smaller than the original figure.

**Reducción** Una reducción es una dilatación con un factor de escala menor que 1. Después de una reducción, la imagen es más pequeña que la figura original.

**Reflection** A reflection, or flip, is a transformation that flips a figure across a line of reflection.

**Reflexión** Una reflexión, o inversión, es una transformación que invierte una figura a través de un eje de reflexión.

**Regular polygon** A regular polygon is a polygon with all sides of equal length and all angles of equal measure.

**Polígono regular** Un polígono regular es un polígono que tiene todos los lados de la misma longitud y todos los ángulos de la misma medida.

**Relate** To relate two different things, find a connection between them.

**Relacionar** Para relacionar dos cosas diferentes, halla una conexión entre ellas.

**Relation** Any set of ordered pairs is called a relation.

**Relación** Todo conjunto de pares ordenados se llama relación.

**Relative frequency** relative frequency

of an event $= \dfrac{\text{number of times event occurs}}{\text{total number of trials}}$

**Frecuencia relativa** frecuencia relativa de un evento $=$

$\dfrac{\text{número de veces que sucede el evento}}{\text{número total de pruebas}}$

**Relative frequency table** A relative frequency table shows the ratio of the number of data in each category to the total number of data items. The ratio can be expressed as a fraction, decimal, or percent.

**Mesa relativa de frecuencia** Una mesa relativa de la frecuencia muestra la proporción del número de datos en cada categoría al número total de artículos de datos. La proporción puede ser expresada como una fracción, el decimal, o el por ciento.

**Remainder** In division, the remainder is the number that is left after the division is complete.

**Residuo** En una división, el residuo es el número que queda después de terminar la operación.

# English/Spanish Glossary

**Remote interior angles** Remote interior angles are the two nonadjacent interior angles corresponding to each exterior angle of a triangle.

**Ángulos internos no adyacentes** Los ángulos internos no adyacentes son los dos ángulos internos de un triángulo que se corresponden con el ángulo externo que está más alejado de ellos.

**Repeating decimal** A repeating decimal has a decimal expansion that repeats the same digit, or block of digits, without end.

**Decimal periódico** Un decimal periódico tiene una expansión decimal que repite el mismo dígito, o grupo de dígitos, sin fin.

**Represent** To represent is to stand for or take the place of something else. Symbols, equations, charts, and tables are often used to represent particular situations.

**Representar** Representar es sustituir u ocupar el lugar de otra cosa. A menudo se usan símbolos, ecuaciones y tablas para representar determinadas situaciones.

**Representative sample** A representative sample is a sample of a population in which the number of subjects in the sample with the trait that you are studying is proportional to the number of members in the population with that trait. A representative sample accurately represents the population and does not have bias.

**Muestra representativa** Una muestra representativa es una muestra de una población en la que el número de sujetos de la muestra que tiene la característica que se estudia es proporcional al número de miembros de la población que tienen esa característica. Una muestra representativa representa la población con exactitud y no está sesgada.

**Rhombus** A rhombus is a parallelogram whose sides are all the same length.

**Rombo** Un rombo es un paralelogramo que tiene todos sus lados de la misma longitud.

**Right angle** A right angle is an angle with a measure of 90°.

**Ángulo recto** Un ángulo recto es un ángulo que mide 90°.

**Right cone** A right cone is a cone in which the segment representing the height connects the vertex and the center of the base.

**Cono recto** Un cono recto es un cono en el que el segmento que representa la altura une el vértice y el centro de la base.

# English/Spanish Glossary

**Right cylinder** A right cylinder is a cylinder in which the height joins the centers of the bases.

**Cilindro recto** Un cilindro recto es un cilindro en el que la altura une los centros de las bases.

**Right prism** In a right prism, all lateral faces are rectangles.

**Prisma recto** En un prisma recto, todas las caras laterales son rectángulos.

**Right pyramid** In a right pyramid, the segment that represents the height intersects the base at its center.

**Pirámide recta** En una pirámide recta, el segmento que representa la altura interseca la base en el centro.

**Right triangle** A right triangle is a triangle with one right angle.

**Triángulo rectángulo** Un triángulo rectángulo es un triángulo que tiene un ángulo recto.

**Rigid motion** A rigid motion is a transformation that changes only the position of a figure.

**Movimiento rígido** Un movimiento rígido es una transformación que sólo cambia la posición de una figura.

**Rotation** A rotation is a rigid motion that turns a figure around a fixed point, called the center of rotation.

**Rotación** Una rotación es un movimiento rígido que hace girar una figura alrededor de un punto fijo, llamado centro de rotación.

**Rounding** Rounding a number means replacing the number with a number that tells about how much or how many.

**Redondear** Redondear un número significa reemplazar ese número por un número que indica más o menos cuánto o cuántos.

## S

**Sale** A sale is a discount offered by a store. A sale does not require the customer to have a coupon.

**Venta** Una venta es un descuento ofreció por una tienda. Una venta no requiere al cliente a tener un cupón.

# English/Spanish Glossary

**Sales tax** A tax added to the price of goods and services.

**Las ventas tasan** Un impuesto añadió al precio de bienes y servicios.

**Sample of a population** A sample of a population is part of the population. A sample is useful when you want to find out about a population but you do not have the resources to study every member of the population.

**Muestra de una población** Una muestra de una población es una parte de la población. Una muestra es útil cuando quieres saber algo acerca de una población, pero no tienes los recursos para estudiar a cada miembro de esa población.

**Sample space** The sample space for an action is the set of all possible outcomes of that action.

**Espacio muestral** El espacio muestral de una acción es el conjunto de todos los resultados posibles de esa acción.

**Sampling method** A sampling method is the method by which you choose members of a population to sample.

**Método de muestreo** Un método de muestreo es el método por el cual escoges miembros de una población para muestrear.

**Savings** Savings is money that a person puts away for use at a later date.

**Ahorros** Los ahorros son dinero que una persona guarda para el uso en una fecha posterior.

**Scale** A scale is a ratio that compares a length in a scale drawing to the corresponding length in the actual object.

**Escala** Una escala es una razón que compara una longitud en un dibujo a escala con la longitud correspondiente en el objeto real.

**Scale drawing** A scale drawing is an enlarged or reduced drawing of an object that is proportional to the actual object.

**Dibujo a escala** Un dibujo a escala es un dibujo ampliado o reducido de un objeto que es proporcional al objeto real.

# English/Spanish Glossary

**Scale factor** The scale factor is the ratio of a length in the image to the corresponding length in the original figure.

**Factor de escala** El factor de escala es la razón de una longitud de la imagen a la longitud correspondiente en la figura original.

**Scalene triangle** A scalene triangle is a triangle in which no sides have the same length.

**Triángulo escaleno** Un triángulo escaleno es un triángulo que no tiene lados de la misma longitud.

**Scatter plot** A scatter plot is a graph that uses points to display the relationship between two different sets of data. Each point can be represented by an ordered pair.

**Diagrama de dispersión** Un diagrama de dispersión es una gráfica que usa puntos para mostrar la relación entre dos conjuntos de datos diferentes. Cada punto se puede representar con un par ordenado.

**Scholarship** A type of monetary award a student can use to pay for his or her education. The student does not need to repay this money.

**Beca** Un tipo de premio monetario que un estudiante puede utilizar para pagar por su educación. El estudiante no debe devolver este dinero.

**Scientific notation** A number in scientific notation is written as the product of two factors, one greater than or equal to 1 and less than 10, and the other a power of 10.

**Notación científica** Un número en notación científica está escrito como el producto de dos factores, uno mayor que o igual a 1 y menor que 10, y el otro una potencia de 10.

**Segment** A segment is part of a line. It consists of two endpoints and all of the points on the line between the endpoints.

**Segmento** Un segmento es una parte de una recta. Está formado por dos extremos y todos los puntos de la recta que están entre los extremos.

**Semicircle** A semicircle is one half of a circle.

**Semicírculo** Un semicírculo es la mitad de un círculo.

# English/Spanish Glossary

**Similar figures** A two-dimensional figure is similar (~) to another two-dimensional figure if you can map one figure to the other by a sequence of rotations, reflections, translations, and dilations.

**Figuras semejantes** Una figura bidimensional es semejante (~) a otra figura bidimensional si puedes hacer corresponder una figura con otra mediante una secuencia de rotaciones, reflexiones, traslaciones y dilataciones.

**Simple interest** Simple interest is interest paid only on an original deposit. To calculate simple interest, use the formula $I = prt$ where $I$ is the simple interest, $p$ is the principal, $r$ is the annual interest rate, and $t$ is the number of years that the account earns interest.

**Interés simple** El interés simple es el interés que se paga sobre un depósito original solamente. Para calcular el interés simple, usa la fórmula $I = crt$ donde $I$ es el interés simple, $c$ es el capital, $r$ es la tasa de interés anual y $t$ es el número de años en que la cuenta obtiene un interés.

**Simple random sampling** Simple random sampling is a sampling method in which every member of the population has an equal chance of being chosen for the sample.

**Muestreo aleatorio simple** El muestreo aleatorio simple es un método de muestreo en el que cada miembro de la población tiene la misma probabilidad de ser seleccionado para la muestra.

**Simpler form** A fraction is in simpler form when it is equivalent to a given fraction and has smaller numbers in the numerator and denominator.

**Forma simplificada** Una fracción está en su forma simplificada cuando es equivalente a otra fracción dada, pero tiene números más pequeños en el numerador y el denominador.

**Simplest form** A fraction is in simplest form when the only common factor of the numerator and denominator is one.

**Mínima expresión** Una fracción está en su mínima expresión cuando el único factor común del numerador y el denominador es 1.

**Simplify an algebraic expression** To simplify an algebraic expression, combine the like terms of the expression.

**Simplificar una expresión algebraica** Para simplificar una expresión algebraica, combina los términos semejantes de la expresión.

# English/Spanish Glossary

**Simulation** A simulation is a model of a real-world situation that is used to find probabilities.

**Simulación** Una simulación es un modelo de una situación de la vida diaria que se usa para hallar probabilidades.

**Sketch** To sketch a figure, draw a rough outline. When a sketch is asked for, it means that a drawing needs to be included in your response.

**Bosquejo** Para hacer un bosquejo, dibuja un esquema simple. Si se pide un bosquejo, tu respuesta debe incluir un dibujo.

**Slant height of a cone** The slant height of a cone, $\ell$, is the length of its lateral surface from base to vertex.

**Altura inclinada de un cono** La altura inclinada de un cono, $\ell$, es la longitud de su superficie lateral desde la base hasta el vértice.

**Slant height of a pyramid** The slant height of a pyramid is the height of a lateral face.

**Altura inclinada de una pirámide** La altura inclinada de una pirámide es la altura de una cara lateral.

**Slope** Slope is a ratio that describes steepness.

$$\text{slope} = \frac{\text{vertical change}}{\text{horizontal change}} = \frac{\text{rise}}{\text{run}}$$

**Pendiente** La pendiente es una razón que describe la inclinación.

$$\text{pendiente} = \frac{\text{cambio vertical}}{\text{cambio horizontal}}$$
$$= \frac{\text{distancia vertical}}{\text{distancia horizontal}}$$

**Slope of a line** slope =

$$\frac{\text{change in } y\text{-coordinates}}{\text{change in } x\text{-coordinates}} = \frac{\text{rise}}{\text{run}}$$

**Pendiente de una recta** pendiente =

$$\frac{\text{cambio en las coordenadas } y}{\text{cambio en las coordenadas } x}$$
$$= \frac{\text{distancia vertical}}{\text{distancia horizontal}}$$

**Slope-intercept form** An equation written in the form $y = mx + b$ is in slope-intercept form. The graph is a line with slope $m$ and $y$-intercept $b$.

**Forma pendiente-intercepto** Una ecuación escrita en la forma $y = mx + b$ está en forma de pendiente-intercepto. La gráfica es una línea recta con pendiente $m$ e intercepto en $y$ $b$.

# English/Spanish Glossary

**Solution of a system of linear equations** A solution of a system of linear equations is any ordered pair that makes all the equations of that system true.

**Solución de un sistema de ecuaciones lineales** Una solución de un sistema de ecuaciones lineales es cualquier par ordenado que hace que todas las ecuaciones de ese sistema sean verdaderas.

**Solution of an equation** A solution of an equation is a value of the variable that makes the equation true.

**Solución de una ecuación** Una solución de una ecuación es un valor de la variable que hace que la ecuación sea verdadera.

**Solution of an inequality** The solutions of an inequality are the values of the variable that make the inequality true.

**Solución de una desigualdad** Las soluciones de una desigualdad son los valores de la variable que hacen que la desigualdad sea verdadera.

**Solution set** A solution set contains all of the numbers that satisfy an equation or inequality.

**Conjunto solución** Un conjunto solución contiene todos los números que satisfacen una ecuación o desigualdad.

**Solve** To solve a given statement, determine the value or values that make the statement true. Several methods and strategies can be used to solve a problem, including estimating, isolating the variable, drawing a graph, or using a table of values.

**Resolver** Para resolver un enunciado dado, determina el valor o los valores que hacen que ese enunciado sea verdadero. Para resolver un problema se pueden usar varios métodos y estrategias, como estimar, aislar la variable, dibujar una gráfica o usar una tabla de valores.

**Sphere** A sphere is the set of all points in space that are the same distance from a center point.

**Esfera** Una esfera es el conjunto de todos los puntos en el espacio que están a la misma distancia de un punto central.

**Square** A square is a quadrilateral with four right angles and all sides the same length.

**Cuadrado** Un cuadrado es un cuadrilátero que tiene cuatro ángulos rectos y todos los lados de la misma longitud.

# English/Spanish Glossary

**Square root** A square root of a number is a number that, when multiplied by itself, equals the original number.

**Raíz cuadrada** La raíz cuadrada de un número es un número que, cuando se multiplica por sí mismo, es igual al número original.

**Square unit** A square unit is the area of a square that has sides that are 1 unit long.

**Unidad cuadrada** Una unidad cuadrada es el área de un cuadrado en el que cada lado mide 1 unidad de longitud.

**Standard form** A number written using digits and place value is in standard form.

**Forma estándar** Un número escrito con dígitos y valor posicional está escrito en forma estándar.

**Statistical question** A statistical question is a question that investigates an aspect of the real world and can have variety in the responses.

**Pregunta estadística** Una pregunta estadística es una pregunta que investiga un aspecto de la vida diaria y puede tener varias respuestas.

**Statistics** Statistics is the study of collecting, organizing, graphing, and analyzing data to draw conclusions about the real world.

**Estadística** La estadística es el estudio de la recolección, organización, representación gráfica y análisis de datos para sacar conclusiones sobre la vida diaria.

**Stem-and-leaf plot** A stem-and-leaf plot is a graph that uses the digits of each number to show the data distribution. Each data item is broken into a stem and into a leaf. The leaf is the last digit of the data value. The stem is the other digit or digits of the data value.

**Complot de tallo y hoja** Un complot del tallo y la hoja es un gráfico que utiliza los dígitos de cada número para mostrar la distribución de datos. Cada artículo de datos es roto en un tallo y en una hoja. La hoja es el último dígito de los datos valora. El tallo es el otro dígito o los dígitos de los datos valoran.

**Stored-value card** A stored-value card is a prepaid card electronically coded to be worth a specified amount of money.

**Tarjeta de almacenado-valor** Una tarjeta del almacenado-valor es una tarjeta pagada por adelantado codificó electrónicamente valer una cantidad especificado de dinero.

# English/Spanish Glossary

**Straight angle** A straight angle is an angle with a measure of 180°.

**Ángulo llano** Un ángulo llano es un ángulo que mide 180°.

**Student Loan** A student loan provides money to a student to pay for college. The student needs to repay the loan after leaving college. Often the student will need to pay interest on the amount of the loan.

**Crédito personal para estudiantes** Un crédito personal para estudiantes le proporciona dinero a un estudiante para pagar por el colegio. El estudiante debe devolver el préstamo después de dejar el colegio. A menudo el estudiante deberá pagar interés en la cantidad del préstamo.

**Subject** Each member in a sample is a subject.

**Sujeto** Cada miembro de una muestra es un sujeto.

**Sum** The sum is the answer to an addition problem.

**Suma o total** La suma o total es el resultado de una operación de suma.

**Summarize** To summarize an explanation or solution, go over or review the most important points.

**Resumir** Para resumir una explicación o solución, revisa o repasa los puntos más importantes.

**Supplementary angles** Two angles are supplementary angles if the sum of their measures is 180°. Supplementary angles that are adjacent form a straight angle.

**Ángulos suplementarios** Dos ángulos son suplementarios si la suma de sus medidas es 180°. Los ángulos suplementarios que son adyacentes forman un ángulo llano.

**Surface area of a cone** The surface area of a cone is the sum of the lateral area and the area of the base. The formula for the surface area of a cone is S.A. = L.A. + $B$.

**Área total de un cono** El área total de un cono es la suma del área lateral y el área de la base. La fórmula del área total de un cono es A.T. = A.L. + $B$.

# English/Spanish Glossary

**Surface area of a cube** The surface area of a cube is the sum of the areas of the faces of the cube. The formula for the surface area, S.A., of a cube is S.A. $= 6s^2$, where $s$ represents the length of an edge of the cube.

**Área total de un cubo** El área total de un cubo es la suma de las áreas de las caras del cubo. La fórmula del área total, A.T., de un cubo es A.T. $= 6s^2$, donde $s$ representa la longitud de una arista del cubo.

**Surface area of a cylinder** The surface area of a cylinder is the sum of the lateral area and the areas of the two circular bases. The formula for the surface area of a cylinder is S.A. $=$ L.A. $+ 2B$, where L.A. represents the lateral area of the cylinder and $B$ represents the area of a base of the cylinder.

**Área total de un cilindro** El área total de un cilindro es la suma del área lateral y las áreas de las dos bases circulares. La fórmula del área total de un cilindro es A.T. $=$ A.L. $+ 2B$, donde A.L. representa el área lateral del cilindro y $B$ representa el área de una base del cilindro.

**Surface area of a pyramid** The surface area of a pyramid is the sum of the areas of the faces of the pyramid. The formula for the surface area, S.A., of a pyramid is S.A. $=$ L.A. $+ B$, where L.A. represents the lateral area of the pyramid and $B$ represents the area of the base of the pyramid.

**Área total de una pirámide** El área total de una pirámide es la suma de las áreas de las caras de la pirámide. La fórmula del área total, A.T., de una pirámide es A.T. $=$ A.L. $+ B$, donde A.L. representa el área lateral de la pirámide y $B$ representa el área de la base de la pirámide.

**Surface area of a sphere** The surface area of a sphere is equal to the lateral area of a cylinder that has the same radius, $r$, and height $2r$. The formula for the surface area of a sphere is S.A. $= 4\pi r^2$, where $r$ represents the radius of the sphere.

**Área total de una esfera** El área total de una esfera es igual al área lateral de un cilindro que tiene el mismo radio, $r$, y una altura de $2r$. La fórmula del área total de una esfera es A.T. $= 4\pi r^2$, donde $r$ representa el radio de la esfera.

**Surface area of a three-dimensional figure** The surface area of a three-dimensional figure is the sum of the areas of its faces. You can find the surface area by finding the area of the net of the three-dimensional figure.

**Área total de una figura tridimensional** El área total de una figura tridimensional es la suma de las áreas de sus caras. Puedes hallar el área total si hallas el área del modelo plano de la figura tridimensional.

# English/Spanish Glossary

**System of linear equations** A system of linear equations is formed by two or more linear equations that use the same variables.

**Sistema de ecuaciones lineales** Un sistema de ecuaciones lineales está formado por dos o más ecuaciones lineales que usan las mismas variables.

**Systematic sampling** Systematic sampling is a sampling method in which you choose every nth member of the population, where $n$ is a predetermined number. A systematic sample is useful when the researcher is able to approach the population in a systematic, or methodical, way.

**Muestreo sistemático** El muestreo sistemático es un método de muestreo en el que se escoge cada enésimo miembro de la población, donde $n$ es un número predeterminado. Una muestra sistemática es útil cuando el investigador puede enfocarse en la población de manera sistemática o metódica.

## T

**Taxable wages** For federal income tax purposes, your taxable wages are the difference between your earned wages and your withholding allowance. Your employer divides your withholding allowance equally among the pay periods of one year.

**Sueldos imponibles** Para propósitos federales de impuesto de renta, sus sueldos imponibles son la diferencia entre sus sueldos ganados y su concesión que retienen. Su empleador divide su concesión que retiene igualmente entre los períodos de paga de un año.

**Tenths** One tenth is one out of ten equal parts of a whole.

**Décimas** Una décima es 1 de 10 partes iguales de un todo.

**Term** A term is a number, a variable, or the product of a number and one or more variables.

**Término** Un término es un número, una variable o el producto de un número y una o más variables.

**Terminating decimal** A terminating decimal has a decimal expansion that terminates in 0.

**Decimal finito** Un decimal finito tiene una expansión decimal que termina en 0.

# English/Spanish Glossary

**Terms of a ratio** The terms of a ratio are the quantities *x* and *y* in the ratio.

**Términos de una razón** Los términos de una razón son la cantidad *x* y la cantidad *y* de la razón.

**Theorem** A theorem is a conjecture that is proven.

**Teorema** Un teorema es una conjetura que se ha comprobado.

**Theoretical probability** When all outcomes of an action are equally likely, $P(\text{event}) = \dfrac{\text{number of favourable outcomes}}{\text{number of possible outcomes}}$.

**Probabilidad teórica** Cuando todos los resultados de una acción son igualmente probables, $P(\text{evento}) = \dfrac{\text{número de resultados favorables}}{\text{número de resultados posibles}}$.

**Third quartile** For an ordered set of data, the third quartile is the median of the upper half of the data set.

**Tercer cuartil** Para un conjunto de datos ordenados, el tercer cuartil es la mediana de la mitad superior del conjunto de datos.

**Thousandths** One thousandth is one part of 1,000 equal parts of a whole.

**Milésimas** Una milésima es 1 de 1,000 partes iguales de un todo.

**Three-dimensional figure** A three-dimensional (3-D) figure is a figure that does not lie in a plane.

**Figura tridimensional** Una figura tridimensional es una figura que no está en un plano.

**Total cost of a loan** The total cost of a loan is the total amount spent to repay the loan. Total cost includes the principal and all interest paid over the length of the loan. Total cost also includes any fees charged.

**El coste total de un préstamo** El coste total de un préstamo es el cantidad total que es gastado para devolver el préstamo. El coste total incluye al director y todo el interés pagó sobre la longitud del préstamo. El coste total también incluye cualquier honorario cargado.

**Transaction** A banking transaction moves money into or out of a bank account.

**Transacción** Una transacción bancaria mueve dinero en o fuera de una cuenta bancaria.

# English/Spanish Glossary

**Transfer** A transaction that moves money from one bank account to another is a transfer. The balance of one account increases by the same amount the other account decreases.

**Transferencia** Una transacción que mueve dinero de una cuenta bancaria a otro es una transferencia. El equilibrio de un aumentos de cuenta por la misma cantidad que la otra cuenta disminuye.

**Transformation** A transformation is a change in position, shape, or size of a figure. Three types of transformations that change position only are translations, reflections, and rotations.

**Transformación** Una transformación es un cambio en la posición, la forma o el tamaño de una figura. Tres tipos de transformaciones que cambian sólo la posición son las traslaciones, las reflexiones y las rotaciones.

**Translation** A translation, or slide, is a rigid motion that moves every point of a figure the same distance and in the same direction.

**Traslación** Una traslación, o deslizamiento, es un movimiento rígido que mueve cada punto de una figura a la misma distancia y en la misma dirección.

**Transversal** A transversal is a line that intersects two or more lines at different points.

**Transversal o secante** Una transversal o secante es una línea que interseca dos o más líneas en distintos puntos.

**Trapezoid** A trapezoid is a quadrilateral with exactly one pair of parallel sides.

**Trapecio** Un trapecio es un cuadrilátero que tiene exactamente un par de lados paralelos.

**Trend line** A trend line is a line on a scatter plot, drawn near the points, that approximates the association between the data sets.

**Línea de tendencia** Una línea de tendencia es una línea en un diagrama de dispersión, trazada cerca de los puntos, que se aproxima a la relación entre los conjuntos de datos.

**Trial** In a probability experiment, you carry out or observe an action repeatedly. Each observation of the action is a trial.

**Prueba** En un experimento de probabilidad, realizas u observas una acción varias veces. Cada observación de la acción es una prueba.

**Triangle** A triangle is a polygon with three sides.

**Triángulo** Un triángulo es un polígono de tres lados.

# English/Spanish Glossary

**Triangular prism** A triangular prism is a prism with bases in the shape of a triangle.

**Prisma triangular** Un prisma triangular es un prisma cuyas bases tienen la forma de un triángulo.

**True equation** A true equation has equal values on each side of the equals sign.

**Ecuación verdadera** En una ecuación verdadera, los valores a ambos lados del signo igual son iguales.

**Two-way frequency table** A two-way frequency table displays the counts of the data in each group.

**Tabla de frecuencia con dos variables** Una tabla de frecuencia con dos variables muestra el conteo de los datos de cada grupo.

**Two-way relative frequency table** A two-way relative frequency table shows the ratio of the number of data in each group to the size of the population. The relative frequencies can be calculated with respect to the entire population, the row populations, or the column populations. The relative frequencies can be expressed as fractions, decimals, or percents.

**Tabla de frecuencias relativas con dos variables** Una tabla de frecuencias relativas con dos variables muestra la razón del número de datos de cada grupo al tamaño de la población. Las frecuencias relativas se pueden calcular respecto de la población entera, las poblaciones de las filas o las poblaciones de las columnas. Las frecuencias relativas se pueden expresar como fracciones, decimales o porcentajes.

**Two-way table** A two-way table shows bivariate categorical data for a population.

**Tabla con dos variables** Una tabla con dos variables muestra datos bivariados por categorías de una población.

## U

**Uniform probability model** A uniform probability model is a probability model based on using the theoretical probability of equally likely outcomes.

**Modelo de probabilidad uniforme** Un modelo de probabilidad uniforme es un modelo de probabilidad que se basa en el uso de la probabilidad teórica de resultados igualmente probables.

# English/Spanish Glossary

**Unit fraction** A unit fraction is a fraction with a numerator of 1 and a denominator that is a whole number greater than 1.

**Fracción unitaria** Una fracción unitaria es una fracción con un numerador 1 y un denominador que es un número entero mayor que 1.

**Unit price** A unit price is a unit rate that gives the price of one item.

**Precio por unidad** El precio por unidad es una tasa por unidad que muestra el precio de un artículo.

**Unit rate** The rate for one unit of a given quantity is called the unit rate.

**Tasa por unidad** Se llama tasa por unidad a la tasa que corresponde a 1 unidad de una cantidad dada.

**Use** To use given information, draw on it to help you determine something else.

**Usar** Para usar una información dada, apóyate en ella para determinar otra cosa.

## V

**Valid inference** A valid inference is an inference that is true about the population. Valid inferences can be made when they are based on data from a representative sample.

**Inferencia válida** Una inferencia válida es una inferencia verdadera acerca de una población. Se pueden hacer inferencias válidas si están basadas en los datos de una muestra representativa.

**Variability** Variability describes how much the items in a data set differ (or vary) from each other. On a data display, variability is shown by how much the data on the horizontal scale are spread out.

**Variabilidad** La variabilidad describe qué diferencia (o variación) existe entre los elementos de un conjunto de datos. Al exhibir datos, la variabilidad queda representada por la distancia que separa los datos en la escala horizontal.

**Variable** A variable is a letter that represents an unknown value.

**Variable** Una variable es una letra que representa un valor desconocido.

**Variable expenses** Variable expenses are expenses that change from one budget period to the next.

**Gastos variables** Los gastos variables son los gastos que cambian de un período económico al próximo.

# English/Spanish Glossary

**Vertex of a cone** The vertex of a cone is the point farthest from the base.

**Vértice de un cono** El vértice de un cono es el punto más alejado de la base.

**Vertex of a polygon** The vertex of a polygon is any point where two sides of a polygon meet.

**Vértice de un polígono** El vértice de un polígono es cualquier punto donde se encuentran dos lados de un polígono.

**Vertex of a three-dimensional figure** A vertex of a three-dimensional figure is a point where three or more edges meet.

**Vértice de una figura tridimensional** El vértice de una figura tridimensional es un punto donde se unen tres o más aristas.

**Vertex of an angle** The vertex of an angle is the point of intersection of the rays that make up the sides of the angle.

**Vértice de un ángulo** El vértice de un ángulo es el punto de intersección de las semirrectas que forman los lados del ángulo.

**Vertical angles** Vertical angles are formed by two intersecting lines and are opposite each other. Vertical angles have equal measures.

**Ángulos opuestos por el vértice** Los ángulos opuestos por el vértice están formados por dos rectas secantes y están uno frente a otro. Los ángulos opuestos por el vértice tienen la misma medida.

**Vertical-line test** The vertical-line test is a method used to determine if a relation is a function or not. If a vertical line passes through a graph more than once, the graph is not the graph of a function.

**Prueba de recta vertical** La prueba de recta vertical es un método que se usa para determinar si una relación es una función o no. Si una recta vertical atraviesa la gráfica más de una vez, la gráfica no es la gráfica de una función.

**Volume** Volume is the number of cubic units needed to fill a solid figure.

**Volumen** El volumen es el número de unidades cúbicas que se necesitan para llenar un cuerpo geométrico.

# English/Spanish Glossary

**Volume of a cone** The volume of a cone is the number of unit cubes, or cubic units, needed to fill the cone. The formula for the volume of a cone is $V = \frac{1}{3}Bh$, where $B$ represents the area of the base and $h$ represents the height of the cone.

**Volumen de un cono** El volumen de un cono es el número de bloques de unidades, o unidades cúbicas, que se necesitan para llenar el cono. La fórmula del volumen de un cono $V = \frac{1}{3}Bh$, donde $B$ representa el área de la base y $h$ representa la altura del cono.

**Volume of a cube** The volume of a cube is the number of unit cubes, or cubic units, needed to fill the cube. The formula for the volume $V$ of a cube is $V = s^3$, where s represents the length of an edge of the cube.

**Volumen de un cubo** El volumen de un cubo es el número de bloques de unidades, o unidades cúbicas, que se necesitan para llenar el cubo. La fórmula del volumen, $V$, de un cubo es $V = s^3$, donde s representa la longitud de una arista del cubo.

**Volume of a cylinder** The volume of a cylinder is the number of unit cubes, or cubic units, needed to fill the cylinder. The formula for the volume of a cylinder is $V = \pi r^2 h$, where $r$ represents the radius of a base and $h$ represents the height of the cylinder.

**Volumen de un cilindro** El volumen de un cilindro es el número de bloques de unidades, o unidades cúbicas, que se necesitan para llenar el cilindro. La fórmula del volumen de un cilindro es $V = \pi r^2 h$, donde $r$ representa el radio de una base y $h$ representa la altura del cilindro.

**Volume of a prism** The volume of a prism is the number of unit cubes, or cubic units, needed to fill the prism. The formula for the volume $V$ of a prism is $V = Bh$, where $B$ represents the area of a base and $h$ represents the height of the prism.

**Volumen de un prisma** El volumen de un prisma es el número de bloques de unidades, o unidades cúbicas, que se necesitan para llenar el prisma. La fórmula del volumen, $V$, de un prisma $V = Bh$, donde $B$ representa el área de una base y $h$ representa la altura del prisma.

**Volume of a pyramid** The volume of a pyramid is the number of unit cubes needed to fill the pyramid. The formula for the volume $V$ of a pyramid is $V = \frac{1}{3}Bh$, where $B$ represents the area of the base and $h$ represents the height of the pyramid.

**Volumen de una pirámide** El volumen de una pirámide es el número de bloques de unidades, o unidades cúbicas, que se necesitan para llenar la pirámide. La fórmula del volumen, $V$, de una pirámide es $V = \frac{1}{3}Bh$, donde $B$ representa el área de la base y $h$ representa la altura de la pirámide.

# English/Spanish Glossary

**Volume of a sphere** The volume of a sphere is the number of unit cubes, or cubic units, needed to fill the sphere. The formula for the volume of a sphere is $V = \frac{4}{3}\pi r^3$.

**Volumen de una esfera** El volumen de una esfera es el número de bloques de unidades, o unidades cúbicas, que se necesitan para llenar la esfera. La fórmula del volumen de una esfera es $V = \frac{4}{3}\pi r^3$.

## W

**Whole numbers** The whole numbers consist of the number 0 and all of the natural numbers.

**Números enteros no negativos** Los números enteros no negativos son el número 0 y todos los números naturales.

**Withdrawal** A transaction that takes money out of a bank account is a withdrawal.

**Retirada** Una transacción que toma dinero fuera de una cuenta bancaria es una retirada.

**Withholding allowance** You can exclude a portion of your earned wages, called a withholding allowance, from federal income tax. You can claim one withholding allowance for yourself and one for each person dependent upon your income.

**Retener concesión** Puede excluir una porción de sus sueldos ganados, llamó una concesión que retiene, del impuesto de renta federal. Puede reclamar una concesión que retiene para usted mismo y para uno para cada dependiente de persona sobre sus ingresos.

**Word form of a number** The word form of a number is the number written in words.

**Número en palabras** Un número en palabras es un número escrito con palabras en lugar de dígitos.

**Work-Study** Work-study is a type of need-based aid that schools might offer to a student. A student must earn work-study money by working certain jobs.

**Práctica estudiantil** La práctica estudiantil es un tipo de ayuda necesidad-basado que escuelas quizás ofrezcan a un estudiante. Un estudiante debe ganar dinero de práctica estudiantil por ciertos trabajos de trabajo.

# English/Spanish Glossary

## X

**x-axis** The x-axis is the horizontal number line that, together with the y-axis, forms the coordinate plane.

**Eje de las x** El eje de las x es la recta numérica horizontal que, junto con el eje de las y, forma el plano de coordenadas.

**x-coordinate** The x-coordinate is the first number in an ordered pair. It tells the number of horizontal units a point is from 0.

**Coordenada x** La coordenada x (abscisa) es el primer número de un par ordenado. Indica cuántas unidades horizontales hay entre un punto y 0.

## Y

**y-axis** The y-axis is the vertical number line that, together with the x-axis, forms the coordinate plane.

**Eje de las y** El eje de las y es la recta numérica vertical que, junto con el eje de las x, forma el plano de coordenadas.

**y-coordinate** The y-coordinate is the second number in an ordered pair. It tells the number of vertical units a point is from 0.

**Coordenada y** La coordenada y (ordenada) es el segundo número de un par ordenado. Indica cuántas unidades verticales hay entre un punto y 0.

**y-intercept** The y-intercept of a line is the y-coordinate of the point where the line crosses the y-axis.

**Intercepto en y** El intercepto en y de una recta es la coordenada y del punto por donde la recta cruza el eje de las y.

## Z

**Zero exponent property** For any nonzero number $a$, $a^0 = 1$.

**Propiedad del exponente cero** Para cualquier número distinto de cero $a$, $a^0 = 1$.

**Zero Property of Multiplication** The product of 0 and any number is 0. For any number $n$, $n \cdot 0 = 0$ and $0 \cdot n = 0$.

**Propiedad del cero en la multiplicación** El producto de 0 y cualquier número es 0. Para cualquier número $n$, $n \cdot 0 = 0$ and $0 \cdot n = 0$.

# Formulas

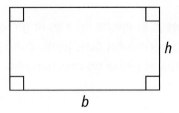

$P = 2b + 2h$

$A = bh$

**Rectangle**

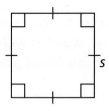

$P = 4s$

$A = s^2$

**Square**

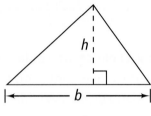

$A = \frac{1}{2}bh$

**Triangle**

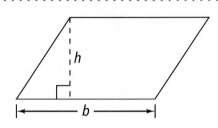

$A = bh$

**Parallelogram**

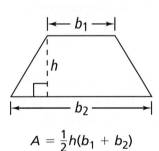

$A = \frac{1}{2}h(b_1 + b_2)$

**Trapezoid**

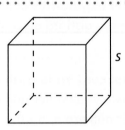

$C = 2\pi r$ or $C = \pi d$

$A = \pi r^2$

**Circle**

$S.A. = 6s^2$

$V = s^3$

**Cube**

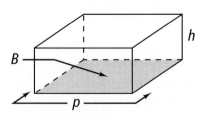

$V = Bh$

$L.A. = ph$

$S.A. = L.A. + 2B$

**Rectangular Prism**

# Formulas

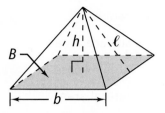

$V = \frac{1}{3}Bh$

L.A. $= 2b\ell$

S.A. $=$ L.A. $+ B$

**Square Pyramid**

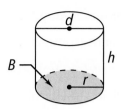

$V = Bh$

L.A. $= 2\pi rh$

S.A. $=$ L.A. $+ 2B$

**Cylinder**

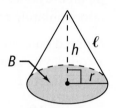

$V = \frac{1}{3}Bh$

L.A. $= \pi r\ell$

S.A. $=$ L.A. $+ B$

**Cone**

$V = \frac{4}{3}\pi r^3$

S.A. $= 4\pi r^2$

**Sphere**

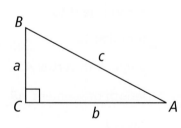

$a^2 + b^2 = c^2$

**Pythagorean Theorem**

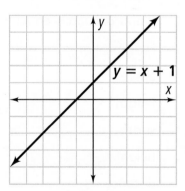

$y = mx + b$, where
$m =$ slope and
$b = y$-intercept

**Equation of Line**

# Math Symbols

| Symbol | Meaning | | Symbol | Meaning |
|---|---|---|---|---|
| $+$ | plus (addition) | | $r$ | radius |
| $-$ | minus (subtraction) | | S.A. | surface area |
| $\times$ , $\cdot$ | times (multiplication) | | $B$ | area of base |
| $\div$ , $\overline{)\phantom{x}}$ , $\frac{a}{b}$ | divide (division) | | L.A. | lateral area |
| $=$ | is equal to | | $\ell$ | slant height |
| $<$ | is less than | | $V$ | volume |
| $>$ | is greater than | | $a^n$ | $n$th power of $a$ |
| $\leq$ | is less than or equal to | | $\sqrt{x}$ | nonnegative square root of $x$ |
| $\geq$ | is greater than or equal to | | $\pi$ | pi, an irrational number approximately equal to 3.14 |
| $\neq$ | is not equal to | | | |
| ( ) | parentheses for grouping | | $(a, b)$ | ordered pair with $x$-coordinate $a$ and $y$-coordinate $b$ |
| [ ] | brackets for grouping | | | |
| $-a$ | opposite of $a$ | | $\overline{AB}$ | segment $AB$ |
| . . . | and so on | | $A'$ | image of $A$, $A$ prime |
| $^\circ$ | degrees | | $\triangle ABC$ | triangle with vertices $A$, $B$, and $C$ |
| $\lvert a \rvert$ | absolute value of $a$ | | | |
| $\overset{?}{=}, \overset{?}{<}, \overset{?}{>}$ | Is the statement true? | | $\rightarrow$ | arrow notation |
| $\approx$ | is approximately equal to | | $a : b, \frac{a}{b}$ | ratio of a to b |
| $\frac{b}{a}$ | reciprocal of $\frac{a}{b}$ | | $\cong$ | is congruent to |
| $A$ | area | | $\sim$ | is similar to |
| $\ell$ | length | | $\angle A$ | angle with vertex $A$ |
| $w$ | width | | $AB$ | length of segment $\overline{AB}$ |
| $h$ | height | | $\overrightarrow{AB}$ | ray $AB$ |
| $d$ | distance | | $\angle ABC$ | angle formed by $\overrightarrow{BA}$ and $\overrightarrow{BC}$ |
| $r$ | rate | | $m\angle ABC$ | measure of angle $ABC$ |
| $t$ | time | | $\perp$ | is perpendicular to |
| $P$ | perimeter | | $\overleftrightarrow{AB}$ | line $AB$ |
| $b$ | base length | | $\parallel$ | is parallel to |
| $C$ | circumference | | $\%$ | percent |
| $d$ | diameter | | $P$ (event) | probability of an event |

# Measures

| Customary | Metric |
|---|---|
| **Length** | **Length** |
| 1 foot (ft) = 12 inches (in.)<br>1 yard (yd) = 36 in.<br>1 yd = 3 ft<br>1 mile (mi) = 5,280 ft<br>1 mi = 1,760 yd | 1 centimeter (cm) = 10 millimeters (mm)<br>1 meter (m) = 100 cm<br>1 kilometer (km) = 1,000 m<br>1 mm = 0.001 m |
| **Area** | **Area** |
| 1 square foot ($ft^2$) = 144 square inches ($in.^2$)<br>1 square yard ($yd^2$) = 9 $ft^2$<br>1 square mile ($mi^2$) = 640 acres | 1 square centimeter ($cm^2$) =<br>$\quad$ 100 square millimeters ($mm^2$)<br>1 square meter ($m^2$) = 10,000 $cm^2$ |
| **Volume** | **Volume** |
| 1 cubic foot ($ft^3$) = 1,728 cubic inches ($in.^3$)<br>1 cubic yard ($yd^3$) = 27 $ft^3$ | 1 cubic centimeter ($cm^3$) =<br>$\quad$ 1,000 cubic millimeters ($mm^3$)<br>1 cubic meter ($m^3$) = 1,000,000 $cm^3$ |
| **Mass** | **Mass** |
| 1 pound (lb) = 16 ounces (oz)<br>1 ton (t) = 2,000 lb | 1 gram (g) = 1,000 milligrams (mg)<br>1 kilogram (kg) = 1,000 g |
| **Capacity** | **Capacity** |
| 1 cup (c) = 8 fluid ounces (fl oz)<br>1 pint (pt) = 2 c<br>1 quart (qt) = 2 pt<br>1 gallon (gal) = 4 qt | 1 liter (L) = 1,000 milliliters (mL)<br>1000 liters = 1 kiloliter (kL) |

| Customary Units and Metric Units | |
|---|---|
| **Length** | 1 in. = 2.54 cm<br>1 mi ≈ 1.61 km<br>1 ft ≈ 0.3 m |
| **Capacity** | 1 qt ≈ 0.94 L |
| **Weight and Mass** | 1 oz ≈ 28.3 g<br>1 lb ≈ 0.45 kg |

# Properties

Unless otherwise stated, the variables a, b, c, m, and n used in these properties can be replaced with any number represented on a number line.

## Identity Properties
**Addition** $\quad n + 0 = n$ and $0 + n = n$
**Multiplication** $\; n \cdot 1 = n$ and $1 \cdot n = n$

## Commutative Properties
**Addition** $\quad a + b = b + a$
**Multiplication** $\; a \cdot b = b \cdot a$

## Associative Properties
**Addition** $\quad (a + b) + c = a + (b + c)$
**Multiplication** $\; (a \cdot b) \cdot c = a \cdot (b \cdot c)$

## Inverse Properties
**Addition**
$a + (-a) = 0$ and $-a + a = 0$
**Multiplication**
$a \cdot \frac{1}{a} = 1$ and $\frac{1}{a} \cdot a = 1, (a \neq 0)$

## Distributive Properties
$a(b + c) = ab + ac \quad (b + c)a = ba + ca$
$a(b - c) = ab - ac \quad (b - c)a = ba - ca$

## Properties of Equality
**Addition** $\quad$ If $a = b$,
$\qquad\qquad$ then $a + c = b + c$.
**Subtraction** $\;$ If $a = b$,
$\qquad\qquad$ then $a - c = b - c$.
**Multiplication** If $a = b$,
$\qquad\qquad$ then $a \cdot c = b \cdot c$.
**Division** $\quad$ If $a = b$, and $c \neq 0$,
$\qquad\qquad$ then $\frac{a}{c} = \frac{b}{c}$.
**Substitution** If $a = b$, then $b$ can
$\qquad\qquad$ replace $a$ in any
$\qquad\qquad$ expression.

## Zero Property
$a \cdot 0 = 0$ and $0 \cdot a = 0$.

## Properties of Inequality
**Addition** $\qquad$ If $a > b$,
$\qquad\qquad\qquad$ then $a + c > b + c$.
$\qquad\qquad\qquad$ If $a < b$,
$\qquad\qquad\qquad$ then $a + c < b + c$.
**Subtraction** $\quad$ If $a > b$,
$\qquad\qquad\qquad$ then $a - c > b - c$.
$\qquad\qquad\qquad$ If $a < b$,
$\qquad\qquad\qquad$ then $a - c < b - c$.
**Multiplication**
If $a > b$ and $c > 0$, then $ac > bc$.
If $a < b$ and $c > 0$, then $ac < bc$.
If $a > b$ and $c < 0$, then $ac < bc$.
If $a < b$ and $c < 0$, then $ac > bc$.
**Division**
If $a > b$ and $c > 0$, then $\frac{a}{c} > \frac{b}{c}$.
If $a < b$ and $c > 0$, then $\frac{a}{c} < \frac{b}{c}$.
If $a > b$ and $c < 0$, then $\frac{a}{c} < \frac{b}{c}$.
If $a < b$ and $c < 0$, then $\frac{a}{c} > \frac{b}{c}$.

## Properties of Exponents
For any nonzero number $n$ and any integers $m$ and $n$:

| | |
|---|---|
| **Zero Exponent** | $a^0 = 1$ |
| **Negative Exponent** | $a^{-n} = \frac{1}{a^n}$ |
| **Product of Powers** | $a^m \cdot a^n = a^{m+n}$ |
| **Power of a Product** | $(ab)^n = a^n b^n$ |
| **Quotient of Powers** | $\frac{a^m}{a^n} = a^{m-n}$ |
| **Power of a Quotient** | $\left(\frac{a}{b}\right)^n = \frac{a^n}{b^n}$ |
| **Power of a Power** | $(a^m)^n = a^{mn}$ |